CANIS MODERNIS

ANIMALIBUS
OF ANIMALS AND CULTURES

Nigel Rothfels, *General Editor*

ADVISORY BOARD:
Steve Baker (University of Central Lancashire)
Garry Marvin (Roehampton University)
Susan McHugh (University of New England)
Kari Weil (Wesleyan University)

Books in the Animalibus series share a fascination with the status and the role of animals in human life. Crossing the humanities and the social sciences to include work in history, anthropology, social and cultural geography, environmental studies, and literary and art criticism, these books ask what thinking about nonhuman animals can teach us about human cultures, about what it means to be human, and about how that meaning might shift across times and places.

OTHER TITLES IN THE SERIES:

Rachel Poliquin, *The Breathless Zoo: Taxidermy and the Cultures of Longing*

Joan B. Landes, Paula Young Lee, and Paul Youngquist, eds., *Gorgeous Beasts: Animal Bodies in Historical Perspective*

Liv Emma Thorsen, Karen A. Rader, and Adam Dodd, eds., *Animals on Display: The Creaturely in Museums, Zoos, and Natural History*

Ann-Janine Morey, *Picturing Dogs, Seeing Ourselves: Vintage American Photographs*

Mary Sanders Pollock, *Storytelling Apes: Primatology Narratives Past and Future*

Ingrid H. Tague, *Animal Companions: Pets and Social Change in Eighteenth-Century Britain*

Dick Blau and Nigel Rothfels, *Elephant House*

Marcus Baynes-Rock, *Among the Bone Eaters: Encounters with Hyenas in Harar*

Monica Mattfeld, *Becoming Centaur: Eighteenth-Century Masculinity and English Horsemanship*

Heather Swan, *Where Honeybees Thrive: Stories from the Field*

Karen Raber and Monica Mattfeld, eds., *Performing Animals: History, Agency, Theater*

J. Keri Cronin, *Art for Animals: Visual Culture and Animal Advocacy, 1870–1914*

Elizabeth Marshall Thomas, *The Hidden Life of Life: A Walk Through the Reaches of Time*

Elizabeth Young, *Pet Projects: Animal Fiction and Taxidermy in the Nineteenth-Century Archive*

Marcus Baynes-Rock, *Crocodile Undone: The Domestication of Australia's Fauna*

Deborah Nadal, *Rabies in the Streets: Interspecies Camaraderie in Urban India*

Mustafa Haikal, translated by Thomas Dunlap, *Master Pongo: A Gorilla Conquers Europe*

Austin McQuinn, *Becoming Audible: Sounding Animality in Performance*

CANIS MODERNIS

Human/Dog Coevolution in Modernist Literature

KARALYN KENDALL-MORWICK

THE PENNSYLVANIA STATE UNIVERSITY PRESS
UNIVERSITY PARK, PENNSYLVANIA

Portions of chapter 2 previously appeared as "Mongrel Fiction: Canine Bildung and the Feminist Critique of Anthropocentrism in Virginia Woolf's *Flush*," *Modern Fiction Studies* 60, no. 3 (2014): 506–26. Copyright © 2014 The Johns Hopkins University Press.

Portions of chapter 4 previously appeared as "Dogging the Subject: Samuel Beckett, Emmanuel Levinas, and Posthumanist Ethics," *Journal of Modern Literature* 36, no. 3 (2013): 100–119. Reproduced with permission from Indiana University Press.

Additional material from chapter 4 previously appeared as "The Face of a Dog: Levinasian Ethics and Human/Dog Coevolution," in *Queering the Non/Human*, edited by Noreen Giffney and Myra J. Hird (Burlington, VT: Ashgate, 2008), 185–204. Reproduced with permission of Informa UK Limited through PLSclear.

Library of Congress Cataloging-in-Publication Data

Names: Kendall-Morwick, Karalyn, author.
Title: Canis modernis : human/dog coevolution in modernist literature / Karalyn Kendall-Morwick.
Other titles: Animalibus.
Description: University Park, Pennsylvania : The Pennsylvania State University Press, [2020] | Series: Animalibus: of animals and cultures | Includes bibliographical references and index.
Summary: "Examines the human-dog relationship in modernist literature, analyzing works by Jack London, Virginia Woolf, Albert Payson Terhune, J. R. Ackerley, Samuel Beckett, and others to show how dogs challenge the autonomy of the human subject and the humanistic underpinnings of traditional literary forms"—Provided by publisher.
Identifiers: LCCN 2020039412 | ISBN 9780271088020 (hardback)
Subjects: LCSH: Dogs in literature. | Human-animal relationships in literature. | Modernism (Literature)
Classification: LCC PN56.D6 K46 2020 | DDC 809/.933629772—dc23
LC record available at https://lccn.loc.gov/2020039412

Copyright © 2021 Karalyn Kendall-Morwick
All rights reserved
Printed in the United States of America
Published by The Pennsylvania State University Press,
University Park, PA 16802-1003

The Pennsylvania State University Press is a member of the Association of University Presses.

It is the policy of The Pennsylvania State University Press to use acid-free paper. Publications on uncoated stock satisfy the minimum requirements of American National Standard for Information Sciences—Permanence of Paper for Printed Library Material, ANSI Z39.48-1992.

Images on page x:
Int. Ch. Bellhaven Laund Logic, out of Florence B. Ilch's famous Bellhaven kennel at Red Bank, New Jersey, circa 1922. Rudolph Tauskey / Courtesy *AKC Gazette*.

CONTENTS

Acknowledgments (vii)

Introduction: Modernism and the Canine Condition (1)

1 Canine Origins: Jack London and Konrad Lorenz (21)

2 Mongrelizing Form: Virginia Woolf's *Flush* (55)

3 The New Dog: Albert Payson Terhune and J. R. Ackerley (92)

4 Dogging the Subject:
Samuel Beckett and Emmanuel Levinas (129)

Coda: Modernism and Literary Canine Studies (166)

Notes (173)
Bibliography (189)
Index (199)

ACKNOWLEDGMENTS

This book would not have been possible without the generous support, fellowship, and guidance of many mentors, colleagues, and friends. I owe an enormous debt of gratitude to Ed Dallis-Comentale, Alyce Miller, Richard Nash, and Stephen Watt for their early support of the project and invaluable role in its conceptualization; to Colin Allen, David Herman, Myra Hird, Daniel O'Hara, Jean-Michel Rabaté, and anonymous reviewers for their constructive feedback on individual chapters and excerpts; to Susan McHugh and an anonymous reviewer for their incisive reading of the manuscript; to Suzanne Wolk for her extraordinarily keen editorial eye; and to Alex Vose, Nigel Rothfels, Laura Reed-Morrisson, Brian Beer, and Kendra Boileau for their patient and expert shepherding of the project through the publication process.

I am grateful to the Animals and Society Institute—particularly Margo DeMello and Kenneth Shapiro—and Wesleyan Animal Studies for selecting me as a recipient of the 2013 Human-Animal Studies Fellowship, during which I benefited enormously from the generous mentorship of Lori Gruen, Susan McHugh, Carrie Rohman, and Kari Weil and the inspiring fellowship of Joel MacClellan, Beatrice Marovich, David Redmalm, Jeanette Samyn, Ann Marie Thornburg, and Zipporah Weisberg. I also gratefully acknowledge the funding for this project provided through the Ruth Neikamp-Cummings Fellowship, awarded by the Indiana University Department of English, and additional research activity funds provided by Indiana University and Washburn University.

Portions of chapters 2 and 4 were previously published as articles in *Modern Fiction Studies* and the *Journal of Modern Literature*, and as part of a chapter in the edited collection *Queering the Non/Human*. I thank Johns Hopkins University Press, Indiana University Press, and the Taylor and Francis Group for permission to reprint them here.

My understanding of the many modes of companion species relating has been enriched and challenged by more people than I can name here, but in addition to those identified above, I particularly thank members of the Society for Literature, Science, and the Arts, the Association for the Study of Literature and Environment, the Animal Studies Workshop at the University of Chicago, and the Modernist Studies Workshop at Penn State; my fellow editors of *Humanimalia: A Journal of Human/Animal Interface Studies*; the staff and volunteers at the Bloomington Animal Shelter in Bloomington, Indiana, Helping Hands Humane Society in Topeka, Kansas, and Lawrence Humane Society in Lawrence, Kansas; the awesomely dedicated volunteers of Topeka Community Cat Fix; and my dear friend Courtney Wennerstrom.

I am profoundly thankful for the unconditional love and support of my husband and best friend, Joey Kendall-Morwick, and my unfailingly supportive parents, Wayne and Chris Kendall, and sisters, Jenny Thomas and Erin Hoffer. Finally, I am grateful beyond the reach of words to Oscar, Benny, Vincent, Ada, Bijou, Zora, Dorian, and most of all my muse and heart-dog, Gatsby, for teaching me what it means to be companion animals.

INTRODUCTION
Modernism and the Canine Condition

One of the most perplexing moments in modernist literature comes at the end of Djuna Barnes's *Nightwood*, when an encounter between protagonist Robin Vote and her ex-lover's dog escalates into a fit of mutual barking, whimpering, grinning, and trembling and ends with both participants prostrate and panting on the floor of an abandoned chapel. The scene is disorienting, not least because of Barnes's dogged refusal to clarify the nature of the encounter; her narrator describes Robin's actions ambiguously as "going down."[1] In a letter to Emily Coleman, a friend who was instrumental in preparing the *Nightwood* manuscript for publication, Barnes writes, "When they see each other Robin goes down with the dog, and thats the end. I do not go any further than this into the psychology of the 'animal' in Robin because it seems to me that the very act with the dog is pointed enough, and anything more than that would spoil the scene anyway; as for what the end promises (?) let the reader make up his own mind, if hes not an idiot he'll know."[2] Despite Barnes's insistence that all but the most obtuse readers should readily grasp what the scene depicts, critics have not reached a consensus about just what this "act with the dog" is. Prior to the so-called animal turn in literary studies, critics interpreted it variously as a thinly veiled representation of bestiality, an empowering reclamation of presymbolic modes of subjectivity, and a violent act of mastery that reinstates phallic order.[3]

With the rapid growth of the interdisciplinary field of animal studies in the past decade or so, recent scholarship has taken more seriously the significance of animality in this scene and in modernist literature more generally. Rather than dismiss literary animals as mere metaphors for repressed sexuality, degeneracy, or the dehumanized modern subject, scholars working at the intersections of modernist and animal studies have revealed a more fundamental decentering of the human at work in texts like *Nightwood*. Carrie Rohman, for example, reads Robin's encounter with the dog as affirming a "radical posthumanism" that "deflate[s] the self-importance of humanism by privileging the nonhuman, the undecidable, the nonlinguistic, the animal." In *Stalking the Subject*, her incisive study of modernism's engagement with the question of the animal, Rohman presents Barnes's "posthumanist triumph" as one of the more radical examples of how modernism, in the wake of Darwin's unprecedented challenge to human exceptionalism, "acknowledges the uncertainty of the species barrier." While writers like T. S. Eliot and Joseph Conrad "cope with that acknowledgment" via a reactionary "displacement of animality onto a disenfranchised [human] other," writers like Barnes and D. H. Lawrence respond with an affirmative "privileging of the animal . . . that disrupts the 'human' at its core." By mapping how "modernist texts variously reentrench, unsettle, and even invert" the traditionally hierarchical relationship between humans and other animals, Rohman reveals the modernist roots of the posthumanist critique of speciesist discourses.[4] Peter Meedom similarly argues that *Nightwood* challenges the human/animal hierarchy by refusing to "present us with a recognizable description of the human as residing above the animal." Rather than posit "the animal [as] a previous state to which the human can 'return,'" Meedom proposes that the novel's final scene presents Robin and the dog as "creatures that are no longer in a binary world but in a world of multiple differences and mutual loss" of the certainty afforded by individuated models of subjectivity.[5]

Yet even these posthumanist readings of *Nightwood*, though consistent with Barnes's desire to challenge "the debased meaning now put on that nice word beast," do not account for the distinctive dogginess of the final scene.[6] While Rohman's reading persuasively demonstrates how Barnes "ultimately *revises* the category 'human'" through "a recuperation of animality," it leaves the corresponding category of "animal" largely intact.[7] Andrew Kalaidjian likewise compellingly demonstrates how Barnes dissolves human fantasies of both domination of and escape into nature—revealing instead that "nature's dark forces are present regardless of how artificially controlled one's environment is"—yet he concludes that "*Nightwood* ends with a 'letting be' of *animal* and human," thereby effacing the particularity of the dog.[8] Such erasures of species difference within the category "animal" bring to mind Derrida's influential critique of that word in *The Animal That Therefore I Am*, a 1997 collection of lectures widely regarded as marking an animal turn in his later work (although Derrida insists that "the question . . . of the living animal . . . will always have been the most important and decisive question," one that he has been addressing all along—"since I began writing, in fact").[9] Western humanism's construction of the animal as a homogenous category neatly separable from the human, Derrida argues, belies the unfathomable diversity and complexity of nonhuman life:

> Beyond the edge of the *so-called* human, beyond it but by no means on a single opposing side, rather than "The Animal" or "Animal Life" there is already a heterogeneous multiplicity of the living, or more precisely . . . a multiplicity of organizations of relations between living and dead, relations . . . among realms that are more and more difficult to dissociate by means of the figures of the organic and inorganic, of life and/or death. These relations are at once intertwined and abyssal, and they can never be totally objectified. They do not leave room for any simple exteriority of one term with respect to another. It follows that one will never have the right to take animals to be the species of a kind that would be named The Animal, or animal in general.[10]

As Barnes signals by adding scare quotes when referencing "the psychology of the 'animal'" in her letter to Coleman, the creature whom Robin encounters at the end of *Nightwood* is not the animal in this generic sense. Rather, he is a member of a species that, Donna Haraway reminds us, exists in an "obligatory, constitutive, historical, protean relationship with human beings"—a relationship in which "none of the partners pre-exist the relating, and the relating is never done once and for all."[11]

Dogs' intimate proximity to the human, as the end of *Nightwood* unnervingly illustrates, means that dogs are uniquely positioned to dismantle the humanist myth of a self-transparent subject differentiated from the animal by its rational autonomy and linguistic ability. While Robin seems to have no difficulty "speaking in a low voice to the animals" as she wanders "the open country" just a few paragraphs before the final scene, it is precisely the encounter with the dog that initiates her descent into what Donna Gerstenberger calls "a world in which human speech is not possible."[12] The positive tenor of interpretations like Rohman's is complicated by the fact that the dog is clearly frightened by Robin's inhuman behavior—he retreats to a corner, "claw[s] sideways at the wall," and bites at her in desperation—and that both woman and beast ultimately "[give] up."[13] The final image of Robin lying on the floor, the dog's "head flat along her knees," suggests that the two achieve a communion of sorts, but the novel remains deeply ambivalent about the nature of their connection. Simultaneously "obscene and touching," this scene evokes, in Haraway's words, the "brutalities as well as multiform beauties" peculiar to the human/dog relationship, making it representative of the complex engagement with the canine spanning modernist literature, science, and philosophy that is the focus of this book.[14]

I read the canine encounter in *Nightwood* as a particularly salient example of a widespread but unexamined tendency in literary modernism: going to the dogs. From the strays wandering the streets of Dublin in James Joyce's *Ulysses* to the highbred subject of Virginia Woolf's *Flush*, dogs populate a range of modernist texts yet remain notably underrepresented in critical accounts of the period. When the figure of the dog has managed to garner critical attention within modernist studies, it has typically been dismissed as a mere metaphor for the fragmentation and degradation of the modern human subject. Dana Seitler, for example, reads the final scene in *Nightwood* as expressing "the dehumanizing effects of modernization" by staging "the corporeal ruination of the human."[15] S. A. Cowan similarly reads a canine image in Eliot's *Waste Land*—in which a dog threatens to "dig ... up" a corpse in an ironic betrayal of his role as "friend to men"—as signifying "the decay and extinction of spirit that is [the poem's] most prominent theme."[16] And Philip Howard Solomon regards the canine figures in the late modernist fiction of Samuel Beckett as "structural device[s]" that reveal the human characters with whom they are associated to be "lowly dogs."[17] Even scholars who resist the temptation to read dogs as ipso facto emblems of degraded humanity tend to regard them as representatives of the animal or animality in the generic sense, emphasizing, as Rohman does, how they blur the species boundary in light of Darwin's revelation of biological kinship between humans and other animals.

Undoubtedly, modernist representations of animals serve in part to register Darwin's challenge to the human/animal binary, and studies like Rohman's lay vital groundwork for understanding modernism's complex and multifaceted engagement with the so-called animal question. The title of Rohman's *Stalking the Subject* encapsulates how "the specter of the animal profoundly threatens the sovereignty of the Western subject of consciousness in modernist literature, and [thus] our understanding of that literature is incomplete without accounting for this complex threat."[18] Recasting Rohman's formulation as "dogging the subject" (the title of my fourth chapter and an implicit theme of the entire book), I build on her work to show how attending to nonhuman animals in their individual and species particularity can yield crucial insight into modernism's response to "the species problematic" that haunts the human subject. In particular, looking at the figure of the dog enables me to go beyond examining modernist critiques of human exceptionalism to highlight another, equally significant implication of evolutionary theory that has been largely ignored within modernist studies: the contingent mutability of species.

By "contingent mutability" I mean something more than what Paul Sheehan has in mind when he notes in *Modernism, Narrative, and Humanism* that the "mechanism of natural selection" explains the human as a product of "chance and necessity rather than divine guidance," with the result that "evolution naturalised the human being by emphasizing its animal origins."[19] Tim Armstrong, too, alludes to but does not fully articulate the contingent nature of species being when he observes in *Modernism, Technology, and the Body* that "Darwinian science suggested a substrata [sic] of primitive material within the body and brain, and aroused widespread fears of regression, destabilizing relations between self and world. The body became a more contingent mechanism, incorporating evolutionary survivals."[20] Left out of these descriptions are the interspecies relations that propel the contingent mechanism of natural selection, with the result that the human body not only evinces its own animal ancestry but also bears traces of the countless other species in whose company it evolved.

The revelation of the human's "animal origins" or "primitive substratum" complicates any rigid distinction between the human and other animals, but its potential to unseat the human from its privileged position atop the species hierarchy is limited. Social Darwinism and the other teleological interpretations of evolutionary processes that proliferated in the late Victorian era, Rohman notes, betray "a residual humanism" insofar as they resituate the human at the pinnacle of "a narrative of purposefulness."[21] Darwin biographer Peter Bowler explains:

> The basic evolutionary position was indeed adopted by a majority of late Victorian thinkers, but their beliefs about *how* we emerged from the apes did not necessarily follow Darwin's own suggestions and certainly did not anticipate the modern viewpoint.... People found that they could reconcile themselves to the prospect of an animal ancestry provided that the evolutionary process was seen as a force driving nature towards a morally significant goal. Instead of seeing ourselves as standing above nature by virtue of our possession of an immortal soul, we became the cutting edge of nature's drive toward the generation of ever-higher mental states.[22]

The humanist frameworks through which evolutionary theory came to be understood in the Victorian era obscure the revolutionary implications of Darwin's ideas—a point Rohman makes via Elizabeth Grosz, who argues that Darwin's understanding of species distinctions as always provisional and unstable "uncannily anticipates Derridean *différance*." By underscoring the arbitrariness with which organisms are classified as species, subspecies, and varieties, Grosz insists, "Darwin inadvertently introduces a fundamental indeterminacy into the largely Newtonian framework he aspired to transpose into the field of natural history: the impossibility of either exact prediction or even precise calculation or designation.... This differentiated his understanding of natural selection from that of his contemporaries and predecessors: [evolutionary] science could not take the ready-made or pregiven unity of individuals or classes for granted but had to understand how any provisional unity and cohesion derives from the oscillations and vacillations of difference. The origin can be nothing but a difference!"[23]

These "oscillations and vacillations of difference" destabilize the human even more fundamentally than does the fact of human/animal kinship. By pointing to the indeterminacy of species difference, Darwin highlights not only the mutability of species, as Grosz notes, but also the role of interspecies relations in shaping all organisms. In *On the Origin of Species*, Darwin calls this implication of his theory of natural selection an insight "of the highest importance": "The structure of every organic being is related, in the most essential yet often hidden manner, to that of all other organic beings, with which it comes into competition for food or residence, or from which it has to escape, or on which it preys." Evolution, in other words, is always *co*-evolution; each species' development is both driven and delimited by "the mutual relations of all organic beings."[24] This insight has profound consequences for post-Darwinian conceptualizations of the human. Darwin's proposition that species—including the human—shape one another through competition, cooperation, parasitism, and predation radically undermines Western humanism's construction of the autonomous, self-authored subject. To extend Armstrong's insight, the human body "harbour[s] a crisis" for modernism not only because it retains traces of its "animal" past but also because it is permeated and perforated by the interspecies relations that enabled its "evolutionary survivals."[25] Herein lies the special significance of the dog for modernism's reconfiguration of the human: as our coevolutionary partners, dogs are specially equipped to expose the human as a contingent being shaped by its material interactions with other species.

Dogs have long been recognized as one of the first domesticated species, yet their coevolutionary relationship with the human complicates even this designation. Domestication is customarily understood as a process of "wild animals' being transformed into something more useful to humans," in the words of *Guns, Germs, and Steel* author Jared Diamond. As this definition indicates, humans tend to think of domestication as something that *happens to* animals; that is, humans actively seek out potentially useful species whose members passively adapt to meet human needs by submitting to selective breeding programs. Thus even while Diamond's study underscores the complexity and limitations of the human role in domestication, his repeated use of the passive voice echoes the familiar narrative of animal submission to human will: "Wolves *were domesticated* . . . to become *our* dogs" (emphasis added). Implicitly, then, domestication remains a process driven by human agency to which animals passively submit. Even those modifications that are not direct results of human intervention are characterized as "automatic evolutionary responses . . . to the altered forces of natural selection operating in human environments as compared with wild environments."[26]

But as Diamond's own account reveals, domestication requires some agency on the part of animals. Cheetahs, for example, "were prized by ancient Egyptians and Assyrians and modern Indians as hunting animals infinitely superior to dogs," yet despite concerted efforts to domesticate such an obviously useful species—rumor has it one of the Mughal emperors of India kept a thousand cheetahs in captivity in a failed attempt to breed them—"cheetahs usually refuse to carry out [their] elaborate courtship ritual inside a cage."[27] Although some individual cheetahs can be tamed, the species has resisted true domestication. The limitations of the domestication model have led cultural theorists and evolutionary biologists to propose that the human/dog relationship is best understood not as a one-way process whereby a fully constituted human species molded the dog to suit its needs, but as what Haraway calls a "still ongoing story of co-evolution."[28] Whereas domestication foregrounds human agency, anthropologist Colin Groves argues that the "human-dog relationship amounts to a very long-lasting symbiosis.... Humans domesticated dogs, and dogs domesticated humans."[29] A host of recent ethological studies have demonstrated how dogs, in their long history as humans' working partners and companions, have developed an apparently innate capacity to interpret human gestures—something neither their closest relatives (wolves) nor ours (chimpanzees) can do without training.[30] But coevolution works both ways. Whereas domestication is often figured as a process of "humanizing" dogs, coevolutionary logic indicates that the human is likewise "dogged," and scientists are beginning to understand dogs' probable role in shaping the course of human biological and cultural development.

Anthropologist Pat Shipman has hypothesized that dogs helped *Homo sapiens* outcompete Neandertals, partially answering the question of why the latter went extinct while the former flourished in the same habitat: "The dominance of modern humans could have been in part a consequence of domesticating dogs—possibly combined with a small, but key, change in human anatomy that made people better able to communicate with dogs." Shipman points to studies that suggest that the emergence of dogs coincided with the period during which Neandertals were in steep decline, and to a study that indicates "that the modern-human population grew so rapidly [during this period] that it overwhelmed Neandertals with its sheer numbers." Noting dogs' likely role in promoting this growth by serving as pack animals and hunting companions, she further speculates that the prominent white sclerae unique to human eyes "could have enhanced human-dog communication," and that this "reciprocal communication" may have proved "instrumental in the survival of our species" by making humans more efficient and effective hunters.[31]

The human brain might even bear physical traces of our evolutionary cooperation with dogs. Domestication often results in reduced brain size because it renders certain energy-expensive neurological functions superfluous. But animal scientist Temple Grandin, citing Groves's research, notes that coevolution may have caused *both* human and dog brains to shrink by 10 percent, with the human brain appearing to have shrunk in areas that manage "emotions and sensory data" (especially olfaction) and the dog brain in areas responsible for "planning and organizing." By enabling each other to develop more "specialized" brains, Grandin explains, "dogs and people coevolved and became even better partners, allies, and friends."[32] While research of this kind is still in its infancy, it is difficult to believe that humans would not be shaped in part by our evolutionary relationship with one of the oldest "domesticated" species. Thus Haraway warns that "it is a mistake to see the alterations of dogs' bodies and minds as biological and the changes in human bodies and lives, for example in the emergence of herding or agricultural societies, as cultural, and so not about co-evolution."[33] Instead, the mutually constitutive nature of the human/dog relationship irreparably dissolves boundaries between nature and culture, evolution and history.

Although such distinctions are untenable, dogs, by virtue of their intimate relationship with the human, are sometimes regarded as confirming John Berger's influential thesis about the disappearance of "real" animals in modernity. Prior to the rise of industrialized capitalism, Berger argues in his 1977 essay "Why Look at Animals?," animals "were with man at the centre of his world."[34] But the nineteenth and twentieth centuries witnessed a "rupture" (3) whereby humans became "irredeemabl[y] . . . isolated" from their animal kin (28). Berger attributes this rupture to the forces of modernization: "During the 20th century, the internal combustion engine displaced draught animals in streets and factories. Cities, growing at an ever increasing rate, transformed the surrounding countryside into suburbs where field animals, wild or domesticated, became rare. The commercial exploitation of certain species . . . rendered them almost extinct" (12–13). The animals who remained in physical proximity to the human—in zoos, industrialized agriculture, research laboratories, and a rapidly expanding pet industry—were not real animals at all but only surrogates for the animal companions whom the forces of modernity had expelled from human routines and consciousness. Unlike the real animals they replaced, they could not "scrutinise" the human, making him "aware of himself returning the look" (5).

For Berger, animals' disappearance is ironically most visible in the distinctly "modern innovation" of the pet, a creature "either sterilised or sexually isolated, extremely limited in its exercise, deprived of almost all other animal contact, and fed with artificial foods" (14). The dog, in this account, is no more capable of scrutinizing the human than is the zoo animal who exists only as a "living monument to [its] own disappearance" (26). Indeed, dogs' unmatched attunement to the human gaze may well underwrite Berger's claim that the pet functions only as a "mirror" that reflects to her owner "the-special-man-he-is-only-to-his-pet" (15). Gilles Deleuze and Félix Guattari similarly dismiss pets as "sentimental, Oedipal animals" who "draw us into a narcissistic contemplation."[35] Yet as Haraway demonstrates in an extended critique of this passage, Deleuze and Guattari's disdain for "little house dogs and the people who love them" exposes how their theory of becoming-animal "feeds off a series of primary dichotomies figured by the opposition between the wild and the domestic." By virtue of their coevolutionary relationship with humans, dogs are uniquely positioned to dissolve such dichotomies; thus in writing them off, Deleuze and Guattari reject potentially ideal accomplices in their "sustained work against the monomaniacal, cyclopean, Oedipal subject"—a project Haraway and her companions take up in *When Species Meet*.[36]

Ironically, the trope of the dog as a mirror for human narcissism has its probable origins in dogs' special adeptness at returning the human gaze. The consequent potency of the canine gaze—itself a product of human/dog coevolution—is evident in Rainer Maria Rilke's short story "A Meeting," in which a stray dog attempts to persuade a man to adopt him. The dog follows the man "unobtrusively, devotedly, without an opinion of his own, the way a dog follows his master," until his "precisely aimed, remarkably sure glances" finally succeed in capturing the man's attention. Yet the man refuses his request, explaining, "Your nature has a tendency to subordinate itself to mine. In the end a responsibility would arise, which I can't accept. You wouldn't notice how completely you had come to trust me; you would overvalue me and expect from me what I can't perform."[37] The pathos of this scene indicates how, even within the already denigrated category of the pet, the dog is frequently singled out for disparagement or pity. Consider, for example, the sharp contrast between the imploring and devoted dog in "A Meeting" and the inscrutable subject of Rilke's poem "Black Cat": "She turns her face to yours; / and with a shock, you see yourself, tiny, / inside the golden amber of her eyeballs / suspended, like a prehistoric fly."[38] While the dog looks at the human and "approve[s] of everything"—his thoughts plain enough for the narrator to report without qualification—the impenetrable (and frequently feminized) gaze of the cat exposes the human's cosmic insignificance.[39] Animals, Rilke proposes in his preface to a book about a cat, are able "to belong our world" to the extent that they "consent . . . to our way of life." In contrast to cats, who belong to a "world . . . which they inhabit exclusively" and that the human cannot access, dogs strive to adapt themselves to the human world: "Their confidential and admiring nearness is such that certain of them seem to have renounced their most ancient canine traditions, in order to adore our habits, and even our errors. This is precisely what makes them tragic and sublime. Their decision to admit us forces them to live, so to speak, at the very boundaries of their nature, which they constantly pass beyond with their humanized gaze and their nostalgic muzzle."[40]

This figuring of the dog as tragically sublime indicates how dogs came to embody the feelings of fragmentation and alienation that accompanied modernity. After all, the rapid urbanization and industrialization that generated a crisis of the human subject in the late nineteenth and early twentieth centuries had a similarly profound impact on man's proverbial best friend. In this period in America and Britain, breed fanciers codified standards that would shape future canine generations, municipalities established animal-control practices that would affect millions of urban dogs, and the now multibillion-dollar pet industry began its rise with the introduction of commercial dog food and mass production of puppies. In many ways, the dog became a potent symbol of the modern condition—facing, like the human species, the challenge of adapting to modernizing forces that relentlessly outpaced it.

In particular, dogs became central to debates about the potentially degenerative effects of modernity. Thus, for example, the bourgeois bohemians for whom the semiautobiographical protagonist of Wyndham Lewis's *Tarr* expresses such disdain are repeatedly described in canine terms. Tarr's antagonist, Otto Kreisler, "a clumsy and degenerate atavism," is nowhere more pathetic than in his desire to assume the role of a woman's pet dog: "He would be her dog! Lie at her feet!" While pondering this wish, Kreisler smiles—in a description that recalls Rilke's excessively approving dog—"with really something of the misplaced and unaccountable pathos and protest of dogs (although still with a slavish wagging of the tail) at some pleasantry of the master."[41] Max Nordau similarly posits a specifically canine atavism as evidence of human enfeeblement in *Degeneration*, his 1892 polemic against decadent art and literature. Disparaging the "aesthetic folly" of writers who assign "high importance" to "the olfactory sensations," he writes, "Smellers among degenerates represent an atavism going back, not only to the primeval period of man, but infinitely more remote still, to an epoch anterior to man. Their atavism retrogrades to animals amongst whom sexual activity was directly excited by odoriferous substances . . . or who, like the dog, obtained their knowledge of the world by the action of their noses."[42]

Dogs' olfactory proficiency likewise explains their prominent role in Freud's theory of organic repression—the rejection of animality that coincided with the transition to erect posture and enabled the rise of human civilization—in *Civilization and Its Discontents*: "It would be incomprehensible . . . that man should use the name of his most faithful friend in the animal world—the dog—as a term of abuse if that creature had not incurred his contempt through two characteristics: that it is an animal whose dominant sense is that of smell and one which has no horror of excrement, and that it is not ashamed of its sexual functions."[43] Of course, dogs are far from the only species to navigate the world with nose to the ground and to copulate without shame, yet their engagement in such behaviors while in intimate proximity to the human serves as a continual reminder of the repressed animality that resides in the human unconscious. The canine thus became a particularly powerful metaphor through which modernist writers expressed anxiety about the return of the repressed in the form of atavistic regression.

Beyond merely symbolizing a primitive substratum perpetually threatening to erupt from within the human, dogs themselves were undergoing dramatic morphological changes that served as material warnings of the unpredictable and potentially degenerative effects of modern sociocultural conditions. As the titles of breed compendia like *The Twentieth Century Dog* (1904) and *The New Book of the Dog* (1907) suggest, early twentieth-century dog fanciers regarded their historical moment as a pivotal one for the human/dog relationship, following the establishment of the (British) Kennel Club in 1873, the New York-based Westminster Kennel Club in 1876, and the American Kennel Club (of which Westminster became a member club) in 1884. The emergence of these clubs as governing authorities of the purebred dog world in the late nineteenth century represented an unprecedented move toward standardization of breeds that were, by and large, not ancient types but recent inventions. The result was, in the words of Michael Worboys, "nothing less than *the invention of the modern dog*, as the species was reimagined and remade into discrete, separated and standard physical forms."⁴⁴ Driving this transformation was a transatlantic purebred dog culture that profoundly reshaped dogs and their place in British and North American societies.⁴⁵ As Herbert Compton explains in *The Twentieth Century Dog*, the show ring came to dictate "the type of perfection to be striven for" in each breed, making "the verdict it issues" of paramount importance for breeders and owners endeavoring to achieve "public fame in the dog-world."⁴⁶ The kennel clubs thus shaped—quite literally—the future of recognized breeds, consequently raising what one breeder called "the much-debated question as to whether the practice of dog-showing tends to the improvement or deterioration of the breed."⁴⁷ Breeders and dog enthusiasts on one side of this debate worried that the aesthetic aims of modern breeding were transforming formerly noble breeds into degenerate caricatures of their predecessors.

Others in the purebred dog world, though, held a considerably more optimistic view of the kennel clubs' impact on the future of dogs. In *The New Book of the Dog*, Robert Leighton notes with approval, "One can nowadays seldom enter a dwelling in which the dog is not recognised as a member of the family, and it is noticeable that the family dog is becoming less of a mongrel and more of a distinguishable and accredited breed."⁴⁸ Compton similarly embraces the transition of dogs from utility animals to household companions and the consequent efforts of breeders to produce more desirable pets. Further, both writers, though expressing occasional concerns about modifications to specific breeds, offer an overwhelmingly positive assessment of the changes to canine bodies and populations achieved through modern breeding. Criticizing past generations of dog owners for permitting "the promiscuous mingling of alien breeds," Leighton praises his contemporaries for exerting more calculated control: "At no other time . . . have the various canine types been kept more rigidly distinct or brought to a higher level of perfection."⁴⁹ Compton not only echoes this sentiment but explicitly aligns the achievements of modern breeding with modernity itself: "The dogs of England have changed almost as much as the map of Europe during the last hundred years. The elaborated type the twentieth century opened upon was as dissimilar to its original family as we to our Saxon ancestors." Placing the dogs of the past "on a par with mail-coaches, mahogany furniture, oil-illumination, and other obsolete and crude examples of the daily life and civilisation of those days," he likens twentieth-century breeds to modern technologies like "motor-cars and Marconigrams."⁵⁰

The phenomenon of the breed dog is itself inextricably linked with industrialized modernity. As Michael Worboys, Julie-Marie Strange, and Neil Pemberton argue in *The Invention of the Modern Dog*, "breed makes dogs modern because it was a new way of thinking about, defining, and increasing the variety of forms within the species *Canis lupus familiaris*."[51] Of course, the long history of human/dog coevolution saw the emergence of numerous canine varieties, but prior to modern dog breeding, differences between these varieties tended to correspond to differences in their environments and the functions they performed for (or in cooperation with) their human companions. As Martin Wallen observes, "pre-nineteenth-century commentators described [dogs] mostly in terms of variability and adaptable utility," but the emergence of the concept of the breed dog beginning in the mid-eighteenth century gave rise to a distinctly "modern dog" and correspondingly novel "human-dog relations."[52] The production of modern breeds accelerated in the nineteenth century, leading Worboys, Strange, and Pemberton to describe them as "thoroughly Victorian inventions, influenced by industrialization, commercialization, class and gender attitudes, the rise of leisure, and evolutionary thinking."[53] It is hardly surprising, then, that purebred dogs—particularly those bred to occupy laps in the upper echelons of human society—soon became emblems of modern decadence and degeneracy.

Yet dogs' coevolutionary relationship with the human means that they are more than just metaphors for the modern condition. Recasting Rilke's characterization of dogs as living "at the very boundaries of their nature," the texts I examine in this book illustrate that the canine encounter persistently pushes the human to the limits of its own nature. The "few moments" during which the man in Rilke's "A Meeting" is "truly unsettled" by the look of the dog, coupled with the "longing" glance he casts back after departing, point to the penetrating and destabilizing power of the canine gaze.[54] And Deleuze and Guattari, despite their wry declaration that "*anyone who likes cats or dogs is a fool*," grant that "any animal" can become one of the "pack or affect animals that form a multiplicity, a becoming, a population, a tale. . . . Even the cat, even the dog."[55] A coevolutionary understanding of the human/dog relationship clarifies why works like "A Meeting" figure dogs as *especially* capable of breaching the borders of the human. Because humans and dogs are reciprocally inscribed with morphological and neurological traces of their shared evolutionary history, the dog is eminently capable of drawing the human *out of* the "narcissistic contemplation" into which the pet ostensibly invites it. As Erica Fudge observes, cohabiting with dogs "requires an imaginative leap. 'What is my dog thinking?' is a question that might only be answered by attempting to think with a dog: something impossible to achieve and yet necessary to attempt by anyone who lives with a dog."[56] The co-constitutive and cooperative nature of the human/dog relationship thus places interpretive and communicative demands on both partners that disrupt human self-absorption. The profound sense of "responsibility" that the narrator of "A Meeting" experiences indicates that even an unknown dog can hail the human and prompt such imaginative leaps. Moreover, dogs' prominent position in the larger web of relations to which the human owes its being means that the canine encounter draws the human beyond the isolated subject position reserved for it by Western humanism and into the radical multiplicity of interspecies life.

By examining how modernist representations of dogs ultimately mongrelize the human, revealing its animal origins in more ways than one, this book builds on scholarship at the intersection of modernist and animal studies that illuminates the modernist beginnings of a posthumanist critique of the subject. Landmark studies like Rohman's *Stalking the Subject* (2009) and Susan McHugh's *Animal Stories: Narrating Across Species Lines* (2011) have done much to challenge a critical tendency to fuse posthumanism with postmodernism. In *The Postmodern Animal* (2000), for example, Steve Baker proposes "that there was no modern animal, no 'modernist' animal." Modernism, it would seem, signals a caesura in the history of animal representation, a gap "between nineteenth-century animal symbolism, with its reasonably secure hold on meaning, and the postmodern animal images whose ambiguity or irony or sheer brute presence serves to resist or to displace fixed meanings." Baker quotes German expressionist painter Franz Marc's criticism of his cubist and futurist contemporaries for reproducing the "poverty-stricken convention" of "project[ing] *their* inner world" onto animals rather than attempting to imagine subjective experience beyond the human.[57] D. H. Lawrence voices a similar sentiment when he dismisses "anthropomorphism [as] a bore. Too much anthropos makes the world a dull hole." Tellingly, Lawrence illustrates his point with an example drawn from the visual arts—in Greek sculpture, he complains, "if it's a horse, it's an anthropomorphised horse"—and Baker is quick to delimit his own hypothesis as "essentially art-historical in its emphases."[58] As Rohman demonstrates, Lawrence is one of numerous writers whose experimental depictions of animals swiftly undercut any attempt to extend

Baker's critique of modernist art to modernist literature. Indeed, Rohman argues, an "antirationalist recuperation of animality" permeates the very language and form of modernist texts as they perform "the perforation of the humanized subject by its evolutionary connection to animality."[59]

While I do not mean to suggest that literary forms, unlike the visual arts, have the capacity to provide unmediated access to animal experience, several of the writers whose work I examine in the following chapters share Marc's keen interest in nonhuman interiority. Jack London, in his limited-omniscient narratives of canine experience, eschews both anthropomorphic projection and the anthropocentric denial of Darwinian continuity, and his exclusion from most studies of literary modernism belies the impact of his innovations on more celebrated writers like Barnes, Faulkner, and Woolf. Moreover, the coevolutionary nature of the human/dog relationship means that modernist experiments with the canine are vital pieces of a broader reconfiguration of the human. As Cary Wolfe argues, "The figure of the 'animal' in the West . . . is part of a cultural and literary history stretching back at least to Plato and the Old Testament, reminding us that the animal has always been especially, frightfully nearby, always lying in wait at the very heart of the constitutive disavowals and self-constructing narratives enacted by that fantasy figure called 'the human.'"[60] Throughout the course of this history, few animals have been as "frightfully nearby" as the dog. The scene from *Nightwood* with which I began, and the similarly destabilizing human/dog interactions I examine throughout this book, demonstrate how the modernist dog, like Baker's postmodern animal, "serves to resist or to displace fixed meanings." In this way, it prefigures the posthumanism of Derrida, Haraway, and Wolfe. This posthumanism, Wolfe clarifies, "isn't posthuman at all—in the sense of being 'after' our embodiment has been transcended"; rather, it is "posthuman*ist*" in that it decenters the human, revealing its "embeddedness" in coevolutionary mechanisms and exposing "humanism as a historically specific phenomenon" rather than an ahistorical truth.[61]

Haraway's *Companion Species Manifesto* (2003) and *When Species Meet* (2008) generated unprecedented interest among humanities scholars in relations between companion species, but this book begins by demonstrating how writers and scientists in the modernist period were already reaching across disciplinary divides to theorize human/dog coevolution and its implications for the human subject. Chapter 1, "Canine Origins: Jack London and Konrad Lorenz," illuminates London's impact on Lorenz, the Austrian biologist and Nobel Prize–winning cofounder of ethology whose pioneering approach to canine evolution and behavior profoundly influenced subsequent generations of canid biologists. I demonstrate that London and Lorenz both take for granted the coevolutionary nature of the human/dog relationship as a logical implication of Darwinian theory. In their respective narratives of canine origins, London and Lorenz dramatize the initial contact between humans and dogs as a formative but problematic moment in the course of human evolution. Cooperation with dogs, they propose, fostered physical and behavioral adaptations that enabled the human to transcend its animal origins. In helping to "civilize" the human, though, dogs accelerated modern humans' much-bemoaned separation from the natural world. The coevolutionary logic of these origin stories thus implicates dogs in broader modernist concerns about the damaging and ultimately degenerative effects of overcivilization. I read London's fiction and Lorenz's popular dog books as attempts to redeem the human/dog relationship from this conundrum. By providing a link to humans' primitive past, both writers ultimately insist, dogs promise to heal the very rupture they helped create.

While chapter 1 concerns a writer not widely hailed as a modernist innovator, the presence of dogs in the more celebrated work of Pound, Joyce, Stein, Faulkner, and others reveals the category of the canine as a particularly rich site for formal experimentation. Chapter 2, "Mongrelizing Form: Virginia Woolf's *Flush*," examines how Woolf uses canine being to reimagine novelistic form and character in her speculative biography of Elizabeth Barrett Browning's cocker spaniel. While *Flush* was long dismissed as a diversion from Woolf's more serious endeavors—or taken seriously only insofar as it could be read as a feminist or antifascist allegory—I read it as Woolf's most genre-bending work, revealing how it strategically mongrelizes the Victorian animal "autobiography" epitomized by Anna Sewell's *Black Beauty* and Marshall Saunders's *Beautiful Joe*, the naturalistic animal story developed by Jack London, and the modernist bildungsromans of writers like Joyce, Lawrence, and Thomas Mann. Ever wary of being dismissed as a "ladylike prattler," Woolf adeptly navigates the literary minefield of animal narratives, resisting both the sentimental anthropomorphism of Victorian animal biographies and the hypermasculine primitivism of London's Darwinian works. I show how Woolf uses the intertwined *Bildung* plots of Flush and Elizabeth to critique the anthropocentrism that underwrites the phallocentric literary tradition against which she positions her own work, and to explore how interspecies entanglements give shape to human and nonhuman character alike.

Moving between Jack London's idealized primitive realm and the cosmopolitan settings of Woolf's fiction, dogs occupy a vexed position in relation to the modern city. Chapter 3, "The New Dog: Albert Payson Terhune and J. R. Ackerley," examines the work of two dramatically different figures united by concerns about the incongruity of canine bodies in urban spaces. In modern America and Britain, rapid rural decline and urban expansion combined to put most working breeds out of a job, raising the question of whether (and how) dogs and the human/dog relationship should adapt to the new economy. Terhune's enormously popular Lad stories—which catapulted both him and his collies to fame and made him the highest-paid writer in America—present the working dog as a defender of rural America from the encroachment of a decadent urban modernity embodied by the dandified pedigree dog. Terhune's collie, like his vision of the human/dog relationship, is thus irreconcilable to the space of the city. Ackerley similarly exposes tensions between working breeds and modern urban life, and his Alsatian heroines in *My Dog Tulip* and *We Think the World of You* figure as excess in the context of postwar London. Yet although Ackerley offers an incisive critique of how city life polices canine bodies, he also insists that dogs read, mark, and shape urban spaces. Whereas Terhune represents the city as a man-made, and therefore unnatural, environment, Ackerley positions dogs as active participants in constructing—and potentially transforming—urban modernity.

Chapter 4, "Dogging the Subject: Samuel Beckett and Emmanuel Levinas," outlines the ontological and ethical challenges that emerge from modernism's reconfiguration of the human/dog relationship and intensify in the aftermath of World War II. Specifically, I examine the destabilizing presence of dogs in Beckett's late-modernist fiction—especially *Watt* and *Molloy*—and in Levinas's neohumanist philosophy. Beckett and Levinas situate the dog in a unique position within what Derrida deems the sacrificial structure of Western humanism, wherein the animal is excluded from subjectivity through both discursive and literal sacrifice. The dog, as animal, belongs to a realm of abjection that defines the humanist subject through negation; yet, as Beckett and Levinas insinuate, dogs also participate in the sacrifice of other animals, complicating the ethical quandary in which Western humanism finds itself vis-à-vis the animal. As humans' longtime hunting and herding partners and as consumers of the by-products of industrialized slaughter, dogs signal the impossibility of a world without sacrifice even as they challenge the sacrificial logic of humanist subject formation. In Beckett's fiction and Levinas's philosophy, dogs disrupt the voice so central to humanist configurations of the subject with their silent call for a posthumanist ethics that accounts not just for the relative alterity of the human other but for the radical alterity and heterogeneity of the animal.

This book foregrounds the novel and its close relatives, the speculative biography and the memoir, not because dogs' presence in literary modernism is limited to these forms—far from it—but because dogs' destabilizing power is especially potent in these ostensibly humanistic representational modes. Rohman discerns a "distinctly modernist formal embodiment of the animal problem" in the innovations of writers like Eliot, Lawrence, Barnes, and Conrad. While Victorian texts register the impact of Darwinian continuity via "a *thematic* and primarily metaphorical interest in animality," modernist texts, she argues, do so via a "breakdown of traditional literary syntax, structure, and narration [and] the introduction of circuitous and unstable narrative devices"—innovations that "line up with the post-Darwinian eruption of 'non-human,' chaotic forces" both within and beyond the human.[62] This "eruption," I argue, reverberates with particular force in narrative forms, whose appeal has long been attributed narrowly to their capacity to give shape to human experience. As Frank Kermode postulates in his 1966 study *The Sense of an Ending*, narrative "humanizes time by giving it form," thus fulfilling a basic need to infuse human experience with order and meaning. We demand stories that "make sense, give comfort ... [and] testify to the continuity of what is called human nature."[63] By this account, narrative forms define and preserve our humanity by obscuring the radical contingency of the human, thereby enforcing the ever-tenuous human/animal boundary.

Yet, as Sheehan notes in *Modernism, Narrative, and Humanism*, the serializing and totalizing forces of narrative mean that it—like the linguistic archive from which it draws—"has the potential to exceed the limits of anthropological mastery."[64] Thus narrative is not necessarily human-shaped; instead, its persistence in the face of the anti- and posthumanisms of the past century demonstrates narrative's potential to transcend the boundaries of human experience, dissolving fantasies of human exceptionalism and rational autonomy. McHugh argues that the appeal of the novel form lies not in its capacity to represent individual human experience—what Georg Lukács famously calls "the autonomous life of interiority"—but instead in "its usefulness for experiments with multiple perspectives and processes that support models centered on agency rather than subjectivity."[65] This capacity, as Ivan Kreilkamp has recently demonstrated in *Minor Creatures: Persons, Animals, and the Victorian Novel*, is partially visible in the Victorian realist novel, which, in its depictions of human-animal relationships, "always contains a creaturely, transspecies presence and potential." Ultimately, though, Victorian realism "hesitates at the boundary of the human, a boundary that it approaches, worries, and at times transgresses but never jettisons entirely."[66]

Beginning in the modernist period, the novel—arguably the most human-shaped of literary forms—has been adapted to the task of deconstructing the category of the human and the assumptions of Western humanism via techniques like multiple and fragmented perspectives, stream-of-consciousness and free indirect narration, and interpenetrating and nonlinear temporalities. In this book, I demonstrate both the thematic and formal "dogginess" of modernist novels, linking it to dogs' special capacity to challenge the humanist underpinnings of traditional literary forms. The modernist techniques in the narratives I examine, moreover, blur disciplinary distinctions by opening up what David Herman calls "a route of access to the strategies for imagining human-nonhuman relationships that are central to multispecies ethnography, trans-species anthropology, cultural ecology and other emergent frameworks for inquiry."[67] As Caroline Hovanec points out, modernism historically was "a period of mutual legibility between literature and science," with fiction writers and scientists alike grappling with the implications of Darwinian theory for understanding and representing animals (including the human). In pursuit of answers, "the scientists found themselves turning to the methods of fiction and poetry to better express animal subjectivity, while the literary writers found themselves adopting the observational techniques of science."[68] My focus on modernist canine narratives, then, reveals modernism's pivotal position not just in literary history but in the continued evolution of modes of inquiry in the natural and social sciences, as well as dogs' vital role in the ongoing project of deconstructing the humanist subject—a role I discuss in the broader context of literary canine studies in the coda. In the chapters that follow, I demonstrate how modernist narratives figure dogs both as instigators of the crisis of the modern subject and as partners uniquely capable of helping the human and its cultural formations adapt to the turbulent and dehumanizing forces of modernization.

CHAPTER 1

CANINE ORIGINS
Jack London and Konrad Lorenz

I begin the story of modernism's reconfiguration of the human/dog relationship by examining a writer generally excluded, like the dog itself, from critical accounts of literary modernism: Jack London. While London's canine-centered work is typically relegated to the realm of American naturalism or even juvenile fiction, this chapter demonstrates his seminal influence on post-Darwinian understandings of dogs and the corollary concept of the human that span modernist literature and science, blurring the "two cultures" divide famously critiqued by C. P. Snow.[1] Since the publication of *The Call of the Wild* in 1903, critics have noted—whether with disdain or admiration—London's commitment to troubling the species boundary. In 1909, Frederic Taber Cooper criticized London's celebration of animality, protesting, "there is a vast difference between thinking of man as a healthy human animal and thinking of him as an unhealthy human beast,—and the Call-of-the-Wild school of fiction is tending toward precisely this exaggerated and mistaken point of view."[2] Just three years earlier, the poet Carl Sandburg had praised London's novella not only as "the greatest dog-story ever written" but also as "a study of one of the most curious and profound motives that plays hide-and-seek in the human soul. The more civilized we become the deeper is the fear that back in barbarism is something of the beauty and joy of life we have not brought along with us."[3]

Despite considerable critical attention to the theme of animality in London's dog stories, the canine protagonists themselves, as Cooper's condemnation and Sandburg's approval of London's portrait of *human* nature suggest, tend not to be read as "real" animals. Indeed, literary critics have dismissed such interpretations as unsophisticated. As Earle Labor and Robert Leitz contend, reading *The Call of the Wild* as an "entertaining" dog story rather than as "a brilliant human allegory" is "tantamount to reading *Moby-Dick* as a long-winded fisherman's yarn."[4] More recently, Michael Lundblad has advocated reading London's dogs as "men in furs," even in the context of animal studies. Observing that anthropomorphic interpretations of erotically charged passages about the love between London's dogs and their masters have generated "interesting and important discussions of . . . homoerotic interactions between men," he postulates that treatments of London's dogs as "real" animals "might not seem very compelling for literary and cultural critics primarily interested in the politics of how various *human* populations are constructed."[5] A central aim of this book, by contrast, is to demonstrate that attending to canine figures in their species particularity is essential to understanding modernist reconceptualizations of the human and its relationship to animality, making London's dogs of great interest to those concerned with the formation of human subjects and cultures.

While literary critics have long dismissed zoocentric interpretations of London's dogs as "not very compelling"—often implicitly, by treating Buck and White Fang as symbols or proxies rather than as "real" animals—readers of a more scientific persuasion have tended to take London's dogs literally, though their conclusions about the value of his work are just as disparate. The environmental writer Barry Lopez, for example, attributes London's wolf "obsess[ion]" to "a neurotic fixation with machismo that has as little to do with wolves as [does] the drinking, whoring, and fighting side of man's brute nature."[6] London's work has endured more than a century of disparagement from both credentialed and self-styled animal behavior experts, beginning with the so-called nature faker controversy of the early twentieth century. This debate, which raged in the pages of popular magazines for the better part of a decade, began with American naturalist John Burroughs's 1903 diatribe against writers of "sham natural history."[7] London was dragged into the fray in 1907, when Theodore Roosevelt accused him of writing "unnatural nature stories" that promulgated distorted views of animal abilities.[8] Characterizations of London as a nature faker have persisted to the present day; dog ethologists Raymond and Lorna Coppinger, for example, have called London's representation of dogs as barely tamed wolves "not just fiction, but awful fiction."[9]

Yet despite this tendency to downplay differences between dogs and their lupine kin, London's largely unexamined influence on the Nobel Prize–winning Austrian biologist Konrad Lorenz—a "truly great scientist" whom the Coppingers credit with pioneering "the first ethological approach to dog behavior"—reveals his pivotal impact on post-Darwinian understandings of the human/dog relationship.[10] Born in 1903, the year *The Call of the Wild* was published, Lorenz later recalled the "romantic enthusiasm I . . . felt as a boy for Jack London's *White Fang*" in his foreword to a collection of work by leading canid biologists of the 1970s.[11] And while Lorenz's language here paints his regard for London as a boyhood diversion, this characterization is somewhat disingenuous. Although by the time of this book's publication Lorenz had abandoned some of the views he had previously shared with London, in his 1949 popular zoology books *King Solomon's Ring* and *Man Meets Dog*, he enthusiastically praises London's "true-to-life depictions" of "behaviour which he has obviously witnessed himself."[12] This praise is noteworthy given Lorenz's general stinginess in acknowledging even recognized animal experts as true "doggy people"—people, that is, "with a real understanding of dogs." So reliable does he consider London's representations that he cites them not only in these texts but as late as 1963 in *On Aggression*, as veritable evidence of how real dogs and wolves behave.[13]

These references, as Susan McHugh observes in *Animal Stories: Narrating Across Species Lines*, treat London's dog stories not just as engaging fictions but "as early documents and models of ethological notation" that prefigure both the literary experiments of writers like Virginia Woolf (as I discuss in chapter 2) and the scientific investigations of Lorenz and his successors. Lorenz's indebtedness to London signals a kinship between ethology (a branch of biology that emerged alongside the literary innovations of the modernist period) and literary representation, prompting McHugh to theorize a "narrative ethology that underscores the ongoing relevance of the humanities to studies of species in the life sciences, and more specifically integrations of narrative practice and research to defy disciplinary divisions of knowledge." McHugh challenges the notion that narrative's appeal lies in its capacity to represent the autonomous human subject, insisting that "the success of the novel form follows instead from its usefulness for experiments with multiple perspectives," including, crucially, those of nonhuman animals.[14] Narrative thus functions as a valuable tool for scientific and literary methodologies alike. In aligning London's "ghastly realism" with his own ethological praxis, Lorenz points to narrative as a way of knowing that cuts across the "two cultures" divide in both directions.[15]

In what follows, I demonstrate London's and Lorenz's shared investment in using narrative to rethink cross-species entanglements and more-than-human agency, showing how their respective narratives of canine origins position dogs as vital and dynamic characters in the story of human evolution. I begin by tracing the narrative of canine domestication that runs through *The Call of the Wild*, *White Fang*, and *Before Adam* (a novel serialized in *Everybody's Magazine* in the midst of the nature faker controversy), demonstrating how London's representation of the intertwined trajectories of human and canine evolution prefigures Lorenz's influential theory of canine origins and positions the human as a contingent being shaped by companion species relations. Next, I explore the role of canine agency in these narratives, examining the extent to which London and Lorenz anticipate the coevolutionary model of the human/dog relationship now espoused by ethologists like the Coppingers and theorists like Donna Haraway. Finally, I discuss the more problematic implications of London's and Lorenz's insistence on the co-constitutive nature of human and canine evolution—specifically, dogs' role in "domesticating" the human and thus fueling modernist anxieties about the potentially degenerative effects of overcivilization for humans and canines alike. Ultimately, I read London's fiction and Lorenz's popular dog books as attempts to redeem the human/dog relationship in light of this conundrum. Both writers intimate that dogs, despite their complicity in instigating the crisis of the modern subject, promise to heal the very rupture they have created by functioning as a vital link to humans' animal past.

Proto-Man Meets Proto-Dog

While London's critics and admirers alike have long observed how his complex portraits of canine experience blur the species divide, thereby undermining human uniqueness, the broader narrative of canine domestication that spans his oeuvre destabilizes the human even more fundamentally. In positing that dogs and humans have shaped each other through their material interactions, London radically undermines cherished beliefs in human autonomy and exceptionalism that persisted even in the wake of Darwin's revelation of human/animal kinship. An episode from *Before Adam* illustrates the significance of canine domestication for London's understanding of human evolution. The novel features a modern American man who relives, in vivid dreams, the experiences of a Mid-Pleistocene ancestor named Big-Tooth. Big-Tooth and his modern counterpart are collapsed into a single narrator who recounts these dreams in a series of loosely connected episodes. Although dogs as such do not appear in this novel, one chapter features an episode in which Big-Tooth kidnaps a wild canid puppy and thus nearly "[brings] about the domestication of the dog"—an achievement that he insists would have constituted "a very great discovery."[16] How great a discovery the reader can only infer, as the pup dies and the novel ends before any human/canine partnership can form, but London indicates the nature of dogs' impact on human evolution when his narrator observes that Big-Tooth's failure to domesticate the dog "possibly set back our social development many generations" (100).

To underscore the potential significance of this discovery, the narrator elaborates at length on humans' primitive status in Big-Tooth's time. There were then three humanoid species: the Tree People, who resemble chimpanzees; the Fire People, who most closely resemble modern humans; and the Folk, the intermediate species to which Big-Tooth belongs. The Folk "were just getting started" and "were without weapons, without fire, and in the raw beginnings of speech. The device of writing lay so far in the future that I am appalled when I think of it" (99). Although the Folk are significantly closer to human than are the Tree People, they lack (or exhibit only rudimentary forms of) characteristics long regarded in Western cultures as evidence of human transcendence of animality. The narrator is particularly disgusted by his ancestors' "inconsequentiality and stupidity" (95). In fact, in a move that recalls London's sometimes clunky attempts to avoid anthropomorphism in his dog stories, the narrator clarifies, "It is I, the modern, who look back across the centuries and weigh and analyze the emotions and motives of Big-Tooth, my other self" (137). Big-Tooth and the rest of the Folk, incapable of such introspection, are essentially animals.

Despite the cognitive simplicity of the Folk and the fact that the Fire People more closely resemble *Homo sapiens*, the novel does not allow modern readers to distance themselves from Big-Tooth and his "inconsequential" brethren. Rather, London explains the survival of Big-Tooth's memories in his narrator's subconscious via "a straight line of descent" from the Folk to modern humans (241). Big-Tooth's experiences, we are told, triggered "molecular changes [that] were transmitted to the cerebral cells of progeny," inscribing in the narrator's subconscious "racial memories" that manifest themselves as dreams (14). In other words, the narrator attributes his dreams, in Lamarckian fashion, to the inheritance of acquired characteristics and behaviors. This explanation deepens the significance of Big-Tooth's attempt to domesticate the dog—something that even the Fire People have yet to accomplish. In a Lamarckian framework, an encounter between an individual humanoid and a wild dog would leave molecular traces on both, transmitting memories of the interaction to subsequent generations. Moreover, the intermediate evolutionary status of the Folk suggests that the domestication of dogs might help complete the untold sequence of events between Big-Tooth's final memory and the emergence of modern *Homo sapiens*. Indeed, the fateful tone of the narrator's recollection of the wild dog episode breaks noticeably with the novel's overarching emphasis on the random and fortuitous nature of evolutionary progress. Despite the narrator's repeated insistence that "our lives and destinies are shaped by the merest chance" (157), he notes, "I had no reason that I knew for wanting to carry the puppy to the cave, except that I *wanted* to; and I stayed by my task" (108). Big-Tooth demonstrates "more pertinacity than the average Folk" in his quest to bring the puppy back to his cave, underscoring the uncharacteristic deliberateness of his actions (109).

Indeed, the narrator's characterization of Big-Tooth's failure as a major setback in the social development of the Folk posits the domestication of the dog as a formative event in human evolution. Comparisons between the novel's three humanoid species repeatedly stress that it is precisely their degree of social development that elevates the Folk above the Tree People and the Fire People above the Folk. This point is made most clearly through Red-Eye, a member of the Folk whom the narrator describes as "an atavism . . . a reversion to an earlier type [whose] place was with the Tree People rather than with us who were in the process of becoming men" (111). Red-Eye's primitivism—marked by his extreme hairiness, awkward carriage, and propensity to "run on all-fours" (59)—appears most tellingly in his antisocial behavior: "Rude as was our social organization, he was, nevertheless, too rude to live in it" (111). By contrast, the Fire People's superior social organization and use of language enable them to become "the most terrible of all the hunting animals that ranged the primeval world" (197). If dogs did facilitate human social development, as the narrator speculates, then their domestication would help explain the leap forward from the increasingly sophisticated social configurations of London's hominid species to those of modern humans.

The physical differences between the Folk and the Fire People, and between these and modern *Homo sapiens*, further suggest that the domesticated dog has quite literally shaped the human, an implication also present in *The Call of the Wild*. Big-Tooth is born in an age during which his species is "in the process of changing our tree-life to life on the ground. For many generations we had been going through this change, and our bodies and carriage had likewise changed" (59). Prefiguring Freud's theory of "organic repression," outlined in *Civilization and Its Discontents*, in which Freud reasons that "the fateful process of civilization would thus have set in with man's adoption of an erect posture," the transition to the upright carriage required for bipedal locomotion is central to the progress narrative that *Before Adam* dramatizes.[17] Just as Red-Eye's hairiness and stooped posture denote his atavistic status, less hair and a more erect posture mark the Fire People as more advanced—further along in the process of "becoming men." The humanoid species that Buck envisions in *The Call of the Wild*, likewise occupying an intermediate position between arboreal and terrestrial life, is a sort of composite that prefigures London's later depictions of the Folk and the Fire People. In dreams akin to the race memories relived by the narrator of *Before Adam*, Buck encounters a "hairy man" who shares traits with both species. Like the Fire People, he builds fires, wears animal skins, carries a weapon, and utters "strange sounds."[18] But, like the Folk, he seems "as much at home among the trees as on the ground" and retains adaptations for arboreal movement: he is "shorter of leg and longer of arm" than modern humans and does "not stand erect but with trunk inclined forward from the hips" (41). Significantly, though, and unlike any of the protohuman species in *Before Adam*, he has a canine companion—the ancestor in whose brain Buck's race memories were first inscribed. By pairing Buck's ancestor with a not-quite-human being, London implies that cooperation with dogs facilitated the adaptations that transformed his hairy man into *Homo sapiens*.

Before Adam's narrator intimates as much when he laments Big-Tooth's failed attempt to domesticate the dog as a significant setback in human social development. Yet how, exactly, might dogs have fostered this development? The narrator fails to explain the underlying mechanism, instead taking for granted the adaptive advantages of canine companionship. Unlike the calorie-conserving efficiency afforded by the Folk's revolutionizing discovery of the "carrying-receptacle" (98), however, the evolutionary benefits of keeping an energy-expensive "plaything" (109) who bites and demands a consistent supply of freshly killed meat appear dubious at best. The narrator alludes to the pup's intelligence—"He learned rapidly" (109)—but otherwise offers no compelling evidence of the potential usefulness of dogs, and Big-Tooth certainly has no practical objectives for his captive. The energy Big-Tooth expends in catching "birds . . . and squirrels and young rabbits" to feed to the pup seems an even greater waste, given that the Folk are omnivores and thus could put this flesh to more immediate use (109). London's canine heroes, by contrast, regard meat as a resource so valuable that they risk violent punishment to steal it from humans. Buck's thievery in *The Call of the Wild* "mark[s] his adaptability . . . the lack of which would have meant swift and terrible death" (21). Given London's usual emphasis on the individual's need to forego moral considerations in the harsh struggle for existence, Big-Tooth's compulsion to acquire and provision the wild pup seems not only pointless but decidedly maladaptive. The behavior of Big-Tooth's friend Lop-Ear seems more in step with London's naturalistic ethos; Big-Tooth returns to his cave one day to find that "Lop-Ear had killed the puppy and was just beginning to eat him" (109).

While the evolutionary benefits of taming wild dogs are far from straightforward in *Before Adam*, Buck's race memories in *The Call of the Wild* offer clues as to why Big-Tooth's descendant regards the introduction of the dog as a pivotal moment for the soon-to-be human species. Closely linked with Buck's visions of the hairy man is a palpable "fear" that seems to him "the salient thing of this other world" and that London associates with the primitive (75). In *Before Adam*, a key indicator of the Fire People's more sophisticated cognitive development is their unique experience of fear. The Folk fear only "the real things, the concrete dangers, the flesh-and-blood animals that preyed," whereas the Fire People have evolved to "[project] this fear into the dark and [people] it with spirits" (185–86). The Folk, "inconsecutive, illogical, and inconsequential" (95), fear nothing more abstract than "the dark," and even this fear is rooted in a concrete, adaptive fear of nocturnal predators (185). Irrational as the Fire People's more abstract fears may be, they signal an advanced capacity for "imagination" that narrows the cognitive gap between London's protohumans and modern *Homo sapiens* (185). This development of the obviously adaptive fear of danger into a less straightforwardly adaptive fear of the unknown,

London suggests, renders the dog a desirable companion. Buck's "memories of nights of vigil spent beneath trees wherein the hairy man roosted" suggest that dogs, by protecting humans from those "flesh-and-blood" dangers feared by the Folk, assuaged the primitive fears that forestalled the development of more sophisticated cognitive abilities (75).

The plots of *The Call of the Wild* and *White Fang* repeatedly emphasize dogs' value as protectors, reinforcing this theory of their coevolutionary impact. The chapter titled "For the Love of a Man" in *The Call of the Wild* details Buck's heroic efforts to protect John Thornton, first by lunging at an "evil-tempered and malicious" man who strikes Thornton in a bar, and later by risking his own life to retrieve Thornton from "a stretch of wild water in which no swimmer could live" (64–65). Finally, Buck's deft and single-handed massacre of the Yeehats—"He plunged about in their very midst, tearing, rending, destroying, in constant and terrific motion which defied the arrows they discharged at him"—confirms that Thornton would have survived their attack had his faithful companion been present when it occurred (84–85). White Fang, for his part, takes "upon himself the guardianship of his master's property," including both material possessions and friends and family.[19] He protects Weedon Scott's cabin from the "bestial" Beauty Smith (248), whose nocturnal prowling recalls the predatory movements of those "denizens of the dark" feared by the Folk in *Before Adam* (254). Even when Scott transports him from the harsh Northland to the considerably less perilous Santa Clara Valley, White Fang continues to demonstrate his value as protector. When Scott is thrown from a horse and breaks his leg, White Fang, in a move befitting Lassie, rushes back to the house to alert his family. Finally, he dispatches another "denizen of the dark": the escaped prisoner and "carnivorous . . . human beast" who tries to murder Scott's father (284). Unlike Big-Tooth's needy puppy, Buck and White Fang demonstrate their worth through feats collectively indicating that the ancestors of domesticated dogs likewise earned their keep.

This theory of human/dog coevolution finds validation in Lorenz's speculative narrative of canine domestication in *Man Meets Dog*. In the opening chapter, "How It May Have Started," Lorenz imagines a band of nomadic hominids taking the first steps toward domesticating the jackal (Lorenz later abandoned the hypothesis that the jackal was the progenitor of most modern dog breeds). Although Lorenz affirms that his hypothetical hominids are "certainly human beings like ourselves, their build no different from that of present-day man," he describes significant behavioral and cognitive differences that align them more closely with London's Folk: they are "unclothed, uncivilized," "careless and unthinking," and exhibit a "child-like, almost ape-like impulsiveness."[20] Their means of communication consist primarily of "chatter [and] laughter" (2), along with occasional "grunt[ing]" (4) or "grumbling" (5). Their rudimentary social development is further reflected in a tendency to gesture with the eyes and head, "not, as we would do it, with the hands" (4).

Despite their superficially human appearance, then, Lorenz's creatures are a far cry from *Homo sapiens*—especially given that behavior, for the ethologist, is no less an indicator of evolutionary change than are physical characteristics. In Lorenz's narrative as in London's novels, the human seems not quite human prior to the domestication of the dog. Moreover, Lorenz echoes London in linking his hominids' primitivism to the state of fear presumed to have governed the lives of our ancestors before dogs became our protectors: "These men are no lords of creation that look out fearlessly into the world; instead, their dark eyes move to and fro restlessly as they turn their heads, glancing from time to time fearfully over their shoulders. They remind one of deer, hunted animals that must always be watchful" (1–2). Explicitly aligning such hypervigilance with animality, Lorenz notes that it "would strike the modern observer as being an animal trait" (1). Thus, while neither London nor Lorenz wants to erect an impenetrable barrier between human and animal, both suggest that movement beyond an existence in which "the salient thing" is fear (to borrow London's words) represents transcendence of a purely animalistic mode of being.

More pragmatically, Lorenz stresses the extent to which fear jeopardizes survival and adaptation in his primordial world. His hominids are undergoing a transition, not just from protohuman to fully human form, but from a territory from which "stronger, more populous tribes" have driven them to "a country which they do not know and where large beasts of prey are much more prevalent" (2). The band must adapt to a new, more dangerous environment if its members—and, more important, their genes—are to survive. Their leader recently killed by a saber-toothed tiger, they are rendered even more vulnerable by an incapacitating fear. Like London's Fire People, Lorenz's hominids are "obsessed by that fear of the unknown which, engraved in bygone eras into the convolutions of our brain, renders even to-day the darkness of night a source of terror [and] symbol of all things evil" (3). Besides echoing London's trope of race memory, Lorenz insists that fear directly threatens the tribe's survival. Sleepless nights during which its members "hardly dared to close an eye" leave them "tired and nervous and thoroughly disconsolate" (3). This combination of fear and fatigue leads to energy-expensive behaviors like scanning constantly for predators and "jumping at every sound"—actions that waste precious calories and exacerbate the group's already "overtaxed" state (3).

Enter canids. Before being driven out of their former territory, Lorenz explains, these hominids "possessed a guard of which, till now, they were unaware. The jackals that followed in the tracks of the human hordes, scavenging the refuse from slaughtered animals, surrounded their camp at night in a close circle" (2). Like London, Lorenz positions canids as humans' protectors, postulating that "the jackals were a definite help to the human beings" in mitigating the maladaptive effects of fear, reducing the need for "setting a watch [each night] since the clamour they set up on the approach of a beast of prey announced from afar the appearance of the marauder" (3). Thus under the jackals' unwitting guard, the equally unwitting band enjoyed more restful nights (and presumably greater energy and sharper hunting skills) in their former territory. Though unaware of this advantage afforded by creatures they formerly regarded as "troublesome," the hominids begin to experience in their new surroundings a longing for the company of jackals (2). While searching for a campsite, they hear a jackal howl, a sound that, unlike the threatening calls of other predators, "seems . . . like a message from home, a reminder of happier and less dangerous times" (4). Lorenz even suggests that the band must suppress a "child-like" impulse to run "in the direction whence the howling proceeds" (4). Even before they can be called domesticated, jackals signify the familiarity and safety of home.

This unconscious desire for proximity to jackals inspires an act that signals the climax of Lorenz's domestication narrative and that, like Big-Tooth's kidnapping of the wild pup, appears simultaneously irrational, fated, and counterintuitively adaptive. Hearing the howl of a nearby jackal, the band's leader, much to the chagrin of his nearest rival, leaves a trail of meat leading to the camp. Lorenz infuses this "remarkable and, to the others, inexplicable" act with an air of predestination, as the howl leaves the rest of the band "strangely moved" and standing "in anticipation" (4). He calls the event "an epoch-making episode, a stroke of genius whose meaning in world history is greater than that of the fall of Troy or the discovery of gunpowder," situating canine domestication atop human history's most momentous developments (5). Moreover, although "not a man"—not even the leader—"is conscious" of the significance of what has taken place,

Lorenz indicates that the act is a natural consequence of the leader's superior instincts and intelligence, both reflecting these traits and securing their continued development in future generations (5).

At this critical juncture, the leader represents the future of his species, a future that hinges on successful cooperation with canids. Though not "so endowed with experience and muscle-power" as his predecessor, "his eyes are brighter and his forehead higher and more arched" (2). Conversely, the rival who challenges his decision to leave the trail of meat is "physically stronger though mentally less active" (4). Lorenz presents the leader's motives for feeding the jackals as both instinctual and adaptive: "He acted on impulse, hardly realizing that the motive for his action was the wish to have the jackals near him. He had instinctively and rightly calculated that since the wind was blowing against them it was bound to waft the scent of the meat into the nostrils of the howling jackals" (5). The heritability of the leader's proclivity for canine companionship is confirmed by Lorenz's description of a man several generations later—"perhaps the great-great-great-grandson of the one who first threw a piece of meat to the jackals"— who displays "intuitive tact" toward the leader of a pack of jackals (9). In this later episode, jackals have for the first time aided hominid hunters by bringing a wild horse to bay. By securing jackals not just as protectors but as hunting partners, the leader's descendant illustrates a clear adaptive advantage for humans instinctually predisposed to form such alliances. In retrospect, then, his ancestor's actions are unquestionably adaptive, and his own gift for interspecies communication affirms London's hypothesis in *Before Adam* that canine domestication facilitated human social development by selecting for such behavior.

From Domestication to Coevolution

A point of tension in London's and Lorenz's domestication narratives is the extent to which dogs function as agents in their own domestication—in other words, the extent to which canine domestication is more accurately understood as human/canine coevolution Big-Tooth's wild dog pup is not, after all, scavenging at the perimeter of the Folk's camp and actively tolerating the presence of hominids when he is captured, but rather playing just outside his own cave, and he makes every effort to escape Big-Tooth's grasp. So uncooperative is the pup that Big-Tooth must forcibly drag him back to camp. He succeeds in this endeavor—"one of the hardest tasks I ever attempted" (107)—only by immobilizing his captive: "Not only did I tie the puppy's legs, but I thrust a stick through his jaws and tied them together securely" (109). The pup has little choice but to remain in Big-Tooth's "high little cave" awaiting the arrival of food (109). That he is ultimately eaten by Lop-Ear further underscores the pup's woeful lack of agency in his ill-fated encounter with hominids.

By figuring Big-Tooth as the sole agent in the first attempt at domestication, London implicitly accepts something like what the Coppingers call the "Pinocchio Hypothesis of dog origin." According to this teleological theory, just as Geppetto wished for a son, carved one out of wood, and lo and behold found himself the proud father of a real boy, primordial humans "took pups from wolf dens and made pets out of them. They tamed them, trained them, and took them out hunting. After many generations of this regime, the wolves evolved into dogs."[21] This hypothesis presupposes extraordinary foresight on the part of primitive humans (or, in Big-Tooth's case, a powerful desire to undertake a difficult, purposeless, and apparently maladaptive enterprise) as well as implausible tractability on the part of wild canids. Further, it rests on the Lamarckian assumption that the tameness acquired by the original captives would have been transmitted to subsequent generations—a premise entirely consistent with London's trope of race memory.

Yet London's insistence on Big-Tooth's unwittingness demonstrates an awareness of the limits of human agency that was probably influenced by Darwin's writings on domestication. In "Variation Under Domestication," a chapter in *On the Origin of Species*, Darwin underscores the distinction between tameness and true domestication: "Nothing is more easy than to tame an animal, and few things more difficult than to get it to breed freely under confinement. . . . How many animals there are which will not breed, though living long under not very close confinement in their native country!" Leaving aside the question of whether early humans could have confined the number of genetically tame canids needed to engage in selective breeding for tameness—an unlikely scenario, as the Coppingers observe—Darwin points here to the necessity of animal agency in the process of domestication. Even if primitive humans consciously set out to domesticate a useful species, they would have been forced to limit their efforts to animals predisposed to survive and reproduce while confined in close proximity to humans. This scenario seemed improbable to Darwin, who doubted that "a savage [could] possibly know, when he first tamed an animal, whether it would vary in succeeding generations," thereby challenging the assumption that our ancestors consciously and intelligently selected species for domestication. Even if several generations of unconscious selection happened to produce an observable, predictable variation that humans then undertook to cultivate further, these enterprising humans, Darwin notes, would no doubt "unconsciously modify other parts of the structure" in selecting for the desired trait. Moreover, before the advent of modern physiology and genetics, humans could select only for "externally visible" traits, and only when such "variations . . . are at first given to [them] in some slight degree by nature."[22]

Traces of the Pinocchio hypothesis, though, remain in both Darwin's and London's accounts. Darwin, despite his warnings about the limits of human agency, figures animals as passively adapting as "man" selects, consciously or unconsciously, traits that suit his "wants or fancies."[23] It is perhaps this underappreciation for animal agency that prevents Darwin from offering a plausible alternative to the Pinocchio hypothesis: he fails to consider how dogs' ancestors may have begun to exhibit variations noticeable to humans only after generations of self-selection for tameness. London likewise emphasizes the limits of human agency but still envisions domestication as something humans did to dogs: Buck's "last wild ancestor," we learn in *The Call of the Wild*, "*was tamed by* a cave-dweller or river man" (28, emphasis added). Like London, Lorenz speculates that a wild puppy could have been carried home and tamed to become a pet—he envisions a "little stone-aged girl" heeding her "maternal instincts" upon discovering an orphaned jackal pup—yet he hypothesizes that such tameness could be achieved only in an animal already predisposed to tolerate the presence of humans (11). At this point in his narrative, jackals have undergone several generations of self-selection for this trait. Moreover, *Man Meets Dog* emphasizes the necessity of canine agency from the start; the jackals actively follow the trail of meat left by the leader and choose to remain at the perimeter of the camp to which it leads: "the party suddenly see a jackal revelling in the pieces of meat. Once he raises his head, glancing apprehensively towards them, but as nobody attempts to move, he returns again to the feast" (6). Like the leader's intuitive decision to leave meat for the jackals, this event constitutes yet another "epoch-making happening: the first time a useful animal has been fed by man!" (6).

In feasting alongside humans, Lorenz's jackal dramatizes the Coppingers' theory of canine domestication—or, more precisely, "the self-domestication of dogs by natural selection." The process whereby some wolves evolved into dogs, they argue, began not with deliberate human attempts at artificial selection but with the emergence of permanent settlements following the last Ice Age, which is "coincidental with the first fossil evidence of dogs as we know them." Early human settlements introduced a valuable new food resource: "the town dump." Genetic variations in tameness enabled some wolves to exploit this resource more successfully than others, leading the successful wolves to produce more offspring that in turn passed genes related to tameness to succeeding generations. As the Coppingers note, wolves are among the many species known to feed at present-day dumps, but they are not efficient dump feeders: "Why are dogs better [than wolves] at feeding in the dump? Partly because dogs are genetically tamer, and outcompete the genetically shy (of people) wolves. Outcompete means that if a dog and a wolf are feeding side by side in a dump, and a person approaches, the wolf would run first and the dog would continue to eat. The dog not only would get more of the dump's resources but wouldn't use up as much energy by running away. A shy animal cannot learn to be tame. Tame is a successful adaptation to feeding in the dump."[24] Lorenz's tame jackal exhibits the precise characteristic the Coppingers credit with enabling some wolves to evolve into dogs: a flight distance ("How shy the animal and how far its retreat") precisely calibrated to allow for eating in proximity to people. The jackal's momentary hesitation serves as a reminder that he *could* flee but, perceiving no threat from the nearby hominids, he consciously chooses to remain. Thus Lorenz identifies canine agency, in the form of tameness, as a prerequisite for domestication.

This agency, moreover, proves beneficial for both canids and hominids. Fast-forwarding "many generations," *Man Meets Dog* portrays the band's descendants not as fearful scavengers but as feared hunters, and the abrupt transition presents their markedly improved state as a direct result of that first feeding (7). The jackals, too, flourish in the company of hominids, "now [surrounding] the camps of man in larger packs" and becoming "tamer and bolder" still (6–7). Generations of proximity have selected for jackals so tame that they now hunt cooperatively with hominids: "now the strongest and cleverest amongst [the jackals] have become diurnal and follow men on their hunting expeditions," enabling both hominids and jackals to consume more calories while expending less energy (7). Canine agency remains integral to their success. In his hypothetical description of the first joint hunting expedition, Lorenz describes the leader of the jackal pack "[shrinking] back a little" when the band's leader offers her a piece of the kill but, "seeing that the man makes no threatening gesture," proceeding to eat it in his presence and even to wag her tail (9). This hunt owes its success to the agency of the jackals, who not only voluntarily accompany the hominids and track the prey but reject the option of flight in favor of remaining with their hunting partners. In *King Solomon's Ring*, Lorenz even suggests that the first cooperatively hunting jackal may, "by a stroke of canine genius, have 'conceived the idea' of calling the hunter's attention to the track," thereby exhibiting autonomous agency. Even without this stroke of genius, Lorenz deems it reasonable to "surmise that, without being consciously trained by man, [jackals] learned to track and bring to bay large game animals."[25] Whether manifested consciously or not, this agency produces a distinctly adaptive advantage for both species: the successful killing of prey that hominids alone could not have tracked and jackals alone could not have killed.

London, despite his tacit acceptance of the Pinocchio hypothesis in *Before Adam*, similarly foregrounds canine agency in *White Fang* and *The Call of the Wild*. The description of the young White Fang's first encounter with humans—a group of Mackenzie Indians that includes his future master, Grey Beaver—establishes his instinctual predisposition to remain in their presence: "Every instinct of his nature would have impelled him to dash wildly away, had there not suddenly and for the first time arisen in him another and counter instinct. A great awe descended upon him" (159). Although his encounter with humans impresses White Fang with "an overwhelming sense of his own weakness and littleness," this feeling arises from his own instinct and not from humans' willful exercise of power over him (159). London likens his voluntary "submission" to Grey Beaver to that of the first wolf who "came in to sit by man's fire and be made warm"—not the first wolf pup whom man forcibly captured and tamed (160). While living in the Indians' camp, White Fang, like Buck, senses "something calling to him" (174) from the woods that repeatedly tempts him to leave, yet an "allegiance to man [that] seemed somehow a law of his being greater than the love of liberty" compels him to stay (195). White Fang's allegiance, moreover, is not blind; though instinctively felt, it is governed by his power of choice, as demonstrated when the Indians move their camp. Having "deliberately... determined to stay behind," White Fang hides in the woods and ignores Grey Beaver's calls (183). Ultimately, though, and just as deliberately, he "[makes] up his mind" (185) to return to Grey Beaver, running continuously for two days and approaching his master despite anticipating a beating (186). White Fang's competing impulses and conscious decision to return to Grey Beaver signal that his actions are guided primarily by his own agency rather than by human will. In surrendering himself to Grey Beaver "voluntarily, body and soul," he dramatizes his species' self-selection for domestication: "Of his own choice, he came in to sit by man's fire and to be ruled by him" (187).

Buck's and White Fang's ability to survive and even thrive without human assistance further underscores that their proximity to humans, like that of Lorenz's jackals, is voluntary. During a period of famine, White Fang leaves the Indian camp to fend for himself in the woods. He not only survives but returns "in splendid condition," having hunted successfully and "eaten his fill" (203). Buck likewise proves a capable hunter, singlehandedly killing "a large black bear" (79) and, even more impressively, a bull moose weighing "more than half a ton" (82). Though still connected to Thornton when he embarks on these hunting expeditions, Buck does not maintain this connection out of necessity. To the contrary, he lives "unaided, alone, by virtue of his own strength and prowess, surviving triumphantly in a hostile environment where only the strong survive" (79). These predatory successes both demonstrate and increase his fitness. So "overspilling with vigor and virility" is Buck that his coat emits "a snapping and crackling" when caressed, "each hair discharging its pent magnetism at the contact" (80). Buck, unlike White Fang, is a full-blooded dog, yet he proves a formidable opponent even for his wild brethren, "breaking the neck" of a wolf who challenges him and subsequently defeating three others "in sharp succession" (86). His supercanine abilities and utter lack of dependence upon Thornton leave no doubt that Buck's residence in the human realm is an act of choice.

Perhaps the most counterintuitive way in which London's dogs exhibit agency in their relations with humans is through their labor, which might initially seem to affirm human power. Having "lived the life of a sated aristocrat" on Judge Miller's Santa Clara Valley estate, Buck transforms into a working dog when Perrault, a courier for the Canadian government, purchases him for use as a sled dog (6). Jonathan Auerbach thus contextualizes *The Call of the Wild* "in an emerging culture of professionalism" in which London sought to establish himself as a writer, likening Buck's carrying of letters to London's "struggle to gain recognition."[26] Although my reading is less allegorical than Auerbach's, I am willing to risk anthropomorphizing in suggesting that Buck and his teammates epitomize professionalism. Buck witnesses how Dave and Sol-leks, the two most sullen dogs on his team, are "utterly transformed by the harness. . . . They were alert and active, anxious that the work should go well, and fiercely irritable with whatever, by delay or confusion, retarded that work" (19). Although they wish only "to be left alone" when at rest, they undertake to teach Buck while in the traces; Perrault need only place him "between Dave and Sol-leks so that he might receive instruction" (17).

Further, London takes care to differentiate sled-pulling from forced or mindlessly conditioned labor. For experienced sled dogs like Dave and Sol-leks, "The toil of the traces seemed the supreme expression of their being, and all that they lived for and the only thing in which they took delight" (19). Their dedication to the work itself overrides obedience to any human master. In one pathos-filled scene, Dave becomes gravely ill but resents being removed from the traces, "whimpering broken-heartedly" and attacking his replacement (43). After chewing through the other dog's traces and obstinately assuming his usual position, Dave is "dragged in the traces" for a full day and, undeterred by physical weakness, attempts by "convulsive efforts" to return to his spot the following morning (44). His persistence leaves the driver with no alternative but to end his suffering with a bullet. Buck, for his part, finds himself "gripped tight by that nameless, incomprehensible pride of the trail and trace"—a pride the text presents as part of "his nature," like White Fang's instinctive desire to surrender himself to Grey Beaver (30). Neither Buck's labor nor White Fang's surrender is motivated by fear of punishment or love for a master; rather, both are internally motivated acts of will.

Of course, Buck and White Fang do find love in the form of John Thornton and Weedon Scott, respectively. While we might read these interspecies romances, as Lundblad does, as veiled representations of human male homoeroticism, they can and should also be regarded more straightforwardly as idealizations of the human/dog bond, which London depicts as more authentic and redemptive than purely human unions.[27] London elevates each relationship precisely by depicting the canine partner as what Keridiana Chez calls a "'bare-dog'—the dog stripped of humanity" and thus capable of assuaging "the degeneration anxieties that dominated the fin de siècle." In contrast to the nineteenth century's "idealized faithful dog on whom so much 'extra' humanity had been inscribed" and who thus generated "debate about whether some intimate human-animal relationships destroyed a distinct 'doggy' essence that was worth preserving," London's bare-dog offers a masculinized alternative that resists the feminizing influence of civilization.²⁸ Significantly, neither Buck nor White Fang is predisposed to love his master. Buck, as noted above, strives for excellence as a sled dog not out of devotion to any of his masters but out of an internal drive. His prior relationship with Judge Miller's family is likewise described as "a working partnership," and his connection to the judge is nothing more than "a stately and dignified friendship" (61). White Fang surrenders himself to Grey Beaver and feels "a certain tie of attachment" (177) to him, but "not love" (219). For members of a species popularly lauded for its unconditionally loving and friendly nature, both dogs prove exceedingly stingy with their affections. Buck comes to love Thornton, but "the rest of mankind was as nothing. Chance travelers might praise or pet him; but he was cold under it all" (63). His behavior toward Thornton's friends is only marginally warmer: "he tolerated them in a passive sort of way, accepting favors from them as though he favored them by accepting" (64). White Fang proves an even tougher case, having become so cynical by the time Scott rescues him from a dogfighting ring that he must suppress "the urges and promptings of instinct and reason, defy experience, give the lie to life itself" to accept Scott's kind overtures (247). Even after his rehabilitation, White Fang behaves as Buck does toward other humans, merely tolerating Scott's friends and family as "possessions of the love-master" (271).

The love that London's dogs come to feel for their masters begins to reveal what is at stake in the question of canine agency in the human/dog relationship: the legitimacy of domestication itself, and consequently of the forms of civilization whose rise dogs facilitated through their vital roles in hunting prey and guarding livestock. Both novels indicate that the first dog "to sit by man's fire and to be ruled by him" may have unwittingly subjected the species to tyranny. Buck and White Fang experience terrible abuse at the hands of owners who regard them as mere property, and Scott views his rehabilitation of White Fang as a means "of redeeming mankind from the wrong it had done White Fang" (248). Even the mutually respectful but loveless relationships that Buck and White Fang experience with earlier masters—Judge Miller and Perrault in the former case and Grey Beaver in the latter—seem to offer woefully insufficient compensation for their species' voluntary surrender to human dominion. The fulfillment that Buck experiences while toiling in the traces seems more than equaled by the satisfaction of his successful hunting endeavors, and the pride he derives from leading the sled team is surely replicated in his eventual leadership of a wolf pack.

The human realm thus seems to offer little to dogs like Buck and White Fang. Yet, as London's description of his "companion-book" to *The Call of the Wild* suggests, "civilization" does offer something beyond material comforts and the satisfaction of labor: namely, "domesticity, faithfulness, love, morality, and all the amenities and virtues" that White Fang cultivates as he reenacts the domestication of his species in a reversal of Buck's devolution.[29] Love, in particular, is a novel and pleasurable experience for both dogs. Buck respects Judge Miller and Perrault, but "love that was feverish and burning, that was adoration, that was madness, it had taken John Thornton to arouse" (61). Not to be outdone, Weedon Scott inspires similar passions in White Fang: "He had gone to the roots of White Fang's nature, and with kindness touched to life potencies that had languished and well-nigh perished. One such potency was *love*. It took the place of *like*, which latter had been the highest feeling that thrilled him in his intercourse with the gods" (247). These idealized man/dog relationships thus illustrate a new breed of dog love—one that evinces a masculinized form of what Alice Kuzniar calls a "melancholic longing for perfect communion with the pet" that haunts modern and contemporary representations of dogs.[30] Stripped of feminized sentimentality, this model reconfigures "canine fidelity [as] a hard-won, masculine achievement" that resists the trappings of overcivilization.[31] Insofar as London depicts love as extraneous—indeed, even inimical—to the Darwinian struggle for survival, the dog love that his ideal masters practice thus legitimizes domestication by proposing that it offers dogs a mode of fulfillment that nature cannot.[32]

Lorenz, too, finds this implication of canine agency particularly compelling. In a chapter in *King Solomon's Ring* called "The Covenant"—also the title of a chapter in *White Fang*—he reflects, "To me it is a strangely appealing and even elevating thought that the age-old covenant between man and dog was 'signed' voluntarily and without obligation by each of the contracting parties" (109). This covenant, he contends, is unique to the human/dog relationship, all other domesticated animals (with the exception of cats) having become domesticated through "true imprisonment" (110). But what makes this covenant so appealing—even elevating? Lorenz clearly wishes to view his personal relationships with his own dogs as bonds between discerning, consenting parties. In *Man Meets Dog*, he describes how he earned the affections of Wolf, a chow who exhibited "the typical, non-infantile, completely independent" qualities that Lorenz then believed to be characteristic of "Lupus" breeds—breeds of wolf and jackal descent, in contrast to the Aureus breeds Lorenz then believed to be descended exclusively from jackals (28). In language that echoes his description of the primitive man whose "intuitive tact" helped forge a hunting partnership between humans and jackals, Lorenz recounts, "Tactfully and unobtrusively, I managed to gain [Wolf's] confidence in so far that he would voluntarily accompany me on long walks" (30).

In securing the voluntary allegiance of a dog whom he describes as "subject to nobody" (28), Lorenz aligns himself not only with the primitive man but also with London. He notes in *King Solomon's Ring* that a Lupus dog who has no master, or who loses his master (as Buck and White Fang do), "becomes as independent and self-sufficient as a cat," thereafter "liv[ing] alongside the human being without ever developing any heart-felt connection with him" (116). By way of illustration, he points to "the North American sledge dogs . . . whose deep qualities of soul are almost never awakened unless a Jack London recognizes and finds access to them" (116). Lorenz thus places himself and London in a select category of men capable of securing the affections of the very dogs who exhibit canine agency most powerfully. As we will see, such men are consequently charged with protecting the human/dog covenant from the existential threat of overcivilized modernity.

Domestication as Degeneration

Part of the appeal of Lorenz's and London's covenant between humans and dogs lies in its capacity to elevate the egos of professed "doggy people" who boast of enjoying unique access to the canine heart. But the implications of their insistence on canine agency in this covenant run much deeper, as evidenced by both writers' profound ambivalence about domestication itself. Lorenz expressed concerns about the degenerative effects of domestication throughout his career, beginning in the early 1930s. As an ethologist, he is most attuned to the impact of domestication on behavior, noting in a 1935 paper "that domestication produces disruptive mutations of fixed action patterns similar to those evident in morphology." These mutations pervert innate behaviors finely tuned by millennia of natural selection, with the result that "if we investigate the underlying principles of the behavior patterns in domesticated animals, we are examining principles which are overlain, and partially reduced, in a completely aberrant manner." Later in the same paper, Lorenz points to the "loss of specificity of the stimulus response" in domesticated animals—in other words, the tendency to display innate behavior patterns in the presence of inappropriate as well as appropriate stimuli—as evidence of their "thoroughly uncharacteristic, debilitated instincts."[33]

Lorenz's views on the degenerative effects of domestication are sometimes attributed to his wartime connection to Nazism. He applied for Nazi Party membership in 1938 and worked as a military psychologist and physician from 1942 until he became a Russian prisoner of war in 1944.[34] Interpretations of Lorenz's relationship to National Socialism vary considerably, with historians of science divided on whether his theory of domestication demonstrates opportunistic complicity with the Nazi rise to power or a sincere embrace of scientific racism. In *Biologists Under Hitler*, Ute Deichmann describes how in 1930s Austria, "owing to the power of the Catholic Church, Lorenz had no prospects of support" for his evolutionarily grounded work.[35] Seeing the rise of National Socialism as an opportunity to bolster his fledgling career, Lorenz emphasized connections between his research and the rhetoric of racial hygiene. For example, his address at the 1938 meeting of the German Society for Psychology, in which he linked the breakdown of instinctive behavior patterns in domesticated animals to the degeneration of civilized humans, impressed the society's president and ardent Nazi Erich Jaensch. Jaensch went on to cite Lorenz approvingly in "The Henhouse as a Means of Research and Explanation in Human Race Questions," a paper that likened behavioral differences between chicken breeds to purported differences between human races.[36] Such endorsements from high-ranking Nazi leaders and scientists had a profound impact on Lorenz's career. Whereas his 1937 application for funding from the German Research Organization failed in large part owing to questions about his ancestry and political leanings, in 1940 he received an appointment under the Third Reich to chair the psychology department at the University of Königsberg.[37]

While Lorenz's writing in the late 1930s undoubtedly reflects his opportunism, Richard W. Burkhardt Jr. concludes in his history of ethology that Lorenz did not view his theory of the degenerative effects of domestication "as a distinctively National Socialist project. In the immediate postwar period, while disavowing he had ever harbored any genuine Nazi sympathies, he continued to rail about the genetic and moral dangers of domestication."[38] His receipt of the 1973 Nobel Prize sparked renewed pressure for Lorenz to apologize for his wartime activities. In an autobiography written for the occasion, he acknowledged, "I did a very ill-advised thing soon after the Germans had invaded Austria: I wrote about the dangers of domestication and, in order to be understood, I couched my writing in the worst of nazi-terminology." Yet even while distancing himself from Nazism in this carefully hedged apology, he took care to separate his theory from his "ill-advised" actions: "I regret those writings not so much for the undeniable discredit they reflect on my person as for their effect of hampering the future recognition of the dangers of domestication."[39] And in his 1975 foreword to *The Wild Canids*, he reiterated his warning that domestication's ill effects "are seriously threatening our culture."[40] Whatever his connection to Nazi ideology might have been in the late 1930s and early 1940s, Lorenz remained convinced of the degenerative effects of domestication for the rest of his career.

Lorenz's view that species—including humans—degenerated under domestication was far from novel in the 1930s. Degeneration theories predated even Darwin's work. In 1835, for example, the American physiologist and vegetarian diet popularizer Sylvester Graham lamented that humans had descended into a state of "degeneracy" and claimed that only humans and domesticated animals suffered from disease.[41] Darwin indicated that domestication might have deleterious effects when he noted that domesticated varieties "often have a somewhat monstrous character." The analogical conflation of human races and nonhuman breeds, which Lorenz would later use to draw comparisons between human and nonhuman domestication, is also evident in Darwin's observation that "one of the most remarkable features in our domesticated races is that we see in them adaptation, not indeed to the animal's or plant's own good, but to man's use or fancy."[42] The concept of race having long encompassed humans, animals, and plants, Lorenz probably would have extended his theory of domestication to human races even without the influence of Nazi politics. Though he would not promote his misgivings about *human* domestication until after the Nazis gained control of Austria in 1938, he implies in the 1935 paper that differences within and between human "races" are analogous to the distinct breeds produced by domestication, with Europeans predictably emerging as the most domesticated race: "We Europeans are in fact much more distinct from one another than are the racially less diverse Negroes or Chinese, and these in their turn differ from one another far more than members of nondomesticated animal species."⁴³ The theory of domestication-induced degeneration, and probably Lorenz's concerns about its implications for humans, thus predates his career under the Third Reich.

Lorenz's ideas about domestication reached a much wider audience with his postwar best sellers *King Solomon's Ring* and *Man Meets Dog*. In *Animals in the Third Reich*, Boria Sax describes *King Solomon's Ring* as "a veritable orgy of cuteness"—both it and *Man Meets Dog* are peppered with whimsical drawings by the author—and reads Lorenz's popular books as part of an effort to "[extend] his rehabilitation beyond the scientific community to the general public." Lorenz's cartoonish drawings of himself, Sax contends, depict "characteristics he previously considered genetically degenerate [and thus] could reflect both pragmatic calculation and sincere regret." Yet Lorenz's repeated valorization of so-called Lupus dogs in both texts seems ill-suited to this purpose, echoing as it does the Nazi "cult of the wolf" that, Sax notes, posited wolves as symbols "of the discipline sometimes associated with 'civilization' without its accompanying decadence."⁴⁴ Before abandoning his theory that all dogs were descended from the golden jackal, Lorenz believed that some breeds—such as huskies, malamutes, and chows—were the result of deliberate crosses between jackal-descended dogs and wolves. The "male dwellers" of the harsh arctic climate, he reasoned in *Man Meets Dog*, "found [it] desirable to introduce as much wolf blood as possible" into their dogs in order to produce "stronger and more hardy" varieties (24–25). This hybridization led to the creation of dogs that Lorenz regarded as significantly less domesticated—and behaviorally "purer"—than their Aureus counterparts.

Lorenz believed that these divergent lines of descent explained behavioral differences between Lupus and Aureus breeds, a theory he presents in "The Covenant" in *King Solomon's Ring* and in a chapter of *Man Meets Dog* titled "Two Origins of Fidelity." Explaining that morphological and behavioral characteristics associated with youth in wild animals "are kept permanently by the domestic form," Lorenz claims that a youthful dependence on and "ardent affection" for the mother "is preserved as a permanent mental trait of all highly domesticated dogs" (*KSR*, 112). The fidelity of Aureus dogs thus arises from their "child-like dependency" (112), and their human masters secure their affection by acting as stand-ins for "parent animals" (*MMD*, 25). Lupus dogs, by contrast, derive their fidelity from the pack organization of their wolf ancestors. Wolf survival, Lorenz explains, depends on an "exacting social organization" in which each individual exhibits "true loyalty to the pack-leader" (25). The master in this scenario thus assumes the role not of parent but of alpha wolf. Insofar as Lupus dogs are less domesticated than their Aureus counterparts, they are also more mature and independent. Not surprisingly, their type of fidelity proves far more appealing to Lorenz. Though professing that his "affections do not belong entirely to Lupus dogs," he repeatedly contrasts the "submissiveness of the childish jackal dog" with the "proud 'man to man' loyalty" of the Lupus dog—punctuating this characterization in *Man Meets Dog* with a drawing of himself and an anthropomorphized Lupus dog clinking foamy mugs of beer over a table in manly camaraderie (25).

Lorenz's preference for Lupus dogs stems from his view of these breeds as closer to nature than the more domesticated Aureus breeds. In a description that uncannily recalls London's Buck and White Fang, Lorenz identifies "the noble qualities of the beast of prey" retained by the Lupus dog: "his profound aloofness toward strangers, his boundless love for his master, and . . . the reticence with which he demonstrates his really deep affection" (*KSR*, 117). Lorenz further credits Lupus dogs with strict social inhibitions stemming not from their refinement through domestication but from their wolf ancestry. Claiming that sled dogs, like wolves, refuse to cannibalize one another "even when at the point of starvation," he insists that "this social inhibition has certainly not been instilled into them by man" (113). He likewise says he does "not hesitate to leave [my grandchildren] unsupervised in the company of our big Chow-Alsatian dogs whose hunting instincts are of the bloodthirstiest." Although the dogs in question are hybrids of a Lupus breed (the chow) and an Aureus breed (the Alsatian, or German shepherd), Lorenz regards the inhibitions that ensure his grandchildren's safety not as qualities "which have been bred into the dog in the course of his domestication" but as "the heritage of the wolf."[45] The Lupus dog's wolf ancestry is also responsible for the "reticent exclusiveness" that guides his behavior toward humans; like London's aloof canine protagonists, he is "for ever a one-man dog and no stranger can win from him so much as a single wag of his bushy tail" (*KSR*, 113). He does not exhibit the indiscriminate affection that Lorenz regards as a marker of domestication, and his fidelity is consequently more valuable to his master: "Nobody who has once possessed the one-man love of a Lupus dog will ever be content with one of pure Aureus blood" (113). For Lorenz, the less adulterated social instincts (and consequently superior fidelity) of Lupus dogs demonstrate their resistance to the degenerative effects of domestication.

Aureus breeds, by contrast, exhibit the juvenile behavior associated with domestication, and their conduct toward humans is consequently more promiscuous than that of Lupus dogs. With his "hail-fellow-well-met" attitude, Lorenz explains, the Aureus dog "will follow any one who holds the other end of the lead in his hand" (113). While "his age-old domestication" thus renders the Aureus dog "a manageable and tractable companion," Lorenz suggests that such a dog is best suited to an equally domesticated master (114). He speculates in *Man Meets Dog* that the (male) primitive humans who first developed Lupus dogs would have experienced "little trouble" in "handling intractable dogs," being "born animal tamers" (25); yet for the modern, inexperienced dog owner, "a good honest Boxer or . . . an Airedale Terrier" will do (78). Lorenz likens the new owner's satisfaction with a ready-made Aureus companion to that of the "beginner in photography [who] will achieve more success with a simple box camera than with a highly complicated apparatus" (78). As this rather condescending analogy suggests, the Aureus dog owner will lose in the richness of his relationship with his companion what he gains in the ease of training such an uncomplicated, eager-to-please pupil. For Lorenz, the Aureus dog's characteristic willingness to "grant you that servitude which . . . awaits your command and even your slightest wish" is cheapened by his concomitant readiness to "follow any man" (*KSR*, 114–15). The superior tameness and tractability that Lorenz ascribes to the "highly domesticated jackal dogs" signal their greater removal from nature (*MMD*, 130). They lack the "charm of the natural" (130) inherent in Lupus dogs, and their fidelity is therefore less desirable: "The less a dog has become altered in type by domestication, the more he has retained the properties of the wild predator, the more wonderful his friendship seems to me" (77). Moreover, Lorenz draws an explicit parallel between the overdomesticated dog and the neurotic modern human, noting that Aureus dogs, owing to "their extraordinary 'humanness'" (130), are susceptible to "Oedipus complexes . . . which convert [the] master to a cross between a father and a god" (26). The Aureus dog owner necessarily becomes entangled in the dog's Oedipus complex and thus cannot claim via the relationship that link to the primitive (in the sense of binary opposition to the modern) available to the Lupus dog owner (130).

But Lorenz's gravest concerns involve the pedigree dog, a creature he regards as a distinctly modern, Western aberration. Expressing dismay (which the Coppingers echo decades later) at the rise of "form-breeding art" in the late nineteenth and early twentieth centuries, Lorenz aligns modern breeding with the feminization and degeneration of Western culture (*KSR*, 120). Though no fan of the "too sentimental" dispositions of sporting breeds (which he classifies as Aureus), Lorenz differentiates the age-old selection of gun dogs "for their fine sense of smell" (*MMD*, 77, 85) from the "modern" practice of breeding "with exclusive consideration for a certain external appearance" (*KSR*, 120). The damage caused by modern breeding far exceeds the dilution of wild traits brought about through the long domestication of Aureus breeds. In abandoning the practice of breeding for a physical and behavioral conformation suited to the performance of certain tasks, Lorenz warns, modern dog breeding allows "fashion, that silliest of all silly females . . . to dictate to the poor dog what he has got to look like" (*MMD*, 85).

For Lorenz, the most disturbing effect of this distinctly modern, feminized shift in breeding practices is the rapid acceleration of mental degeneration in recognized breeds: "there is no single breed of dog the originally excellent mental qualities of which have not been completely destroyed as a result of having become 'fashionable'" (85). Here, Lorenz has in mind not only the obviously fashionable, nonfunctional toy breeds, but also dogs like the Saint Bernard—the breed of Buck's father in *The Call of the Wild*—whose central European members have been reduced through "modernization" to "degenerate mental cripples" (86). Another of his preferred Aureus breeds, the Scottish terrier, has been subjected to rapid "mental degeneration" since the 1910s (87). Even Lupus breeds are at risk of becoming mere "caricatures" of themselves; chows, Lorenz laments, "were still natural dogs" as recently as the 1920s but have since become "stodgy teddy bears," both physically and "mentally" (87). The deterioration of dogs' mental capacities is particularly troubling for Lorenz, both as an ethologist and as a dog lover deeply invested in legitimizing the human/dog relationship by portraying it as a product of mutual agency. Modern breeding, by irrevocably damaging dogs' minds, effectively negates the voluntary covenant into which humans and dogs have entered. Thus Lorenz implicates modern breeding practices in undermining the integrity of domestication itself.

London shares Lorenz's distaste for these excesses of domestication, reserving special contempt in his dog stories for overcivilized humans and either pity or indifference for overdomesticated dogs, whom modern civilization has rendered unfit for Northland survival. *White Fang* opens with a team of dogs transporting a coffin containing one such effete man across the desolate Yukon landscape. From the two experienced drivers, we learn that the deceased was a wealthy man—"a lord or something in his own country"—whose vanity trip to the Northland cost him his life and now endangers theirs (97). Indeed, one of the drivers dies while transporting the coffin and the other narrowly escapes the same fate, their vulnerability in spite of experience only underscoring the ludicrousness of an uninitiated outsider fancying himself sufficiently fit to traipse about "the God-forsaken ends of the earth" (97). Even more ridiculous are Hal and Charles, the Southland degenerates who purchase Buck and his team in *The Call of the Wild*. London introduces them before they have occasion to travel in coffins, thus affording himself the opportunity to link their poor survival skills explicitly with morphological evidence of their excessive refinement:

> Charles was a middle-aged, lightish-colored man, with weak and watery eyes and a mustache that twisted fiercely and vigorously up, giving the lie to the limply drooping lip it concealed. Hal was a youngster of nineteen or twenty, with a big Colt's revolver and a hunting-knife strapped about him on a belt that fairly bristled with cartridges. This belt was the most salient thing about him. It advertised his callowness—a callowness sheer and unutterable. Both men were manifestly out of place, and why such as they should adventure the North is part of the mystery of things that passes understanding. (47)

Charles's pale skin, weak eyes, and droopy mouth signal degeneracy, and while both men attempt to advertise themselves as fit and virile—Charles with his erect moustache and Hal with his weapon-laden belt—their innate deficiency gives the lie to these adornments. Buck intuits as much, regarding them "apprehensively" as they prepare to set off on the trail with their newly purchased team (47).

London implicitly links Charles's and Hal's ineptitude to the decadence of the civilization of which they are products, embodied most potently in their insufferable female traveling companion. Mercedes, Charles's wife and Hal's sister, epitomizes the excesses of feminized, decadent modernity. She insists upon overloading the sled with frivolous luxuries—hotel-quality blankets, dishes, a tent, and altogether too much clothing—the resulting awkward, immobile load signifying all of the trappings of modern civilization. Only when the sled proves too heavy for the dogs is Mercedes persuaded to part with "the superfluous," and the sacrifice of her beloved commodities elicits hysterical emotion: "She cried in general, and she cried in particular over each discarded thing. She clasped hands about knees, rocking back and forth broken-heartedly . . . finally wiping her eyes and proceeding to cast out even articles of apparel that were imperative necessities" (50). As her outburst suggests, Mercedes represents a feminine excess fundamentally at odds with the masculine economy of efficiency that governs London's Yukon. Her continual "flutter[ing] in the way of her men and . . . unbroken chattering of remonstrance and advice" cost Charles and Hal valuable time and energy in loading, unloading, and reloading the sled to appease her (47–48). Moreover, in adding herself as "a lusty last straw to the load" and remaining there even when the dogs are "weak and starving," Mercedes quite literally becomes an excess—little more than "one hundred and twenty pounds" of luggage (54). Hardly more bearable than her weight is her feminized sentimentality. Mercedes's saccharine affection for the dogs, exposed as superficial when her "own misery" eventually renders her (like the men) "callous to [their] suffering" (50), hastens their starvation when she begs Hal to feed them more than their ration of a rapidly dwindling supply of fish and secretly feeds them "still more" (52). In this way, Mercedes is aligned with those "ladies" whom fin-de-siècle commenters had blamed for ruining dogs through capricious and sentimental pet-keeping practices.[46]

Mercedes is only the most extreme member of a party of overcivilized travelers. As Buck observes, "There was a great deal of effort about their manner, but no businesslike method" (47). Even Charles and Hal's arguments, like their sled, are encumbered by civilization. They might begin by disagreeing about a pressing matter of survival, but "presently would be lugged in the rest of the family . . . people thousands of miles away" and topics ranging from "Hal's views on art, or the sort of society plays his mother's brother wrote," to "Charles's political prejudices" (53). These preoccupations extend to their method of travel in the Northland. After a failed attempt to set out with their overburdened sled, they purchase additional dogs and feel "proud" to be "doing the thing in style, with fourteen dogs" (51). Motivated solely by appearances—traveling the Northland "in style"—they overlook the fundamental incompatibility of civilization's excesses with survival: "In the nature of Arctic travel there was a reason why fourteen dogs should not drag one sled, and that was that one sled could not carry the food for fourteen dogs" (51). Driven by the fantasy of a Northland adventure full of "glamour and romance," Charles, Hal, and Mercedes are manifestly out of place in London's text (53). Even when the Northland exhibits its own brand of excess—the "bursting, rending, throbbing of awakening life" that signals the welcome arrival of spring— they stagger "like wayfarers to death" alongside the overtaxed team, their incompetence again placing them out of step with their surroundings (56).

Charles, Hal, and Mercedes lack the intuitive understanding of dogs that London sees as essential to human survival in the harsh and indifferent Yukon. John Thornton, who nurses Buck back to health and secures his love and fidelity, stands in sharp contrast to the effete Southlanders. In the tradition of masculine self-reliance, he asks "little of man or nature.... With a handful of salt and a rifle he could plunge into the wilderness and fare wherever he pleased" (73). Whereas Charles and Hal naively assume that survival in a brutal climate requires equally brutal treatment of one's dogs, Thornton, an "ideal master," cares for his dogs not "from a sense of duty and business expediency" but "as if they were his own children" (61). These opposing attitudes toward dogs lead to dramatically different outcomes. Hal, failing to earn Buck's respect, finds his lead dog "[refusing] to move" when he commands him to lead the team across thin ice. Rather than heed Buck's implicit warning of "impending doom," he drives the rest of the team (and himself, Charles, and Mercedes with it) to certain death (58). By contrast, Thornton's faith in Buck motivates the latter to perform a series of heroic acts, including saving Thornton's life and pulling a thousand-pound sled to win a wager, its winnings enabling Thornton not just to survive but to venture into new territory in pursuit of further prosperity. The relationship, moreover, is mutually beneficial. Under Thornton's care, Buck flourishes: "He was in perfect condition, without an ounce of superfluous flesh, and the one hundred and fifty pounds that he weighed were so many pounds of grit and virility" (70). Both man and dog thus epitomize the efficiency and interspecies cooperation required for Northland survival—qualities that Charles and Hal lack precisely because of their ties to the excesses of modern civilization.

The link between human overcivilization and canine overdomestication becomes apparent when Charles and Hal demonstrate their poor understanding of dogs by adding "six Outside dogs" to the team: three short-haired pointers, one Newfoundland, and two "mongrels of indeterminate breed" (50). The purebred additions exhibit the characteristic deficiencies Lorenz associates with "modernized" dogs. Their inferiority is apparent in the contrast between Buck's rapid adaptation, despite having lived in the lap of Southland luxury prior to his immersion in the North, and their woeful inability to adapt. Buck, though an experienced leader, cannot "teach them what to do" because they lack the instinctive propensity for "trace and trail" that he and the huskies possess (51). In contrast to Buck, whose "stomach extracted the last least particle of nutriment" (22) from each meal, the purebred dogs quickly confirm the "saying of the country that an Outside dog starves to death on the ration of the husky" (53). Moreover, they lack Buck's mental resilience. While Buck's "heart [is] unbreakable" (55), the purebred outside dogs are "bewildered and spirit-broken by the strange savage environment in which they found themselves and by the ill treatment they had received" (51). Physically and mentally, these Southland dogs are as manifestly out of place as their incompetent owners. The mongrels prove unfit for different reasons. Unlike Buck, whose hybridity gives him the appearance of a "gigantic wolf" and the advantageous mixture of "wolf cunning" with "shepherd . . . and St. Bernard intelligence," the mongrels are too diluted in their makeup to benefit from their mixed ancestry (79). Wholly "without spirit" (51), they cling "more grittily on to life" but perish soon after the purebred dogs (53). Collectively, the outside dogs thus represent two trajectories of canine degeneration: excessive domestication and excessive mongrelization. Conversely, Buck's hybridity and eventual return to the wild help mitigate the potentially degenerative effects of domestication for himself and his offspring.

Conclusion

As both writers' concerns about the deleterious effects of domestication indicate, the coevolutionary narrative that grounds London's and Lorenz's understanding of the human/dog relationship ultimately implicates dogs in the intertwined processes of overcivilization and degeneration, with troubling implications for both species. If dogs facilitated crucial adaptations that produced *Homo sapiens*, then they are not only symbolically linked to Freud's theory of organic repression (as creatures who have "incurred [man's] contempt" by persisting in the olfactory mode that humans have ostensibly transcended) but embroiled in the evolutionary changes that precipitated it—most notably, the transition to erect posture that "paved the way to civilization."[47] Consequently, London's and Lorenz's understanding of human/dog coevolution also implicates dogs in the repression of human animality that produces the unconscious. As Carrie Rohman explains, "Freud's theory of organic repression can be read as an originary narrative of the human unconscious that outlines the initial attempt to suppress instinctual drives out of the conscious mind—a mind that is coded as human—into a separate psychic region that remains aligned with the animal. In other words, Freud's narrative suggests that an attempted rejection of humanity's own animality created the human unconscious."[48] Significantly, this rejection is merely "attempted"; it is never complete. Caroline Hovanec points out that "the primitive animal self remains potent in the unconscious, resurfacing in dreams, art, and neuroses."[49] Thus as London's and Lorenz's fictional hominids dramatize the species' transition to erect posture under the watchful eyes of their canid companions, they recapitulate the very rupture that alienated the human from the nonhuman world and from its own animality, ultimately producing the neuroses of the overcivilized modern subject—what Lorenz calls "hurried, worried, modern man" (*MMD*, 140).

Despite exposing the canine origins of human civilization and its discontents, both London and Lorenz remain invested in legitimizing the phenomenon of canine domestication and, through it, the human/dog relationship. London's hybrid heroes assuage modernist anxieties about degeneration by continually crossing the boundaries between modern and primitive, culture and nature. Even before Thornton's death severs "the last tie" connecting him to civilization, Buck undergoes an "instant and terrible transformation" (86) each time he crosses from his master's camp into the surrounding forest: "He no longer marched. At once he became a thing of the wild, stealing along softly, cat-footed, a passing shadow that appeared and disappeared among the shadows" (80). While Thornton's love exerts a "soft civilizing influence," Buck retains "the strain of the primitive, which the Northland had aroused in him" (62). If Buck's devolution from pampered pet to primordial beast underscores the permeability of the barrier between civilization and the primitive, Thornton's death seems to impose a limit on the modern human's access to the latter realm. The search for "a fabled lost mine" that culminates in his murder by the Yeehats undermines Thornton's status as an ideal master by revealing an all-too-human materialism that ultimately links him to the same civilizing forces that produced Charles,

Hal, and Mercedes (73). Only Buck succeeds in "link[ing] the past with the present," maintaining his tie to the primitive and thereby resisting the enfeebling effects of civilized modernity (63). Thornton, inextricably tied to human economies, cannot accompany Buck into "the younger world" to which the dog ultimately returns, and his death serves as a reminder of what humans lost in the transcendence of animality that dogs enabled them to achieve (88).

Lorenz echoes this familiar refrain, lamenting humans' separation from nature and contrasting "the almost film-like flitting-by of modern life" (*KSR*, 120) with "the thoughtless happiness of pre-human paradise" (*MMD*, 140). This primordial past became a "paradise lost" with the advent of human "culture and civilization" and the irrevocable "severing of [the] bond" with nature (*KSR*, 120). Although Lorenz regards this loss to some extent as a "liberation" that enabled "new ways of acting," he emphasizes its more problematic outcomes—in particular, the alienation of modern humans from their animal origins (*MMD*, 132). The ever-proliferating amenities of modern life, as his film metaphor indicates, exert a "mental strain" that only dogs can alleviate (140). But the conditions of modernity require a particular kind of dog—"a natural being with an undistorted soul," not a "triumph" of modern breeding (*KSR*, 120). Lorenz offers his Lupus/Aureus hybrids as ideal candidates. Like London's protagonists, these dogs maintain a proximity to nature that makes them "specially capable of supplying that which poor, civilized, city-pent man is so badly in need of!" (120). The dog who remains uncorrupted by modern breeding, "and thus does not spoil the landscape by its civilized appearance," retains his status as "a rightful participant" in the natural realm (*MMD*, 140). It is via just such a dog that the modern human can access, albeit fleetingly, Lorenz's (and London's) paradise lost.

In theorizing the human/dog relationship as a coevolutionary entanglement rather than a one-way process of canine domestication, London and Lorenz cannot avoid implicating dogs in the civilizing processes that led to modern humans' much-bemoaned estrangement from nature. Yet dogs' pivotal role in facilitating human evolution simultaneously positions them as partners uniquely equipped to help humans reclaim their animal origins while adapting to the turbulent forces of modernization. Dogs, Lorenz insists, are uniquely capable of facilitating "a re-establishment of the immediate bond with that unconscious omniscience that we call nature" (*KSR*, 120). For London, too, the mode of interspecies intimacy modeled by Buck and Thornton constitutes a privileged means by which modern humans can access their primordial past, all the while retaining the mark of civilization demonstrated by love for the dog. In Lorenz's words, the canine companion who remains "a piece of unwarped nature" (*MMD*, 77) reminds the human "that he is still himself"—that he remains a product of nature in a period in which the excesses of modernity threaten to blot out the instincts that mark him as such (*KSR*, 121). It is precisely London's and Lorenz's view of dogs as agents in human/dog coevolution that makes this reassurance possible.

CHAPTER 2

MONGRELIZING FORM
Virginia Woolf's Flush

The backlash that Jack London and other American nature writers faced during the nature faker controversy discussed in chapter 1 powerfully demonstrates the stigma that hounds efforts to represent animal worlds—a stigma that resurfaces across the Atlantic and three decades later in the diary of Virginia Woolf. Anticipating the 1933 publication of *Flush*, her biography of Elizabeth Barrett Browning's cocker spaniel, Woolf writes, "Flush will be out on Thursday & I shall be very much depressed, I think, by the kind of praise. They'll say its 'charming' delicate, ladylike. And it will be popular. Well now I must let this slip over me without paying it any attention.... I must not let myself believe that I'm simply a ladylike prattler: for one thing its not true. But they'll all say so. And I shall very much dislike the popular success of Flush."[1] Indeed, a canine biography was a hazardous undertaking for a female writer perpetually wary of being dismissed as sentimental. The book represents a series of historical events—most notably, the storied love affair of Elizabeth Barrett and Robert Browning—from a canine perspective, following Flush through his puppyhood with Mary Russell Mitford, his early years in the Barrett home on London's aristocratic Wimpole Street, and his later years with the married Brownings in Italy. As an account of the life of a dog, *Flush* unavoidably joins a tradition of female-authored animal (auto)biographies like Anna Sewell's 1877 *Black Beauty* and (Margaret) Marshall

Saunders's 1893 *Beautiful Joe*, which feature liberally anthropomorphized protagonists whose first-person descriptions of cruel treatment at the hands of humans were calculated to evoke sympathy for animals. And as Bonnie Kime Scott points out, the children's stories written by Woolf's mother, Julia Stephen, "featured talking and thinking animals . . . [who] teach that good children are sensitive to kind treatment of animals."[2] Thus the popular association of animal narrative with feminine sentimentality and children's moral education was well established by the time Woolf undertook to write a canine biography.[3]

That Woolf consequently approached this project with trepidation is evident in her letters, which are peppered with references to her "little joke" of a book, and in her diary, in which she wonders whether Flush is "worth writing."[4] Her fears about its reception were largely realized. While *Flush* became an international best seller and received a handful of positive reviews (one tellingly titled "Brown Beauty"), most early critics dismissed it either as a charming diversion from Woolf's more serious endeavors or as a piece of second-rate literature, beneath its author's eminent position within a burgeoning modernist canon. Frank Chapman, writing for the *Granta*, declared that its "deadly facility [and] popular success" spelled "the end of Mrs Woolf as a live force."[5] *Flush*'s continued marginalization in critical accounts of Woolf's work suggests that many scholars continue to regard it as a "trivial potboiler." *The Cambridge Companion to Virginia Woolf*, for example, contains only two passing references, and most studies of Woolf's oeuvre mention it briefly, if at all. As Craig Smith notes in a 2002 essay, a survey of the scholarship suggests that "*Flush* may be accepted as a serious object of study only to the extent that it may be represented as being not really about a dog."[6] Until recently, allegorical readings have reigned, with Flush standing in for an array of marginalized humans and the book itself presenting a veiled critique of Victorian sexual mores, urban class divisions, or fascist ideology.[7] Even among such readings—which implicitly posit *Flush* as deserving of critical attention—Smith detects "a faint odor of professional embarrassment": "It is as if, in writing about a dog, Woolf were doing something not merely atypical but unworthy of a great writer—one, moreover, whose reputation bears the burden of proving that it is possible for a woman to be a great writer within the configuration of high modernism."[8]

The emergence of literary animal studies around the turn of the twenty-first century saw Smith and other scholars begin the project of reevaluating *Flush* "as what it declares itself to be: the biography of a dog."[9] In *Dog Love*, for example, Marjorie Garber declares *Flush* "a masterpiece in its own terms" that "explores the mind of a dog" in order to interrogate the categories of "the 'human' and the 'literary.'"[10] Yet in productively situating *Flush* within a cross-disciplinary and transhistorical tradition of animal narrative, such readings tend to downplay the modernist scene of its creation, obscuring its connection to the body of work that established Woolf's reputation as a major modernist innovator. Smith notes that Woolf "exercise[s] modernist literary techniques in the mapping of a canine subjectivity," but the bulk of his essay positions *Flush* alongside late twentieth-century zoological findings about animal behavior and cognition to show how the protagonist's rich inner life challenges anthropocentrism and the Cartesian human/animal divide.[11] I concur, but in what follows I want to move beyond reading *Flush* simply as an admirable attempt to represent nonhuman experience—an interpretation that perhaps rescues it from literary obscurity but does not contextualize it within the larger project of narrative innovation undertaken by Woolf and her contemporaries. In *Animal Stories: Narrating Across Species Lines*, Susan McHugh underscores *Flush*'s significance for critical accounts of literary modernism by connecting it to Woolf's famous declaration that "on or about December 1910, human character changed."[12] By narrating agency beyond the human, McHugh contends, "this canine biography intimates why, when human nature changed . . . it could never do so alone"; however, she goes on to note, the entrenched disciplinary habit of reading literary animals allegorically means that "few of Woolf's critics have wanted to follow her to this conclusion."[13]

Woolf's own tendency to dismiss *Flush* as "a waste of time" no doubt helped set the tone for its long-uncelebrated status within modernist studies.[14] Yet it would be a mistake to accept this characterization at face value, especially given that Woolf recognized her misgivings about *Flush* as typical of her "self-admonishments previous to publishing a book." Derek Ryan points out that two of Woolf's most oft-cited descriptions of *Flush* as a "joke" appear in letters to a friend (Ethyl Smyth) whom "she had earlier worried would 'hate' the book" and a publisher (Donald Brace) whose reaction she was "apprehensive of."[15] In fact, Woolf seems to have taken her ostensibly "silly book" rather more seriously than her characteristic self-deprecation indicates.[16] Early in its composition, she describes "writing Flush of a morning, half seriously to ease my brain, knotted by all that last screw of The

Waves"; however, later diary entries contradict Chapman's insinuation that so trivial a project must have been completed with ease, instead revealing Woolf's growing frustration with "trying to re-write that abominable dog Flush." In one entry, she declares herself in "a tremor" at having "botched the last—penultimate chapter." Months later, she complains of being unable to "dispatch [Flush]" because "I always see something I could press tighter, or enwrap more completely. There's no trifling with words—cant be done: not when they're to stand 'for ever.'" In the days following its release, moreover, she is pleased to discover that "some obscure journalist detects no signs of whimsicality" and that another recognizes *Flush* as a "new venture." In a letter to a friend, she writes, "I'm so glad that you liked Flush. I think it shows great discrimination in you because it was all a matter of hints and shades, and practically no one has seen what I was after."[17]

What, then, was Woolf after? Why would a writer excruciatingly wary of being labeled a "ladylike prattler" risk venturing onto the literary minefield of animal narrative? I propose that a partial answer is found in her famous call for a radically new approach to the novel in the 1921 essay "Modern Fiction." There, Woolf expresses her dissatisfaction with the conventional novel, which, in its insistence on linear causation and detached narration, fails to record the "myriad impressions" received by "an ordinary mind on an ordinary day." In an "attempt to come closer to life," the new generation of novelists must "discard most of the conventions" associated with the form.[18] Strictly speaking, of course, *Flush* is a biography, written in part as a parody of the new breed of life writing developed by Woolf's friend and Bloomsbury associate Lytton Strachey. Yet the task of piecing together a full canine life from fragments of Barrett Browning's poetry and correspondence forced Woolf to "invent a good deal" in hopes of "throw[ing] some light upon [Flush's] character."[19] Thus *Flush* is perhaps best classified with Strachey's *Eminent Victorians* and *Queen Victoria* as what Marjorie Garber calls "speculative biography," a genre that, like the novel, "imputes motives, intentions, and causes, linking historical events in an arc of character intentionality that is a fictional construct."[20] As a speculative biography of a dog, *Flush* is a direct response to the challenge Woolf presents to the modern novelist: "Let us record the atoms as they fall upon the mind in the order in which they fall, let us trace the pattern, however disconnected and incoherent in appearance, which each sight or incident scores upon the consciousness. Let us not take it for granted that life exists more fully in what is commonly thought big than in what is commonly thought small."²¹ Woolf's warning against dismissing subject matter conventionally regarded as trivial resonates not only with her innovative representations of women's experience in novels like *The Voyage Out*, *Mrs. Dalloway*, and *To the Lighthouse* but also with her portrait of an ordinary canine mind in *Flush*.

That *Flush* cannot be disentangled from Woolf's more renowned modernist achievements is evident in her diary, where she muses, "It is a good idea I think to write biographies, to make them use my powers of representation reality accuracy; & to use my novels simply to express the general, the poetic. Flush is serving this purpose."²² Although she differentiates between biography and novel here, a later entry indicates that canine experience muddies such formal distinctions: "I must write off my dejected rambling misery—having just read over the 30,000 words of Flush & come to the conclusion that they won't do. . . . Its not the right subject for that length: its too slight & too serious. Much good in it but would have to be much better."²³ Several scholars have invoked Woolf's characterization of her subject as "too slight & too serious" to confirm *Flush*'s inconsequential status (usually leaving out the qualifying sentence that follows), yet her indication that it is too slight and too serious *for its length* suggests not the triviality of her subject but the inadequacy of traditional literary forms to represent it.²⁴ The challenge of recording "the atoms as they fall" upon an ordinary *canine* mind pushes Woolf to expand her "powers of representation," reimagining novelistic form and character in the process. We might, in fact, view *Flush* as Woolf's most genre-bending work, mongrelizing as it does several strains of the animal narrative and bildungsroman traditions. By strategically amalgamating the Victorian animal biography, the naturalistic animal story, the speculative biography, and the modernist bildungsroman, Woolf reveals the power of canine experience to propel modernist reconfigurations of form and character and demonstrates that even the task of "bring[ing] before us a real human being" requires a rigorous engagement with the realities of interspecies life.²⁵

To trace the impact of canine experience on literary form, I begin by discussing *Flush*'s complex relationship to an animal narrative tradition that encompasses both the anthropomorphic "autobiographies" written by Woolf's Victorian predecessors and the hypermasculine Darwinian narratives epitomized by London's canine bildungsromans. I then reexamine the much-discussed connection between Flush and the woman writer, demonstrating how Woolf uses the figure of the dog not merely to stand in for the woman writer but to expose how anthropocentrism underwrites the phallocentrism of the literary canon. Finally, I show how Woolf uses the intertwined self-cultivation plots of Flush and Elizabeth to develop a modernist understanding of literary character that reflects humans' entanglement in the more-than-human contexts of multispecies life.

Flush and the Animal Narrative Tradition

No doubt mindful of the charges of anthropomorphism that plagued her predecessors in the animal narrative tradition, Woolf strategically employs and discards conventions of the Victorian animal autobiography throughout *Flush*, refusing to dismiss animal experience as inherently trivial even as she resists sentimentalizing her subject. Following Sewell and Saunders, she frankly depicts the animal suffering that supports human social and economic structures when she imagines the historical Flush's experience of being stolen by dognappers in a chapter called "Whitechapel."[26] Just as Sewell documents the abusive working conditions endured by cab horses and human drivers alike in Victorian London, Woolf reveals how the criminal enterprise of stealing valuable pets and holding them for ransom links the "respectability" of Wimpole Street to the "filth" and suffering of the Whitechapel slums where Flush is held hostage.[27] The Whitechapel chapter opens with the heterodiegetic narrator recounting scenes from Thomas Beames's 1850 exposé *The Rookeries of London*, revealing "sights and ... smells, not a stone's-throw from Wimpole Street, that threw doubts upon the solidity even of Wimpole Street itself" (78). Anna Snaith, one of several scholars to examine how this chapter critiques London class hierarchies, proposes that Woolf presents "Whitechapel as the unsaid of Wimpole Street: the latter's purity relying on its perceived separation from the former."[28] Indeed, the fragile boundary between Wimpole Street and Whitechapel collapses in Flush's mind when, following his safe return, he experiences traumatic repetitions of his ordeal: "As he lay dazed and exhausted on the sofa at Miss Barrett's feet the howls of tethered dogs, the screams of birds in terror still sounded in his ears. When the door opened he started, expecting a hairy man with a knife" (101). Flush's perception of his captors, Snaith argues, evokes the "middle-class reformer's language of depravity and savagery" and recalls Jack London's descriptions of the London slums in *The People of the Abyss*. "By attributing the 'bestial' view of Whitechapel to an aristocratic *dog*," she insists, "Woolf exposes the ridiculousness of the hierarchies" implicit in such accounts.²⁹

While Snaith implies that the canine perspective is inherently trivial—a mere vehicle for Woolf's ironic critique of human socioeconomic disparity—the sober tone of the passages in question challenges this assumption. In these scenes, Maureen Adams observes, "the book's ironic humor vanishes." Although Woolf's knowledge of Flush's experience is filtered through the lens of Barrett Browning's letters, which foreground "her distress over Flush's disappearance and her anger at those who take dogs and hold them for ransom," the biographer's empathy is with Flush.³⁰ Flush's difficulty distinguishing "beast" from "human being" in the "low dark room" (83) where he is held captive echoes Beames's horror upon discovering "ruined sheds in which human beings lived herded together above herds of cows" (78). But even as Woolf deconstructs the class hierarchies of Victorian London through Flush's perspective, she resists the speciesist hierarchy of interests implicit in readings like Snaith's. Flush's suffering, though less visible than the human suffering Beames witnessed "in the course of an afternoon's walk through some of the most aristocratic parishes in London," is described with an empathic vividness reminiscent of scenes from *Black Beauty* and *Beautiful Joe* (78–79). In particular, Flush's fear of being "hauled off by a ruffian" (88) to have his "head and paws" (81) severed as a warning to Wimpole Street evokes Beautiful Joe's mutilation at the hands of his original owner, who chops off the dog's ears and tail with a hatchet in an enraged display of mastery. Much of the chapter represents an attempt—returning to Woolf's challenge in "Modern Fiction"—to "record the atoms" as they may have fallen on the mind of the historical Flush during the longest of his three captivities. Woolf's Flush is "bewildered in the extreme" (82), assaulted literally by the "heavy hand [that] beat[s] him over the head" (83) and figuratively by the "racket, the hunger and the thirst, [and] the reeking smells of the place" (88). The frenzied cries of other animals, coupled with his own suffering, leave "myriad impressions," which his enduring trauma confirms are "engraved with the sharpness of steel" (to borrow Woolf's words in "Modern Fiction").³¹ Like Sewell and Saunders, Woolf foregrounds animal suffering even as she remains aware of the intersecting oppressions that shape spaces as socioeconomically and biologically diverse as the modern city.

But Woolf also departs from the Victorian animal autobiography in significant ways. Rejecting the pretense of unmediated access to the canine mind, she dispenses with the first-person narration employed not only by Sewell and Saunders but also by Rudyard Kipling in his 1930 *Thy Servant a Dog*. Kipling's Aberdeen protagonist, Boots, relates his experiences in what early critics described as "dog-language"—a sort of child-speak-meets-pidgin-English that simultaneously reflects the infantilization of companion animals and the animalization of marginalized humans.[32] By contrast, Woolf's patently human narrator ranges from confidently reporting Flush's thoughts to professing an inability to represent certain aspects of canine experience (especially olfaction, as we shall see). This is not to say that Woolf eschews anthropomorphism; rather, as Kari Weil argues, Woolf resists what primatologist Frans de Waal calls "anthropodenial"—the anthropocentric refusal "to acknowledge the ways that nonhuman and human animals (or men and women) are alike."[33] For example, as the courtship between Robert and Elizabeth intensifies, Flush understandably develops "an intense dislike for Mr. Browning" (61) that motivates him to attempt two violent (albeit ineffectual) attacks on "his enemy" (69). The biographer's descriptions of Flush's "jealousy," "rage," and "disappointment" (62–63) in these scenes are representative of a broader pattern of what David Herman calls "unhedged attributions of experiences for which there is no evidentiary backing." From the standpoint of anthropodenial, these attributions might be regarded as an indirect means of commenting on matters presumed more important (read: human-centered) than canine phenomenology. Yet by peppering the narrative with plausible characterizations of Flush's mental state, Woolf "hold[s] up for scrutiny normative assumptions bound up with judgments about what constitutes a falsifiable claim concerning animal minds."[34]

Woolf's rejection of anthropodenial works in tandem with her critique of what de Waal calls "anthropocentric anthropomorphism"—the uncritical projection of "our own inner lives" onto animals.[35] When a distracted Elizabeth allows Flush's paw to be shut in a door, the narrator's commentary challenges her anthropomorphic interpretation of his response. After she answers his whimpers with mocking laughter, he dashes across the park, leading her to conclude that "'he is of the Byronic school—*il se pose en victim.*' But here Miss Barrett, absorbed in her own emotions, misjudged him completely. If his paw had been broken, still he would have bounded. That dash was his answer to her mockery; I have done with you—that was the meaning he flashed at her as he ran" (65–66). By juxtaposing competing interpretations of Flush's "meaning," Woolf underscores the limits of even Elizabeth's insight into her companion's mind. The possibility that the narrator's interpretation is yet another anthropomorphic projection only reinforces Woolf's two-pronged critique of anthropocentrism; regardless of the actual reason for Flush's sprint across the park, Woolf satirizes the certitude with which humans impute motives to animal behavior.

Sewell and Saunders likewise challenge the anthropocentrism behind the exploitive practices they document, but their protagonists' status as furry Uncle Toms—perpetual victims with a selfless desire to please their masters—reinforces another brand of anthropocentrism. Black Beauty heeds his mother's advice "always to do my best to please my master," in part because "the better I behaved, the better I should be treated," but primarily to uphold what she describes as a proud family tradition of exemplary service to humans. "You have been well bred and well born," she tells her colt; "your father has a great name in these parts . . . and I think you have never seen me kick or bite. I hope you will grow up gentle and good, and never learn bad ways; do your work with a good will, lift your feet up well when you trot, and never bite or kick even in play."[36] And while Saunders's overt aim in writing *Beautiful Joe* was to foster sympathy for abused animals, her protagonist has very different reasons for "writing, or rather getting a friend to write, the story of my life. I have seen my mistress laughing and crying over a little book that she says is a story of a horse's life. . . . I love my dear mistress . . . and I think it will please her if I write the story of a dog's life." Echoing the literary horse explicitly invoked in the novel's opening lines, Beautiful Joe closes his narrative with a plea to the reader to "be kind to dumb animals," insisting that "dogs and many other animals love their masters and mistresses, and live only to please them."[37] Of course, it is difficult to fault Sewell and Saunders for couching their appeals for compassion in these terms given their shared goal of improving animal welfare in deeply anthropocentric cultures. The result, though, is that Black Beauty's and Beautiful Joe's status as individual animals is subordinated to their role as proxies for their respective species—even for "the whole animal kingdom," according to a member of the committee that chose Saunders's manuscript as the winner of a contest sponsored by the Humane Society.[38]

Woolf, by contrast, takes a more individualized interest in her subject and playfully inverts the expectation of canine fidelity idealized in Beautiful Joe's dedication to his mistress. In a letter to a friend that is otherwise dismissive of *Flush*, she compellingly explains her inspiration: "I lay in the garden and read the Browning love letters, and the figure of their dog made me laugh so I couldn't resist making him a Life." Another letter to a fan reads, "I am very glad to think that you share my sympathy for Flush. The idea came to me that he deserved a biography last summer when I was reading the Browning letters. But in fact very little is known about him."[39] She goes on to express her hope of having "thrown some light on his character," placing the burden of fidelity squarely on the shoulders of the canine biographer. The vivid depiction of Flush's suffering at the hands of dognappers notwithstanding, *Flush* is not a didactic tale of the evils of cruelty to animals, and its aristocratic protagonist is hardly representative of his entire species, let alone "the whole animal kingdom." As Flush discovers soon after his move to Wimpole Street, "there is no equality among dogs: there are high dogs and low dogs. . . . Heaven be praised, he was a dog of birth and breeding!" (32). As both victim and beneficiary of Victorian class and social norms, Flush is no more representative of all dogs than Elizabeth is of all women.

In endeavoring to impart truth to individual canine experience, Woolf comes closer to Jack London than to her Victorian predecessors in the animal narrative tradition. Both writers privilege the development of canine character over the cultivation of sympathy via descriptions of human cruelty and animal suffering. To this end, they employ the hybrid narrative voice of the speculative biographer, alternating between free indirect speech and detached narrative commentary. "The effect of this style," Garber notes, "is to produce ironic disjunction and implicit commentary at the same time that it offers an opportunity for narrative identification with fictional or historical characters."[40] By moving strategically in and out of their protagonists' minds, London and Woolf underscore distinctions between canine and human perspectives, not to diminish the former but to satirize the follies and limits of the latter. *The Call of the Wild* opens with the narrator's wry observation that "Buck didn't read the papers" and is thus unaware that "trouble was brewing" for dogs like himself "because men, groping in the Arctic darkness, had found a yellow metal."[41] Just as Buck is immune to the uniquely human affliction of gold fever, Flush is bewildered by the passion of Elizabeth and her friends for gathering around tables to summon spirits during the heyday of Victorian mysticism. When Flush inexplicably finds the table above him "swaying violently from side to side," the narrator intervenes to supply "a few facts"—actually several pages describing the fervor for spiritual communion in 1850s London that made its way to the Brownings' home in Italy (149). Flush's assessment of this craze is drolly rational: "Whatever the ladies and gentlemen round the table could hear and see, Flush could hear and see nothing. True, the table was standing on one leg, but so tables will if you lean hard on one side. He had upset tables himself and been well scolded for it" (153–54).

Buck and Flush may be indifferent to yellow metal and moving tables, but they are adept at reading other signs in their environments. Buck, though he does not understand the value of the money that strangers give to the dog breaker who introduces him "to the reign of primitive law," quickly learns what it signifies for dogs. Seeing "money pass" between the dog breaker and the dog driver Perrault, he is "not surprised" to find himself being "led away" by Perrault.[42] Flush, for his part, can "make no sense of the words that Miss Barrett was murmuring to herself" while reading and replying to Robert Browning's letters, but he knows, "just as well as if he could read every word, how strangely his mistress was agitated as she wrote; what contrary desires shook her" (53–54). Flush's canine perceptiveness accentuates the "obtuseness" of the imposing Mr. Barrett, who carefully monitors his daughter's activities but "notice[s] nothing" while sitting "in the very chair" that Robert has recently occupied (58). Mr. Barrett's "astonishing blindness" to his daughter's growing resolve to leave her sickroom and elope with Robert prompts one of the text's few uses of direct speech to convey Flush's thoughts: "'Don't you know,' Flush marveled, 'who's been sitting in that chair? Can't you smell him?'" (58). Flush is keenly aware both of Elizabeth's growing "vigour" (56) and of "where her strength came from" (58). Woolf, like London, thus calls into question the glorified status of human communication, privileging instead the sensory cues that dogs easily interpret.

As these passages also illustrate, Woolf follows London in representing canine character as the product of a complex interplay between species and individual experience—the combination of instinct and the capacity for learning ("simple reasoning") that London attributes to dogs in his response to naturalist John Burroughs in the nature faker debate.[43] Buck's devolution reflects his ability to "learn by experience," but his learning is accelerated by the awakening of "instincts long dead" that "forgotten ancestors" have "stamped into the heredity of [his] breed."[44] Thus the collective agency of his species reverberates in his individual actions: "He sat by John Thornton's fire, a broad-breasted dog, white-fanged and long-furred; but behind him were the shades of all manner of dogs, half-wolves and wild wolves, urgent and prompting, tasting the savor of the meat he ate, thirsting for the water he drank, scenting the wind with him, listening with him and telling him the sounds made by the wild life in the forest, dictating his moods, directing his actions, lying down to sleep with him when he lay down, and dreaming with him and beyond him and becoming themselves the stuff of his dreams."[45] Through the trope of race memory, London reimagines character as the literary equivalent of nesting dolls, each individual consciousness containing the cumulative experiences of the species. London's construction of character thus resembles the understanding of individuality proposed by Henri Bergson—whose thought, as Paul Sheehan and others have noted, shares "numerous striking parallels and coincidences" with Woolf's literary imagination.[46] In attempting to delineate the borders of the individual, Bergson insists in *Creative Evolution*, "gradually we shall be carried further and further back, up to the individual's remotest ancestors: we shall find him solidary with each of them, solidary with that little mass of protoplasmic jelly which is probably at the root of the genealogical tree of life."[47]

In *Flush*, Woolf employs London's trope of race memory to illustrate the multilayered nature of canine interiority. Flush remembers not back to the experiences of his lupine ancestors but to the early days of his breed. During an outing with Miss Mitford, "the smell of hare, the smell of fox ... ripped across his brain stirring a thousand instincts, releasing a million memories" (12). In what will become a recurring motif, he hears "dark men cry 'Span! Span!'" (12)—a reference to the theory put forth in the opening pages that the spaniel derives its name from the Carthaginians, who, upon arriving in ancient Spain, found the land teeming with rabbits and cried out "*Span*"—or "Rabbit"—when their dogs gave chase (3). Like Buck's visions of the hairy man discussed in chapter 1, Flush's memories constitute a living archive of the coevolutionary entanglements that have made his species "highly sensitive to human emotions" (47). Further, race memory powerfully influences how Buck and Flush perceive and adapt to their respective environments. Buck experiences his relocation to the Northland as a kind of homecoming; following his initial bewilderment at being "jerked from the heart of civilization," he soon feels "the ancient song" surge through him and comes "into his own again." His instincts and learning thus combine to transform him into "as formidable a creature as any that roamed the wild."[48] Conversely, Flush's race memories complicate his adaptation to life "in the heart of civilisation" (27). Visitors usher in sounds and smells that remind Flush "of forests and parrots and wild trumpeting elephants" and "dark men cursing in the mountains," prompting him to bite one guest in a fit of "ancestral rage" (36) before he learns "the prime lesson of the bedroom school": "To resign, to control, to suppress the most violent instincts of his nature" (34–35).

The processes of education narrated in both *The Call of the Wild* and *Flush* point to the overlapping ways in which London and Woolf use canine experience to reimagine that most humanistic of literary genres: the bildungsroman. As Jonathan Auerbach argues of London's novella, "Buck's character develops along the lines of a traditional nineteenth-century bildungsroman, in which identity is a process of becoming via moral education: a portrait of the dog as a young artist, if you will. . . . Learning his many 'lessons,' knowing his proper place, disciplining his body, and struggling for approval, Buck fulfills a higher calling."[49] Buck's transformation from "sated aristocrat" to "dominant primordial beast" echoes key elements of the prototypical *Bildung* plot of Goethe's novel *Wilhelm Meister's Apprenticeship*, in which the eponymous protagonist abandons a comfortable future as a bourgeois businessman to pursue a risky but intrinsically rewarding project of self-cultivation. By learning and ultimately transcending the Yukon's "law of club and fang" to assume leadership of a wolf pack, Buck finds personal fulfillment while also contributing to the future of his species, thus achieving a dialectical harmony between self and (canine) society. The final image of Buck "running at the head of the pack . . . leaping gigantic among his fellows, his great throat a-bellow," epitomizes the ideal of the self-constituted person whose socialization, like that of Goethe's Wilhelm, culminates in finding a calling that promotes the greater good of his society. Buck's positive impact on dog-kind is visible in the subsequent flourishing of the pack, accompanied by a "change in the breed of timber wolves; for some were seen with splashes of brown on head and muzzle, and with a rift of white centring down the chest."[50]

As Buck's severing of ties with the human realm suggests, however, his devolution undermines the humanistic underpinnings of the traditional bildungsroman. E. L. Doctorow proposes that "*The Call of the Wild* may well constitute a parody of the bildungsroman, the novel concerned with the sentimental education of its hero, not only because the hero in question is a dog but also because his education decivilizes him to the savage wolfhood of his ancestors."[51] Indeed, Buck comes by his education largely through what London's narrator describes as "the decay or going to pieces of his moral nature, a vain thing and a handicap in the ruthless struggle for existence."[52] Rather than affirming the humanist ideal of a moral education, as Auerbach suggests, Buck's transformation is marked by a gradual abandonment of human moral codes that culminates in his brutal massacre of the Yeehat Indians who kill John Thornton. Like the hero who frees himself from bourgeois values and expectations by acquiring knowledge through personal experience, Buck grows increasingly independent, finally revolting against human sovereignty in a passage that graphically celebrates his inhumanity: "He had killed man, the noblest game of all, and he had killed in the face of the law of club and fang."[53] While this scene problematically exploits the Yeehats' status as racial others in order to justify Buck's revenge, it also underscores the novella's implicit critique of the humanist values of the traditional bildungsroman. Buck quickly learns from the dog breaker that club trumps fang, and his ultimate rejection of this uneven law challenges the anthropocentric logic that valorizes civilization and reason while devaluing nature, instinct, the primitive, and the animal.

Flush's self-cultivation is, of course, considerably less violent than Buck's. Whereas "experience gained in the fiercest of schools" molds Buck into a fearsome predator "overspilling with vigor and virility,"[54] Flush's education has the opposite effect. Flush's biographer, while ironically echoing London's insistence on his protagonist's exceptionality, acknowledges the softening influence of the "bedroom school":

> Such an education as this, in the back bedroom at Wimpole Street, would have told upon an ordinary dog. And Flush was not an ordinary dog. He was high-spirited, yet reflective; canine, but highly sensitive to human emotions also. Upon such a dog the atmosphere of the bedroom told with peculiar force. We cannot blame him if his sensibility was cultivated rather to the detriment of his sterner qualities. Naturally, lying with his head pillowed on a Greek lexicon, he came to dislike barking and biting; he came to prefer the silence of the cat to the robustness of the dog; and human sympathy to either. (47)

Insofar as he undergoes a process of civilization in the domestic confines of Elizabeth's bedroom, Flush has more in common with the eponymous hero of London's *White Fang* than with Buck. As London explains, his "companion-book" to *The Call of the Wild* is its "complete antithesis": "Instead of devolution or decivilization of a dog," *White Fang* charts "the evolution, the civilization of a dog—development of domesticity, faithfulness, love, morality, and all the amenities and virtues."⁵⁵ The last four chapters in particular narrate an educational process whereby White Fang learns the social and moral "intricacies" of his new Santa Clara Valley home and cultivates the "restraint" needed to "[qualify] himself for civilization."⁵⁶

Yet while Woolf shares London's investment in repurposing the bildungsroman to narrate the development of nonhuman character, she challenges his representation of animality as a masculine force opposed to the feminizing influence of modernity. In chapter 1, I discussed how London represents human Southlanders as emasculated by the decadence and degeneracy of modern culture and domestication. As a wolf-dog who elects "to sit by man's fire and to be ruled by him," White Fang, like Buck, retains the wildness that inoculates him against the deleterious effects of domestication that afflict both the modern human and the overbred dog. Even as he becomes civilized, he "never chum[s]" with his fellow canines or becomes "a common dog, loving here and loving there, everybody's property for a romp and good time. He loved with a single heart and refused to cheapen himself or his love."⁵⁷ With his singular love for Weedon Scott and consequent aloofness toward all other humans, he epitomizes what ethologist Konrad Lorenz calls the "proud 'man to man' loyalty" of the Lupus (wolf-descended) dog.⁵⁸ In Italy, by contrast, Flush grows increasingly independent from Elizabeth—their "relations" having become "far less emotional now than in the old days"—and takes daily walks with his former enemy Robert (117). And while White Fang remains different from (and implicitly superior to) other dogs, the formerly aristocratic Flush becomes "daily more and more democratic" as he takes to cavorting with mongrels in the streets of Florence: "He was the friend of all the world now. All dogs were his brothers" (117).

Thus while Woolf situates *Flush* within the broader animal narrative tradition by echoing tropes and conventions of existing subgenres, she takes care to differentiate her canine protagonist both from the furry Uncle Toms of the Victorian animal autobiography and the hypermasculine Überhunds of London's dog stories. Moreover, although Woolf joins London in critiquing the anthropocentrism of the traditional bildungsroman, she exposes the phallocentrism of both that form and the naturalistic animal story epitomized by London's twin narratives of canine (d)evolution. As I discuss in the next section, her representation of canine development under circumstances that parallel those of the woman writer challenges the traditional bildungsroman's depiction of self-cultivation as an ideal achieved in the public sphere through prototypically male experience—a feature that persists in London's antihumanist appropriation of the form. This model, she intimates, is problematic for women and dogs, whose experiences are constrained in different but equally significant ways by their subordinate positions in patriarchal structures.

The Writing Woman and the Dancing Dog

Woolf's critique of the privileging of male experience in both the traditional bildungsroman and London's zoocentric variant becomes apparent in Flush's first visit to Regent's Park, which closely resembles an experience of the fictional woman writer who narrates Woolf's *A Room of One's Own*. Seeing before him a vast expanse of "grass, flowers and trees," Flush "dashe[s] forward to run as he had run in the fields at home," only to find himself checked by his collar and lead (30). Perplexed, Flush begins to notice differences between the open fields of his puppyhood and the more regimented space of the urban park: flowers, rather than dotting the landscape haphazardly, are confined to "narrow plots" framed by "hard black paths" upon which "men in shiny top-hats [march] ominously" (30). He quickly comes to regard these features not as isolated but as interrelated parts of a system that governs canine bodies: "Where there are flower-beds there are asphalt paths; where there are flower-beds and asphalt paths, there are men in shiny top-hats; where there are flower-beds and asphalt paths and men in shiny top-hats, dogs must be led on chains" (30). Taken together, these features signify to Flush precisely what "the placard at the gate" communicates to dog owners (31).

While this scene demonstrates Flush's capacity for what London calls "simple reasoning," it also parallels the experience of Woolf's narrator in the opening pages of *A Room of One's Own*, thus signaling Woolf's critique of the privileging of male experience, which is as evident in London's zoocentric narratives as it is throughout the literary canon. Sitting on a riverbank in the fictional Oxbridge, she is contemplating the situation of the woman writer when "the sudden conglomeration of an idea" prompts her to rush unthinkingly "across a grass plot." Much like the personified smells that "came tearing . . . down the wind," "thrilled [Flush's] nostrils," and "ripped across his brain" during his off-leash outings with Miss Mitford (12), the *Room of One's Own* narrator's idea "darted and sank, and flashed hither and thither, set up such a wash and tumult of ideas that it was impossible to sit still." And just as Flush plunges spontaneously off the path in Regent's Park, the narrator, spurred on by her "exciting" idea, unconsciously finds herself "walking with extreme rapidity" across the lawn, where she is immediately intercepted by "a man's figure" no less ominous than the men in top hats who send Flush shuddering back to Elizabeth's side.[59]

Their respective encounters with the male policing of public space serve to remind Flush and the narrator in *A Room of One's Own* of their subordinate roles within a culture dominated by the intertwined forces of anthropocentrism and patriarchy. Like Flush, the narrator quickly discerns the rule conveyed by the man's look of "horror and indignation": "he was a Beadle; I was a woman. This was the turf; there was the path. Only the Fellows and Scholars are allowed here; the gravel is the place for me. Such thoughts were the work of a moment." And while the narrator attributes her sudden realization to "instinct rather than reason"—invoking the irrationality ascribed to women and animals alike by patriarchal discourses—instinct alone cannot account for her ready grasp of the culturally constructed rules and hierarchical relations communicated through her silent exchange with the beadle.[60] Rather, the similarities between her situation and Flush's underscore the arbitrariness of social codes in a culture that mandates the leashing of dogs and women alike, prompting Donna Haraway to allude to the opening scene of *A Room of One's Own* in *The Companion Species Manifesto*: "Woolf understood what happens when the impure stroll over the lawns of the properly registered. She also understood what happens when these marked (and marking) beings get credentials and an income."[61]

That both woman and dog intuit their subordinate positions within phallo- and anthropocentric social configurations reflects not their acceptance of a natural order but their internalization of power structures that privilege the male (and thus fully human) subject. Their parallel encounters affirm Cary Wolfe's observation that "the humanist discourse of species" naturalizes the oppression of "the social other of *whatever* species—or gender, or race, or class, or sexual difference."[62] Indeed, Woolf's narrator attributes to a common source the possessive impulse that every "Alf, Bert, or Chas" experiences in the presence of "a fine woman . . . or even a dog" or "a piece of land or a man with curly black hair": "Ce chien est à moi."[63] *Flush* thus joins *A Room of One's Own* in exposing how speciesism and phallocentrism work together, helping to co-constitute patriarchy itself. Woolf signals the connection between the dog and the woman as writer via the narrator's characterization of her subject—"women and fiction"—as a "collar" that "bowed my head to the ground,"[64] recalling the "heavy weight" that "jerk[s] at [Flush's] throat" and prevents him from sprinting across the grass in Regent's Park (30). By emphasizing the parallel positions of the dog and the woman writer, as Jane Goldman notes, Woolf appropriates for feminist purposes a tradition of "misogynist . . . canine troping" extending from the fictional Elizabethan actor Nick Greene's assertion "that a woman acting put him in mind of a dog dancing" to the very real Samuel Johnson's infamous declaration—cited favorably, Woolf's narrator observes, as recently as 1928—that "a woman's preaching is like a dog's walking on his hinder legs. It is not done well; but you are surprised to find it done at all."[65]

In noting the similarities between Flush and the narrator in *A Room of One's Own*, I am not suggesting that *Flush* is simply a feminist allegory, as other critics have argued. In one of the earliest studies of *Flush*, Susan Squier contends that it marks a return "to the theme of *A Room of One's Own*" in that its protagonist "operates as a stand-in for the woman writer: for the woman poet who was his historical mistress . . . and for the woman writer who was his creator."[66] Certainly, as Squier notes, the first encounter between Flush and Elizabeth establishes their "uncanny resemblance": "Heavy curls hung down on either side of Miss Barrett's face; large bright eyes shone out; a large mouth smiled. Heavy ears hung down on either side of Flush's face; his eyes, too, were large and bright: his mouth was wide. There was a likeness between them" (23). But this likeness is quickly undercut:

> As they gazed at each other each felt: Here am I—and then each felt: But how different! Hers was the pale worn face of an invalid, cut off from air, light, freedom. His was the warm ruddy face of a young animal; instinct with health and energy. Broken asunder, yet made in the same mould, could it be that each completed what was dormant in the other? She might have been—all that; and he—But no. Between them lay the widest gulf that can separate one being from another. She spoke. He was dumb. She was woman; he was dog. Thus closely united, thus immensely divided, they gazed at each other. (23)

As this passage suggests, the inevitable disparities of interspecies life complicate any simple equation of Flush's position with that of Elizabeth. Flush is the picture of unbounded vitality, while Elizabeth is a fragile "bird in a cage" (35). The freedom that Flush must "forfeit" to be her companion only underscores the suffocating conditions to which patriarchal culture subjects the woman writer (35).

Indeed, Woolf's critique of patriarchal structures hinges as much on the differences between Elizabeth and Flush as it does on their similarities. As a sexually intact male dog, Flush enjoys a relative freedom from the moral constraints imposed on female humans, and in this respect "he is the envy of the woman writer," as Scott observes.[67] In her 1918 essay "Women Novelists," Woolf laments the burden of respectability that weighs disproportionately on women, to the detriment of their writing: "The problem of art is sufficiently difficult in itself without having to respect the ignorance of young women's minds or to consider whether the public will think that the standard of moral purity displayed in your work is such as they have a right to expect from your sex."[68] Unfettered by such constraints, Flush engages in promiscuous sex before coming to live with Elizabeth and also during his later years in Italy, and the narrator underscores the species and gender disparities that permit him to do so with impunity: "Such conduct in a man even, in the year 1842, would have called for some excuse from a biographer; in a woman no excuse could have availed; her name must have been blotted in ignominy from the page. But the moral code of dogs, whether better or worse, is certainly different from ours, and there was nothing in Flush's conduct in this respect that requires a veil now, or unfitted him for the society of the purest and the chastest in the land then" (13).

Flush's promiscuity evokes what Patricia Alden calls the "sexual Bildung" typical of narratives of male identity formation in late Victorian and modernist bildungsromans like George Moore's *Confessions of a Young Man* (1886), James Joyce's *A Portrait of the Artist as a Young Man* (1916), and D. H. Lawrence's *Sons and Lovers* (1913), in which women play a largely instrumental role in the male protagonists' moral and intellectual development.[69] Lawrence's protagonist Paul Morel, for example, regards "sex desire" as "a sort of detached thing, that did not belong to a woman."[70] Flush evinces total detachment in his sexual relations and so realizes, as Alden notes in reference to Paul, "a full experience of individuality without costly estrangement, guilt, self-betrayal, or disillusionment":[71] "So variously, so carelessly Flush embraced the spotted spaniel down the alley, and the brindled dog and the yellow dog—it did not matter which. To Flush it was all the same" (119). As a purebred cocker spaniel who departs from the human norms associated with breed coupling, he mirrors the male hero who resists the socially sanctioned union of heterosexual marriage. Woolf underscores the centrality of sexual liberation to Flush's self-cultivation by drawing an explicit parallel between it and Elizabeth's own means of development: "It cannot be doubted that Mrs. Browning and Flush were reaching different conclusions in their voyages of discovery—she a Grand Duke [a reference to her support for Italian nationalism], he a spotted spaniel" (122–23). Flush's sexual education is part of what enables him to detect upon his return to London "a certain morbidity . . . among the dogs," who regard him just as their human counterparts would "an English peer who has lived a lifetime in the East and contracted some of the habits of the natives—rumour hints indeed that he has turned Moslem and had a son by a Chinese washerwoman" (138–39).[72]

While Flush's sexual awakening might seem merely to parody that of the white male protagonist whose violation of taboos against miscegenation signifies his worldliness, Woolf further discerns in canine desire a queer potential to subvert the sexual mores that tug like a collar at the throat of the woman writer. The narrator might decline to judge whether dogs' "moral code" is "better or worse" than its human counterpart, but an air of sincere approval mingles with irony in the idealized descriptions of Flush experiencing "what men can never know—love pure, love simple, love entire; love that brings no train of care in its wake; that has no shame; no remorse; that is here, that is gone, as the bee on the flower is here and gone" (119). Woolf's own mixed feelings about literary obscenity might explain why Flush's sexual exploits are, as Smith notes, couched "in elaborate metaphor and euphemism," but personal correspondence reveals her delight at watching her own cocker spaniel, Pinka, offend public decency (a delight also evident in the dog's provocative nickname, Pinker).[73] One letter informs Clive Bell that Pinka "is violently on heat, yet must be exercised, and if you consider that there are ten fox terriers in the Square, all belonging to old, and mostly maiden, ladies, you can forgive the gusto with which, when I've written this, I must take her out." In another, to Quentin Bell, after insisting that "nothing is too small, remote, large, or obscene" to satisfy her "appetite for facts," Woolf laments, "Beauty shines on two dogs doing what two women must not do. Thats a fact—Pinker got enmeshed with a fox terrier this very afternoon. Can you blame them?"[74] Thus, while Woolf's approach in *Flush* "lacks the frankness of the later dog biographer J. R. Ackerley"—whose graphic depictions of canine intercourse in *My*

Dog Tulip continue to polarize readers—her letters indicate that she shares Ackerley's interest in the "fact" of canine sexuality.[75]

Pinka served as a source of inspiration for *Flush* and as a sign of the queer power of canine desire in more ways than one, as she was a gift from Vita Sackville-West—Woolf's lover and the subject of her first speculative biography, *Orlando*. Woolf's correspondence with Sackville-West is rife with erotically charged canine imagery, and both women aligned themselves with real and imaginary dogs to express desire, affection, and resentment.[76] The slippage between literal and figurative dogs in these letters indicates that for Woolf, dogs' power to undermine the "prevailing models of socialization" that the traditional bildungsroman upholds is not merely metaphorical.[77] While both women sometimes adopt canine personas, more often they position dogs not as emissaries of human desire but as what McHugh, in her analysis of Ackerley's oeuvre, calls "queer comrades"—animals whose triangulating presence in human interpersonal configurations implicitly challenges the expectation of heterosexual coupling.[78] When Sackville-West took an extended trip to Persia, for example, both women envisioned Woolf's mongrel Grizzle as a participant in their longed-for reunion. Anticipating her lover's return, Woolf writes, "Grizzle and Virginia will rush down to meet you—they will lick you all over."[79] Sackville-West replies, "The next thing you know of me, will be that I walk in and fondle Grizzle."[80] Following Grizzle's death, the highbred Pinka assumed the role of the queer comrade: "Please Vita dear dont forget your humble creatures—Pinker and Virginia. Here we are sitting by the gas fire alone. Every morning she jumps on to my bed and kisses me, and I say thats Vita." The "joke" of *Flush*, then, overlaps with that of Woolf's earlier portrait of her "dearest creature."[81] In a letter urging Sackville-West to sell the manuscript of *Orlando*, she promises to "write another book and give you the MS. instead—about turning into a rusty, clotted, hairy faithful blue-eyed sheepdog."[82]

The apparent mislabeling of her protagonist as a sheepdog signals yet another model for Flush: Gurth, a merle-colored dog who belonged to Woolf's sister, Vanessa Bell, but was Woolf's constant companion during her early years in Bloomsbury. Woolf's diary entries at times convey her frustration with the unblinking vigilance of "that ubiquitous dog"—a description Maureen Adams attributes to the "particularly penetrating stare known as the 'eye-stalk'" common among herding breeds—but they also reveal why Woolf would later use "sheepdog" as a term of endearment for both her lover and her sister.[83] She documents numerous outings with Gurth during which she dispensed with the "botheration" of the leash and chose routes that promised "a variety of street smells" for him to investigate.[84] Adams proposes that Gurth came to embody freedom for Woolf at a time when she was "fettered by her doctor's rules," which included strict limits on the time she could devote to reading and writing.[85] Her amusement at Gurth's indifference to human behavioral codes is evident in her descriptions of him "disgracing" her by barking in a shop "like a Lion roaring in a Cave" and interrupting a concert at Bechstein Hall "with a voluntary bass of his own composition."[86] Beyond modeling an enviable disregard for human social constraints, Gurth enabled Woolf to venture out without her sister and the other human companions she had formerly relied on "to act as a buffer between her and the rest of the world."[87] It is hardly surprising, then, that she later borrowed Gurth to accompany her on a solitary walking tour of Wales and, upon her return, was reluctant to return him to Vanessa: "I will send you your dog. I should be glad to keep him, for he is really rather an engaging beast."[88]

But while Woolf's relationship with Gurth no doubt informs the sharp contrast between Flush's freedom to indulge his animal appetites and Elizabeth's confinement under the watchful eye of the Victorian patriarch, the *Flush* narrator takes care to avoid depicting canine experience as an unfettered "orgy of pleasure" (132). Satirizing the "idealization of animality" that Carrie Rohman finds in the work of some of Woolf's modernist peers— especially the antihumanist aesthetics of Lawrence—the narrator refuses to indulge the fantasy of animal being as "a Paradise where essences exist in their utmost purity and the naked soul of things presses on the naked nerve" (132).[89] Ursula in Lawrence's *Women in Love* exemplifies this view: "She loved the horses and cows in the field. Each was single and to itself, magical. It was not referred away to some detestable social principle."[90] Flush, by contrast, "lived in no such Paradise. The spirit, ranging from star to star, the bird whose furthest flight over polar snows or tropical forests never brings it within sight of human houses and their curling wood-smoke, may, for anything we know, enjoy such immunity, such integrity of bliss. But Flush had lain upon human knees and heard men's voices" (132–33). Flush's evolutionary and personal entanglement with the human species deconstructs the nature/culture binary implicit in Lawrence's ideal. If the comparison between the pet dog and the woman writer underscores the moral and social constraints imposed on the latter, it also reveals the inadequacy of traditional literary modes for representing character as it emerges in what Haraway calls the "contact zones" of interspecies life.[91] As I discuss in the next section, the limits of literary characterization are especially evident in the bildungsroman, which, with its emphasis on the individual realization of human potential, isolates the protagonist from the interspecies relations that give rise to this potential.

Canine *Bildung*

Woolf's implicit critique in *Flush* of the intertwined anthropocentrism and phallocentrism of the bildungsroman tradition brings this once-marginalized text into conversation with her more widely recognized feminist novels. In his study of the modernist bildungsroman, Gregory Castle argues that modernism's critique of the "Enlightenment thinking" that underwrites the conventional bildungsroman plot does not constitute a rejection of the genre itself; rather, modernist writers "recuperat[e] a classical notion of Bildung [the process of self-cultivation] that incorporates the crucial elements of individual freedom and aesthetic education." He sees Woolf's *Voyage Out* and *Mrs. Dalloway* as "radical feminist Bildungsromane" that "reclaim and reconfigure classical, aesthetic-spiritual Bildung to serve the developmental needs of women" who aspire to more than the "quietist piety, moral perfection, and marital security" promoted by the so-called female bildungsroman of the nineteenth century. *Flush* similarly reclaims the zoocentric gestures of the Victorian animal autobiography and the naturalistic animal story even as it eschews the sentimental anthropomorphism of the former and the phallocentrism of the latter. Thus, just as any attempt to establish *Flush*'s significance by divorcing it from the animal narrative tradition would obscure how it both participates in and critiques that tradition, Castle insists that efforts to situate Woolf's novels of female development within "a separate tradition" uncoupled from the "male-oriented discourse of Bildung" are deeply problematic. Such a redrawing of boundaries, he warns, "reinscribes the very gender and genre differences that a writer like Virginia Woolf seeks so brilliantly to overcome, for her novels do not so much discover a separate space of female self-development as occupy a common space that is seen in a radically different fashion from the men who share it."[92]

While *The Voyage Out* and *Mrs. Dalloway* represent domestic and public spaces from the female perspectives so woefully underrepresented in the literary canon, *Flush* brings to light an even more marginalized perspective. Like Elizabeth Barrett Browning's servant Lily Wilson—whose "extremely obscure" life, the narrator insists in a lengthy endnote, "cries aloud for the services of a biographer" (168n)—Flush offers a radically different view of the spaces he cohabits with the woman writer, thereby exposing the anthropocentric privilege and limitations of Elizabeth's perspective. As I noted earlier, his difficulty adjusting to the stifling environment of the bedroom, signified by the overpowering "smell of eau de cologne" that continually "lacerate[s] his nostrils," serves partially to highlight the injustice of Elizabeth's circumstances (27). As a dog, however, Flush experiences the constraints of domestic life even more acutely. Having spent his puppyhood enjoying "with all the vivacity of his temperament most of the pleasures and some of the licenses natural to his youth and sex" (11), he finds "all his instincts ... thwarted and contradicted" as he adapts to "a life of complete seclusion" with Elizabeth interrupted only by "brief and perfunctory" outings with Wilson (32–33). The sound of "autumn winds," for example, prompts Elizabeth merely to ask Wilson "to see to the fastenings of the window," but for Flush it stirs race memories, recalling all that he has sacrificed in exchange for bourgeois domesticity: "He could not help dancing round the room on a windy autumn day when the partridges must be scattering over the stubble. He thought he heard guns on the breeze" (33–34).

Elizabeth's own confined situation fosters a partial appreciation for the effects of Flush's deprivation: "She was too just not to realize that it was for her ... that he had sacrificed the sun and the air" (48). Her historical counterpart recognized the similarities in their circumstances: "Why, what *is* Flush, but a lapdog? And what am *I*, but a woman? I assure you we never take ourselves for anything greater."[93] Yet Barrett Browning also recognized that these circumstances would weigh differently, and in some respects more heavily, on a dog. When her friend Mary Russell Mitford first offered her the young Flush as a gift, she was reluctant to accept, in part because of the monetary value of a purebred cocker spaniel puppy but also because she doubted whether she could give a young, energetic dog a fulfilling life. When Barrett Browning finally consented to receive Flush, she strove to provide whatever enrichment she could. Although ill health prevented her from maintaining the level of activity he enjoyed with Mitford—with whom he took the daily off-leash walks that Woolf's Flush remembers when he first glimpses Regent's Park—Barrett Browning kept Flush mentally occupied, endeavoring to teach him numbers, letters, and games using the positive-reinforcement methods now advocated by professional dog trainers. During his "arithmetic lessons," she would hold up "pieces of cake while Flush barked out the correct number," rewarding his successes with tidbits and praise.[94] Woolf's Elizabeth exhibits a similar faith in Flush's intellectual potential and does "her best to refine and educate his powers still further" (47).

Indeed, in her efforts to introduce Flush to a harp and a mirror, Elizabeth strives to facilitate the "aesthetic education" and "self-cultivation" that, according to Castle, remain central to modernist recuperations of the bildungsroman plot.[95] While Flush briefly examines the harp but loses interest once he concludes that it is not alive, the mirror proves more unnerving: Elizabeth "would make him stand with her in front of the looking-glass and ask him why he barked and trembled. Was not the little brown dog opposite himself? But what is 'oneself'? Is it the thing people see? Or is it the thing one is? So Flush pondered that question too, and, unable to solve the problem of reality, pressed closer to Miss Barrett and kissed her 'expressively.' *That* was real at any rate" (47–48). As a number of critics have noted, in this scene Woolf anticipates Lacan's theory of the mirror stage as a formative moment in the process of self-realization.[96] But the competing definitions of selfhood here, coupled with the uncertainty as to whether these are the thoughts of Elizabeth, the narrator, or Flush, undermine the anthropocentric assumption that recognizing oneself in a mirror is a universal sign of self-awareness. As Weil argues, Flush's expressive kiss "pits the 'real' body language of affection against the often unreal signs of identity that otherwise structure human relations and human-animal relations alike."[97] That Flush discovers "reality" not in the illusion of autonomous identity but in his embodied relationship with Elizabeth—a theme to which I will return—indicates the limitations of compartmentalized models of the self for both human and nonhuman animals.

Flush's barking and trembling aside, dogs have not been shown to respond to their reflections in ways that demonstrate self-awareness (as defined, of course, by human inquirers). In *Inside of a Dog*, comparative psychologist Alexandra Horowitz offers a compelling theory of dogs' failure to pass the so-called mirror test, in which researchers place a mark on an animal, present a mirror, and watch for outward signs thought to indicate whether the subject recognizes the image as his or her own reflection and thus possesses a sense of self. While chimpanzees, dolphins, and elephants have evinced something like self-awareness by investigating the new mark on their bodies when presented with their reflections, dogs "never examine themselves in the mirror"; instead, they "look at it idly" or, like Flush, respond "as though it were another animal." Horowitz proposes that a "possible explanation for the dogs' behavior is that the lack of other cues—specifically olfactory cues—coming from the mirror image leads dogs to lose interest in investigating it. Some fantastical odor-mirror that wafts the dog's own scent while reflecting the dog's own image would be a better medium" for gauging canine self-awareness. Further compounding the test's emphasis on sight is its presumption of "a specific kind of curiosity about oneself: one that leads humans to examine what is new on our own bodies. Dogs may be less interested in what is visually new than what is tactually new: they notice strange sensations and pursue them with nibbling mouth or scratching paw. A dog is not curious why the tip of his black tail is white, or what the color of his new leash is." In other words, dogs' apparent failure to demonstrate self-awareness via the mirror test might instead reflect a human failure to recognize how species differences influence whether a mark is "noticeable, and also worth noting."[98]

A more accurate measurement of canine self-awareness would require a more rigorous attempt to imagine the canine *Umwelt*—ethologist Jakob von Uexküll's term for an organism's perceptual world. This is precisely what Woolf endeavors to do in scenes like the one describing Flush's first entrance into Elizabeth's room, which stresses the olfactory and tactile nature of his *Umwelt* (though the limitations of human perception mean that Flush's sensations can only be approximated through analogy):

> Only a scholar who has descended step by step into a mausoleum and there finds himself in a crypt, crusted with fungus, slimy with mould, exuding sour smells of decay and antiquity, while half-obliterated marble busts gleam in mid-air and all is dimly seen by the light of the small swinging lamp which he holds, and dips and turns, glancing now here, now there—only the sensations of such an explorer into the buried vaults of a ruined city can compare with the riot of emotions that flooded Flush's nerves as he stood for the first time in an invalid's bedroom in Wimpole Street, and smelt eau de cologne. (19–20)

The very structure of this sentence, which distends to the point that it must start anew following one of Woolf's characteristic dashes, illustrates the inadequacy of human representational modes—like the mirror itself—to portray the room as Flush perceives it. By piling on descriptive phrases and figurative appeals to humans' limited senses of smell and touch, passages like this push the reader to imagine sensations beyond human capabilities. Indeed, Flush acclimates himself to Elizabeth's room largely through the overlooked (by humans) senses of smell and touch: "Very slowly, very dimly, with much sniffing and pawing, Flush by degrees distinguished the outlines of several articles of furniture" (20). And although he is eventually "amazed" to see "staring back at him from a hole in the wall another dog with bright eyes flashing, and tongue lolling," the mirror is one of the last objects to attract his notice (21). It was only with considerable difficulty and persistence that the historical Barrett Browning managed to persuade Flush to acknowledge the mirror, and even when he did, his "barking & howling & gnashing" could well have signaled his frustration at having an uninteresting object repeatedly placed in his path rather than what she interpreted as his "rage" upon seeing "the brown dog in the glass."[99]

By imagining the distinctly canine ways in which the historical Flush might have experienced the environments he cohabited with Barrett Browning, Woolf arguably exhibits keener insight into the canine *Umwelt* than does Uexküll himself, demonstrating the adeptness of what Derek Ryan has called "Woolf's nonanthropocentric theorising."[100] Despite his groundbreaking theorization of perceptual worlds beyond human comprehension—an insight that profoundly influenced not only the emerging field of ethology but also the anti- and posthumanist thought of figures like Heidegger, Deleuze, and Agamben— Uexküll's illustrations depicting the same room through the eyes of a human, a dog, and a fly in *A Foray into the Worlds of Animals and Humans* affirm a rather conventional view of animal experience as impoverished, prefiguring Heidegger's characterization of "the animal" as "poor in world."[101] The images use different colors to denote the "effect tones" of the room's furnishings—that is, the subjective meanings they signify as a result of their use value to the perceiver. In the image representing the human *Umwelt*, Uexküll assigns an effect tone to nearly every object in the room. An array of colors designates the "reading shade" of the bookshelf, the "writing shade" of the desk, the "light tone" of the lamp, the "walking shade" of the floor, the "sitting shade" of the chairs, sofa, and stool, and the "eating and drinking tones" of the plates and glasses and the table on which they sit; only the walls have a neutral "obstacle shade."[102]

The dog's view of the same room is stark by comparison (though considerably less so than the fly's view, which includes only light and eating shades). While Uexküll includes walking, sitting, eating, and light shades in the canine *Umwelt*, he assigns an obstacle shade to the objects that emanate reading and writing shades to the human. In representing the canine *Umwelt* as a mere subset of its human counterpart—indeed, he notes that "the number of dog objects [is] far less than the number of human objects"—Uexküll fails to imagine specifically canine ways of acting in and on this environment. We might reasonably surmise that the floor, for example, would have a lying as well as a walking shade for the dog. Further, given Uexküll's astute observation that dogs "learn to handle certain objects useful to human beings insofar as [humans] make them into things of use to dogs," dogs' perceptions of the room might vary widely based on their experiences, age, and size.[103] For a puppy, books and chair legs might have a chewing shade, and for attention-seeking dogs, the sofa might have something like a humans-at-petting-level shade. Dogs with messy or indulgent owners might perceive the eating shade as extending from the plates to the table, chairs, and surrounding floor, yet even the table lacks an eating tone—perhaps because Uexküll assumes that the dog views it only as an obstacle that bars the way to food. By contrast, Flush is bewildered to see "that article of furniture, whose chief function it was to provide shade, kicked on the floor" during a séance at the Brownings' Florence home (155). While the table acquires what we might call a spiritual-communion tone for Elizabeth when she is swept up in the Victorian craze for mysticism, Flush quite reasonably perceives a shade tone.

Even in the relatively stable environment of Elizabeth's Wimpole Street bedroom, objects' effect tones are in flux and not securely tied to any practical value they might have for Flush. In contrast to the relatively barren room that Uexküll imagines for the dog, Elizabeth's bedroom is filled with objects that fascinate Flush precisely because their appearances fail to intimate their functions: "That huge object by the window was perhaps a wardrobe. Next to it stood, conceivably, a chest of drawers. In the middle of the room swam up to the surface what seemed to be a table with a ring round it; and then the vague amorphous shapes of armchair and table emerged. But everything was disguised" (20). Even after he learns to "identify [and] distinguish ... all the different articles he saw there," their effect tones remain contingent and unstable—particularly with the (for Flush) intrusive arrival of Robert Browning (27). Earlier, we saw how Robert's visits change what the chair opposite Elizabeth's sofa signifies for Flush, although it retains only a sitting tone for Mr. Barrett. Even objects that have only a symbolic connection to Robert—the bookcase and busts of famous poets—become "alien" and "severe" in his presence (56). Indeed, from Flush's predominately olfactory perspective, the entire room is transformed anytime a visitor interrupts his "long hours" of quiet seclusion with Elizabeth: "The handle was seen to spin round; the door actually opened; somebody came in. Then how strangely the furniture changed its look! What extraordinary eddies of sound and smell were at once set in circulation! How they washed round the legs of tables and impinged on the sharp edges of the wardrobe!" (39). Whereas Uexküll pictures the canine *Umwelt*, like the human one, as a collection of discrete objects, Woolf's characterization of Flush's *Umwelt* as a swirl of smells suggests a different, potentially less human-centered strategy for representing nonhuman worlds.

Insofar as Elizabeth and Flush inhabit the same space but perceive dramatically different worlds, the text points to "vast gaps in their understanding" that mark crucial distinctions in their development (36). Elizabeth cannot smell the distant mutton bones and passing dogs that prompt Flush to "tremble suddenly, and whimper and start and listen," nor can he comprehend why she spends "hour after hour passing her hand over a white page with a black stick" (36). And while Elizabeth's reading and writing enable her to cultivate a rich inner life and participate in a vibrant intellectual community even while confined to her sickroom, Flush has no such outlet. At first, he envies Elizabeth's access to the realm of language so privileged in both traditional and modernist modes of *Bildung*: "When he heard her low voice syllabling innumerable sounds, he longed for the day when his own rough roar would issue like hers in the little simple sounds that had such mysterious meaning. And when he watched the same fingers for ever crossing a white page with a straight stick, he longed for the time when he too should blacken paper as she did" (38–39). Here, the narrator attributes to Flush a desire to speak and write that might seem to affirm the humanist—and anthropocentric—ends of the prototypical bildungsroman plot. However, the abrupt shifts from free indirect speech to narrative commentary in the longer passage from which this passage is extracted persistently undermine the fantasy of the talking dog: "But suppose Flush had been able to speak—would he not have said something sensible about the potato disease in Ireland? . . . And yet, had he been able to write as she did?—The question is superfluous happily, for truth compels us to say that

... Flush was not a poet but a red cocker spaniel" (38–39). The anthropocentric underpinnings of this fantasy later become apparent in Elizabeth's desire that a distraught Flush give voice to her own feelings for Robert—the very feelings that render her oblivious to Flush as he lies at her feet in "tense and silent agony" (56) during his rival's lengthy visits: "And smiling, she gave him the oddest look—as if she wished that he could talk—as if she expected him too to feel what she felt. And then she laughed, pityingly; as if it were absurd—Flush, poor Flush could feel nothing of what she felt" (57). Only from a human-centered perspective can the absence of speech from Flush's communicative repertoire be viewed as a pitiable deprivation. As Horowitz reminds us, "it is not the animals who desire to speak and cannot"; rather, "it is that we desire them to talk and cannot effect it."[104]

In fact, the "vast gaps in understanding" that sometimes divide Flush and Elizabeth also underscore the remarkability of their communicative successes. Just as Flush can "read signs that nobody else could even see" (51) and so predict the arrival both of Robert's letters and of the man himself, he adeptly employs body language and vocalization to make his feelings and intentions understood, however imperfectly. Flush's barking and biting convey his antipathy to Robert in no uncertain terms, while "the fixity with which [he] gaze[s] at Elizabeth" after she has "inflicted upon him the worst punishment he had ever known" moves her to forgive him for biting Robert (63). Her description of the "beseeching eyes" that persuade her to relent signals a popular anthropomorphic projection—that of the guilty dog (64). As Horowitz explains, recent research indicates that the submissive canine posture so often interpreted a "guilty look"—dropped ears, tucked tail, and hunched, slinking body—is not an outward sign of a troubled conscience but a gesture to appease an angry human.[105] Whatever the feelings or motives behind Flush's pitiable expression, he succeeds in persuading Elizabeth to welcome him back to her side. Later, when he stands before the empty chair that holds "the shape of his enemy" and looks at the now-stale cakes Robert has left for him, "Flush's meaning [is] plain" (71). In eating the cakes, which are "bereft of any carnal seduction" but undoubtedly retain the scent of his rival, Flush "signified" to Elizabeth his acceptance of Robert as a "friend" (72). Both Elizabeth's and the narrator's interpretations of Flush's gestures are, of course, open to the charge of anthropomorphism, as Horowitz's refutation of the "guilty dog" fallacy demonstrates. Yet, as Weil argues, Woolf uses anthropomorphism consciously and strategically "to dislodge the reader and author from an objective standpoint from which to judge what is exclusively human or animal."[106] Woolf's strategic anthropomorphism, combined with the free indirect discourse that continually blurs distinctions between the perspectives of the narrator, Flush, and Elizabeth, reminds us that there is no unmediated access to other minds, whether human or non.

Further, the text's recurrent critique of language challenges the assumption that human systems of signification are any less opaque than the canine gaze: "'Writing,'—Miss Barrett once exclaimed after a morning's toil, 'writing, writing . . . ' After all, she may have thought, do words say anything? Can words say anything? Do not words destroy the symbol that lies beyond the reach of words?" (37–38, ellipsis in original). Woolf again anticipates Lacan in proposing that language inevitably distorts the reality it purports to represent. Flush's and Elizabeth's reliance on the "body language of affection," to borrow Weil's phrase, thus leads "to much misunderstanding" but also produces "a peculiar intimacy" for which language cannot account (37). The limits of language are perhaps most apparent in the narrator's attempt to describe Italy as Flush experiences it:

> Here, then, the biographer must perforce come to a pause. Where two or three thousand words are insufficient for what we see . . . there are no more than two words and perhaps one-half for what we smell. The human nose is practically non-existent. The greatest poets in the world have smelt nothing but roses on the one hand, and dung on the other. The infinite gradations that lie between are unrecorded. Yet it was in the world of smell that Flush mostly lived. Love was chiefly smell; form and colour were smell; music and architecture, law, politics, and science were smell. To him religion itself was smell. To describe his simplest experience with the daily chop or biscuit is beyond our power. . . . Confessing our inadequacy, then, we can but note that to Flush Italy, in these the fullest, the freest, the happiest years of his life, meant mainly a succession of smells. (129–30)

This passage breaks with an entire humanist tradition that prizes language as evidence of a human surpassing of the animal; as Derrida observes, thinkers as diverse as Aristotle, Descartes, Kant, Heidegger, Lacan, and Levinas "all say the same thing: the animal is deprived of language."[107] For Woolf's narrator, by contrast, language confirms the severe limits of the human *Umwelt*, inverting the view of the animal as deprived. Seen in this way, language both reveals and compounds a human lack. By assigning one of a paltry assortment of words to each smell within his limited reach, the poet (Woolf offers Swinburne and Shakespeare as examples) restricts his olfactory repertoire further still, effectively plugging his nose to the "infinite" variety of smells that "lie beyond the reach of words." Even the suggestion of a vast continuum of smells ranging from pleasing to offensive reveals humans' limited criteria for evaluating scents. Underscoring how language both reflects and exacerbates humans' sensory impoverishment, the narrator reports approvingly that "not a single one of [Flush's] myriad sensations ever submitted itself to the deformity of words" (132).

Woolf's emphasis on Flush's olfactory and tactile experiences forms a crucial part of the text's critique not only of language but also of existing models of the bildungsroman. As Elizabeth Abel and her co-editors argue in *The Voyage In: Fictions of Female Development*, "The fully realized and individuated self who caps the journey of the *Bildungsroman* may not represent the developmental goals of women, or of women characters."[108] Building on this insight, Castle contends that the "mutually embedded Bildung plots" of Clarissa and her daughter, Elizabeth, in *Mrs. Dalloway* challenge both the privileging of male experience in the bildungsroman tradition and the "socially pragmatic Bildung deemed appropriate for young women" in the female bildungsroman.[109] I would add that Woolf's strategy of embedding the famed narrative of Barrett Browning's liberation from her domineering father within Flush's own *Bildung* plot radically undermines the status of human modes of identity formation as privileged—indeed, exclusive—means of achieving developmental maturity, reminding us that processes we have come to class under the rubric of self-cultivation always take place within what David Herman calls the "wider webs of creatural life."[110] In addition to highlighting how patriarchal structures hinder both characters' attempts at self-cultivation, the narrator repeatedly compares Elizabeth's writing to Flush's olfactory aesthetics, thereby marking their means of fulfillment as distinct but equally legitimate. Whereas, for Elizabeth, "the beauty of the Apennines brought words to birth in such numbers that they positively crushed each other out of existence," Flush takes no notice of such visual spectacles: "Beauty, so it seems at least, had to be crystallised into a green or violet powder and puffed by some celestial syringe down the fringed channels that lay behind his nostrils before it touched Flush's senses; and then it issued not in words, but in silent rapture. Where Mrs. Browning saw, [Flush] smelt; where she wrote, he snuffed" (128–29).

Flush's development accelerates in Italy, where the aesthetic education he began under Elizabeth's tutelage takes a distinctly canine turn: "Mr. Browning wrote regularly in one room; Mrs. Browning wrote regularly in another.... But Flush wandered off into the streets of Florence to enjoy the rapture of smell" (130–31). Roaming the streets "with his nose to the ground, drinking in the essence" (131), he comes to know Florence "as no human being has ever known it; as Ruskin never knew it or George Eliot either" (132). In addition to developing a detailed olfactory and tactile knowledge of the city—a canine version of what Castle identifies as "an aesthetics of everyday life" cultivated by Woolf's female protagonists—he gains a "new conception of canine society" (116–17).[111] The mongrels he encounters in the streets of Florence force him to confront "the curious and at first upsetting truth that the laws of the Kennel Club are not universal" (116)—a realization that ultimately proves liberating when Robert takes a pair of scissors to Flush's coat to combat a flea infestation, clipping away "the insignia of a cocker spaniel" in the process (135). Like the modernist bildungsroman's hero, for whom "Bildung so often turns out to be a dissent from social order, from the bourgeois appropriation of self-cultivation," Flush rejects the entrenched ideology of breed and embraces his rebirth as a mongrel.[112] His acceptance of this transformation ironically echoes an earlier passage in which Elizabeth watches him gazing at the mirror in Wimpole Street and prematurely dubs him "a philosopher"—an attribution undercut by the narrator's insistence that "on the contrary, he was an aristocrat considering his points" (32). By contrast, when Elizabeth calls Flush "wise" after Robert has clipped him "into the likeness of a lion," the narrator concurs: "The true philosopher is he who has lost his coat but is free from fleas" (136).

Flush, then, realizes a specifically canine form of *Bildung* by shedding the "pedigree" thrust upon him by human breed standards and embracing the species identity that unites him with the mongrels of Florence—a shift that echoes Jack London's zoocentric model of canine development (134). Yet whereas London's Buck cannot fully self-actualize until the deus ex machina of John Thornton's death severs the "last tie" binding him to humanity, the tie that joins Flush and Elizabeth is "undeniably still binding" right up to the moment of Flush's death in the book's final paragraph (123).[113] In declining to represent canine fulfillment as a liberation from human influence, Woolf refuses to reinscribe the nature/culture boundary that London's vision ultimately necessitates. While Buck retains the wildness that helps him return to the primitive, Flush is irrevocably transformed by the fact of companion-species entanglements; his "flesh [is] veined with human passions" (133), and the "pads of his feet" are "stamp[ed]" with the "proud Latin inscriptions" that pave the streets of Florence (132). Far from forsaking human society altogether, he comes to regard not only "all dogs" but "all men" as "his brothers" (117, 137). Thus Flush achieves *Bildung* not by answering the call of a natural realm separated from human culture but by immersing himself in the multispecies community of Florence, as portrayed in a vignette of the marketplace in the book's penultimate scene: "The market women were sitting beside baskets of fruit; pigeons were fluttering, bells were pealing, whips were cracking. The many-coloured mongrels of Florence were running in and out sniffing and pawing. . . . [Flush] flung himself down beside his friend Catterina, under the shadow of her great basket. . . . He guarded her melons and she scratched his ear. . . . The flies buzzed on the great pink melon that had been sliced open to show its flesh" (157–58). Woolf's portrait of an old dog as part of a broader scene in which the "snarling and biting" of street dogs blend with the "fluttering" of pigeons and the "perpetual buzz and hum of human voices" reveals that, contrary to the anthropocentric assumptions of the traditional bildungsroman, the social configurations within which character develops are never exclusively human.

Conclusion

While species and sex differences mean that Flush and Elizabeth occupy distinct perceptual worlds and thus reach "different conclusions in their voyages of discovery," their developmental journeys remain deeply interdependent (122–23). Elizabeth plays a vital role in Flush's education, but Flush's impact on her deferred development is no less profound. Just as his historical counterpart empowered Barrett Browning to leave her sickroom—"Aspiring to the pure heroic . . . [I] called Flush, & walked down stairs & into the street . . . in glorious independence"—Woolf's Flush becomes Elizabeth's coconspirator "in defiance of [the] black and beetling tyranny" (73) of patriarchy embodied by the domineering Mr. Barrett.[114] Castle argues that in the case of the intertwined trajectories of Clarissa and Elizabeth in *Mrs. Dalloway*, "this mutual embeddedness testifies [to] the complexity of the relations between mothers and daughters, which has a particularly subversive resonance in any discussion of the Bildungsroman."[115] The mutually embedded plots of *Flush*, I would add, testify to the complexity of interspecies relations, reminding us that processes we have come to class under the rubric of self-cultivation always take place within what Haraway calls the "mortal world-making entanglements" of human/animal relations.[116] By reimagining social and personal development as a multispecies process, Woolf, in Ryan's words, "draws out the complexity of materially involved entanglements between companion species, which include the possibility for the movements of becoming rather than a fixed and defined dividing line."[117]

Indeed, the central insight Flush takes from "the bedroom school"—as illustrated in the aftermath of his long-anticipated confrontation with Robert—is an understanding of character as contingent and relational. After Robert departs, Flush's conjectural train of thought includes the realization that "things are not simple but complex. If he bit Mr. Browning he bit her too. . . . Mr. Browning was Miss Barrett—Miss Barrett was Mr. Browning" (69–70). This realization prompts Flush to reject jealousy and swear "to love Mr. Browning," a decision he signals to Elizabeth by humbly consuming the stale cakes (72). The rare shift to direct speech in the passage that follows underscores the multispecies model of the bildungsroman, and of character more generally, presented in the book as a whole: "I need all the things that you both need. We are all three conspirators in the most glorious of causes. We are joined in sympathy. We are joined in hatred. We are joined in defiance of black and beetling tyranny. We are joined in love" (73). Flush's epiphany, like the book itself, affirms not a narrowly humanist project of self-cultivation but an ongoing process of intersubjective becoming that exceeds the boundaries and potential of the individual human.

In this way, Woolf's portrait of canine experience epitomizes what Castle regards as a distinctly "modernist . . . notion of 'Bildung' as multiple and (de)constructed subjectivities," subverting not only the phallic "I" of the traditional hero but the fantasy of the self-authored human subject that underwrites conventional notions of literary character.[118] Flush's observation that Elizabeth is changing "in every relation" (62) and that he, too, is no longer "the same dog" (71) after Robert comes into their lives echoes Clarissa's reflections on human character in *Mrs. Dalloway*:

Clarissa had a theory in those days—they had heaps of theories, always theories, as young people have. It was to explain the feeling they had of dissatisfaction; not knowing people; not being known. For how could they know each other? You met every day; then not for six months, or years. It was unsatisfactory, they agreed, how little one knew people. But she said, sitting on the bus going up Shaftesbury Avenue, she felt herself everywhere; not "here, here, here"; and she tapped the back of the seat; but everywhere. She waved her hand, going up Shaftesbury Avenue. She was all that. So that to know her, or any one, one must seek out the people who completed them; even the places. Odd affinities she had with people she had never spoken to, some woman in the street, some man behind a counter—even trees, or barns. It ended in a transcendental theory which, with her horror of death, allowed her to believe, or say that she believed (for all her scepticism), that since our apparitions, the part of us which appears, are so momentary compared with the other, the unseen part of us, which spreads wide, the unseen might survive, be recovered somehow attached to this person or that, or even haunting certain places after death ... perhaps—perhaps.[119]

The question posed by Woolf's narrator during the first meeting between Flush and Elizabeth—"Could it be that each completed what was dormant in the other?"—uncannily recalls Clarissa's observation that to know someone, "one must seek out the people who completed them; even the places." "Even the dogs," *Flush* seems implicitly to add, expanding Clarissa's theory of character to account for the companion species whose marginal status throughout much of the literary canon belies their omnipresence in social configurations that are by no means exclusively human. Woolf's diary entries following Pinka's unexpected death in 1935 affirm dogs' place in the network of relations that shapes "the unseen part of us": "8 years of a dog certainly mean something. I suppose—is it part of our life thats buried in the orchard? That 8 years in London—our walks—something of our play private life, thats gone?" The "intensity" with which Woolf experienced the intermingling "sense of death" and the "feeling of [Pinka's] character" signals her alertness to how the entanglement of human and canine subjectivities undermines the phallo- and anthropocentric subject of the traditional bildungsroman. By publishing *Flush* despite her characteristic "fear of [the] sentimentality" that pervades popular understandings of the human/dog relationship, Woolf recognized the extraordinarily high stakes of her experiment in animal narrative, in which she uses the intimate and vital role of companion species to engage in nothing less than a radical reconceptualization of human identity itself.[120]

CHAPTER 3

THE NEW DOG
Albert Payson Terhune and J. R. Ackerley

The entanglement of human and canine lives becomes particularly (and often humorously) vexed in the space of the modern city, as indicated by the gossip circulating among the dogs of London in Virginia Woolf's *Flush*: "It was common knowledge that Mrs. [Jane Welsh] Carlyle's dog Nero had leapt from a top-storey window with the intention of committing suicide. He had found the strain of life in Cheyne Row intolerable, it was said. Indeed Flush could well believe it now that he was back again in Welbeck Street. The confinement, the crowd of little objects, the black-beetles by night, the bluebottles by day, the lingering odours of mutton, the perpetual presence on the sideboard of bananas—all this, together with the proximity of several men and women, heavily dressed and not often or indeed completely washed, wrought on his temper and strained his nerves."[1] As Flush is acutely aware, urban modernity imposed new constraints that underscored the interspecies nature of social life and demanded a dramatic reconfiguration of the human/dog relationship. This much is evident in reference books by early twentieth-century breed fanciers, which reveal deep-rooted ambivalence in the purebred dog world regarding dogs—particularly those bred for work—inhabiting urban spaces. Those who fancied working dogs lamented the degraded, artificial existence to which urban life subjected members of their favorite breeds.[2] In *The New Book of the Dog*, a 1907 encyclopedia of

"British dogs and their foreign relatives," collie fancier James C. Dalgliesh complains that "the townsman who knows the shepherd's dog only as he is to be seen, out of his true element, threading his confined way through crowded streets where sheep are not, can have small appreciation of his wisdom and his sterling worth."[3] Deerhound enthusiast Robert Leighton bemoans the relegation of "one of the grandest of hunting dogs" to "the life of a pedestrian pet" and pities the "town dog" whose exercise is limited to a "sober walk at the end of a lead in crowded streets."[4] Such accounts portray the large, athletic bodies of working dogs as wholly incongruous in the city.

These critiques of urban life as unsuitable for working breeds are frequently accompanied by acknowledgments that the conditions of modernity have rendered these breeds' special talents largely superfluous. "Gone are the good romantic days of [deer] stalking," Leighton admits, and his deerhound's "vocation, therefore, has undergone a change" from specialized hunter to domestic companion or show specimen. Dalgliesh similarly holds that one can come to know the collie "properly" only by seeing him "at work in a country where sheep abound," yet he also asserts that "the show Collie of the present period," though "produced from the old working type, . . . is now practically a distinct breed. His qualities in the field are not often tested, but he is a much more handsome and attractive animal."[5] As spaces "where sheep abound" become increasingly scarce, Dalgliesh's collie, like Leighton's deerhound, finds himself in search of a new occupation—one for which his working abilities are not his chief qualifications.

Dalgliesh's appeal to the show collie's beauty as compensation for his lack of utility points to a central tension in the purebred dog world produced by the transition of the working dog from rural laborer to urban or suburban pet. Fanciers of breeds like the collie fell largely into two camps, one insisting upon the primacy of working ability in determining a dog's quality, the other regarding aesthetic enhancement as the chief goal of modern breeding. As Dalgliesh explicitly acknowledges, "What is aimed at is something beautiful; a head that will cause the observer to linger in admiration."[6] Those who regarded working ability as paramount (like ethologist Konrad Lorenz, discussed in chapter 1) feared that breeding for aesthetics would dilute or pervert the physical and mental qualities required for herding, flushing, and retrieving. Yet the rapidly declining need for dogs to perform such tasks placed the future of working breeds in jeopardy, prompting many enthusiasts to regard beautification as a wholly justifiable aim for modern breeders. Thus Herbert Compton reasons in his 1904 compendium *The Twentieth Century Dog*, "it may be argued that the collie, to the non-pastoral community that owns it, is not a sheep-dog at all, but a companion, prized for its beauty and intelligence, and not for working qualities which it has ceased to be trained to, and has no opportunity of exercising or displaying; and that under these conditions and circumstances breeders are justified in focussing their attention on those two points, head and coat, which undoubtedly constitute its chief glory when it is expatriated from its native folds." Though professing neutrality on the question of form versus function, Compton reminds his readers that "we are dealing with the dog as he exists for the multitude and not merely for the shepherd," and he stresses the consequent need to "adapt ourselves . . . to the idiosyncrasies of fashion and the insistence of craze as reflected in results."[7] Form *is* functional, he intimates, when the dog is essentially a companion or ornament kept for human pleasure. By working to enhance physical beauty, breeders of the period molded dogs into more enjoyable pets for the "non-pastoral" majority who had no need for their more specialized skills.

At stake in the form-versus-function debate is the question of how (or how much) dogs and the human/dog relationship should be transformed in order to adapt to the shifting landscapes of urban industrial modernity. It is this question that connects the two otherwise profoundly different writers whose work this chapter examines: Albert Payson Terhune and J. R. Ackerley. Terhune, an American journalist, prolific fiction writer, and hobby breeder, is best known for his enormously popular stories about a heroic collie named Lad, a precursor to British writer Eric Knight's even more famous Lassie. The success of the original Lad stories, published beginning in 1915 and compiled in the 1919 collection *Lad: A Dog*, established Terhune's position as what biographer Irving Litvag calls "unquestionably the most famous, the most productive, and the best-compensated writer of dog stories that ever lived."[8] Part of Lad's appeal, no doubt, was Terhune's decidedly antimodern idealization of the human/dog relationship—informed by Jack London's primitivism but ultimately more indicative of reactionary longing for a vanishing past, as reflected in Terhune's description of the thoroughbred collie as "an ultraconservative" who "loathe[s] change of any sort."[9] The setting for the Lad stories, called simply "The Place," is an idyllic rural estate modeled after Sunnybank, the Terhune family home in Pompton Lakes, New Jersey, which Terhune dreamed of inheriting while working as a reporter for the *Evening World* and living in a series of cramped Manhattan apartments. As "official guardian of The Place" (302), Lad serves chiefly to protect this "paradise on earth" from the encroachment of decadent, urban modernity.[10]

Whereas Terhune imagines an idealized human/dog relationship far removed from the modern city, Ackerley, writing several decades later, narrates his efforts to provide his Alsatian bitch, Queenie, with a fulfilling and decidedly "doggy" life in postwar London. Despite his history as a self-described "querulous dog denouncer," Ackerley acquired the high-strung, possessive Queenie in the mid-1940s, during his twenty-four-year tenure as editor of the BBC's literary magazine the *Listener*.[11] The 1956 memoir *My Dog Tulip* (in which Queenie was renamed at the recommendation of editors who feared that her real name would draw attention to Ackerley's homosexuality) recounts Ackerley's life with Queenie, while the 1960 novel *We Think the World of You* fictionalizes the events that led Ackerley to acquire Queenie from his sometime lover Freddie Doyle, a working-class petty thief. In sharp contrast to Terhune, who held a "generally Victorian outlook toward everything," Ackerley delighted in offending "the philistines," and originally planned for *My Dog Tulip* to include photographs of Queenie "micturating, crapping, and conversing with other dogs" on the streets of London.[12] Although he consented to pull the photographs, Ackerley made no attempt to shield his readers from the indelicate realities of canine life; *My Dog Tulip* includes detailed accounts of Tulip's bodily functions and ill-fated sexual encounters. Whereas the commercial success of *Lad: A Dog* prompted parents from all over the country to bring their children to Sunnybank (much to Terhune's irritation), the blurb for the first edition of *My Dog Tulip* included a warning that parents "should not present it to their children without a previous careful reading themselves."[13]

Taken together, Terhune and Ackerley bookend modernism's reconfiguration of the human/dog relationship. Terhune's Lad stories encapsulate a reactionary vision of this relationship that is implicitly challenged by the modernist writers I discuss in other chapters, while Ackerley, coming on the heels of the Bloomsbury group, inherits literary modernism's fascination with the category of the canine and adapts it to the task of cultivating a postmodern pluralism that embraces diversity both within and beyond the human species. Both Ackerley and Terhune, through their interactions with the purebred dog world as amateur breeders, grew highly skeptical of modern breeding's promise to reconcile canine bodies to the constraints of the city and the whims and tastes of its human inhabitants.

Yet whereas Terhune's antimodern vision of the human/dog relationship depends upon an absolute (and ultimately impossible) separation of working dogs from urban spaces, Ackerley's depictions of Queenie expose the anthropocentrism that underpins Terhune's critique of the city as a wholly human-created—and therefore artificial—space. Although Queenie's fictional counterparts figure initially as excess in the context of modern London, they read, mark, and shape this environment, giving the lie to Terhune's view of the city. In the words of Ackerley's longtime friend E. M. Forster, Tulip represents "the New Dog—a creature comparable to the New Woman who disturbed our grandparents.... Where she innovates, where she rebels, is in demanding to be treated as a creature in her own right, as a dog of dogdom, and not as an apanage of man."[14] Like the New Woman, Tulip not only enters the ostensibly man-made space of the city but also transforms that space and demands a reassessment of her place in it. Thus where Terhune clings to an outmoded vision of the human/dog relationship that cannot be reconciled to the space of the modern city, Ackerley reimagines this relationship, thereby revealing the interspecies nature of urban modernity itself.

"Thoroughbred in Body and Soul": Terhune's Collie

Terhune's antiurbanism and antimodernism help explain his complex relationship with, and ambivalent attitude toward, the purebred dog world. In the Lad stories and elsewhere, he rails against the aims of modern breeding and the practice of dog showing, calling the latter "a form of unremitting torture" (101). Yet despite his apparent disdain for "the fancy"—purebred dog enthusiasts' term for their hobby—Terhune not only owned, bred, and showed American Kennel Club–registered dogs but also served in the 1920s as a member of that organization's board of directors, even judging collies in an honorary capacity. He also played a central role in improving the *Gazette*, the AKC's official magazine, contributing articles and stories without payment—practically unheard of for Terhune, who, as Litvag notes, lived in perpetual fear of descending into poverty and "was never above haggling over the sale price of something he had written" even after the success of the Lad stories placed him among the highest-paid writers in the country.[15] Following his scathing depiction of the Westminster Kennel Club's annual show in *Lad: A Dog* (discussed below), Terhune's stance on dog fancy softened somewhat in the course of his involvement with the AKC, and even in the midst of his most vehement critique he acknowledges the exhibition of dogs to be "the straightest sport on earth. Not an atom of graft in it, and seldom any profit" (112).

However, Terhune's rapid rise to fame, the resulting public perception of him as a preeminent authority on dogs, and his ongoing protest against what he perceived as inordinate grooming and modification of show dogs made him a controversial figure among fanciers. No doubt irked by the unflattering portrayals of dog shows and their human participants in the Lad stories, many breeders, owners, and handlers further resented the throngs of Terhune fans who descended upon each show he attended, hoping to catching a glimpse of the author and his Sunnybank collies. Many—especially among "the collie people"—opposed his election to the AKC board, protesting that he "knew next to nothing about dogs" and that his collies were unfit for the show ring, despite public demand that prompted buyers to drive from "as far away as California" to purchase a Sunnybank puppy.[16] In fact, such accusations seem to have motivated Terhune to begin exhibiting his dogs in the 1920s, first at local kennel club shows and later at Westminster, after his initial success prompted his critics to retort that his dogs could win only at small-time shows. Yet even the championships earned by at least four Sunnybank collies failed to silence Terhune's opponents in the dog fancy world, and he remains a problematic figure in AKC history.

That Terhune proved unable to ignore his critics' provocations and ultimately succumbed to what he calls "the Show Germ" (99) demonstrates his affinity for dog fancy's commitment to cultivating and preserving distinct breeds through artificial selection. Further, the Lad stories, although they contain Terhune's most adamant denunciations of dog fancy, also reveal that his investment in the breed dog predates his official involvement with the AKC. The real Lad, a collie who served as a watchdog and companion at Sunnybank from 1902 to 1918, was not a show dog and appears never to have been registered with the AKC.[17] The fictional Lad, however, boasts a "certified pedigree, abristle with the red-letter names of champions"; and the impressive collection of cups, medals, and "bit[s] of silk" displayed in the study of "the Master" (Terhune's fictional counterpart) attests to his success in the show ring (297). Detailed descriptions of Lad's physical conformation also form a central motif in Terhune's stories, mirroring dog fancy's practice of "viewing dogs' bodies as being made up of quantifiable parts (so-called points)" by dwelling most insistently on characteristics that are likewise underscored in collie breed standards.[18] For example, the standard reproduced in *The Twentieth Century Dog* calls for brown eyes that impart an "expression full of intelligence."[19] Lad's eyes are "seal-dark and sorrowful—eyes that proclaimed not only an uncannily wise brain, but a soul as well" (219). References to Lad's "deep chest" (118), "snowy and absurdly small" paws (219), "shaggy burnished coat" (131), and "ease" of movement further echo key points delineated in the breed standard (153).

Yet Terhune's persistent use of the term "thoroughbred" in place of the more common "purebred" begins to reveal the difference between his vision of the breed dog and that of modern dog fancy, which his Lad stories align with urban decadence. While descriptions of Lad frequently highlight his external beauty, even more emphatic are Terhune's assertions about the collie's exceptional mental and physical abilities. Lad's dark, intelligent eyes not only mark him as a "well-bred dog" but also make him "skilled in reading human faces" (161) and signal that he possesses "the mysterious foreknowledge of the best type of thoroughbred collie" (100). In addition to his impressive mental traits, Lad—like Jack London's Buck—exhibits a useful knack for tapping into his wolf or collie ancestry as circumstances require. In one story, a mongrel watchdog, unprovoked, attacks a muzzled Lad, only to discover belatedly that "a collie down is not a collie beaten. The wolf-strain provides against that" (150). In contrast to the mongrel, whose "savagely inefficient hold" (151) only temporarily inconveniences his opponent, Lad, miraculously freed from the debilitating muzzle, wins the battle "with ridiculous ease," slashing the mongrel "as the wolf and the collie alone can slash" (153). Lad's exceptional mental and physical capacities mark him as thoroughly bred—that is, bred for brains, strength, and skill rather than for beauty alone.

As the emphasis on Lad's breed heritage suggests, a key dimension of Terhune's investment in the concept of the thoroughbred dog is its association with the Victorian aristocracy—a connection particularly strong for the collie, which enjoyed distinction as "Queen Victoria's favorite breed." In *The Animal Estate*, Harriet Ritvo demonstrates how dog fancy emerged in the Victorian era as a key means through which a growing middle class sought to align itself with "the upper ranges of society": "The structures that evolved in the third quarter of the nineteenth century to regulate the breeding and showing of pedigreed dogs figuratively expressed the desire of predominantly middle-class fanciers for a relatively prestigious and readily identifiable position within a stable, hierarchical society."[20] This same desire underpins Terhune's idealization of the thoroughbred dog. Unlike London, whose initial description of Buck as a "sated aristocrat" only underscores the pampered, overcivilized life from which the plot of *The Call of the Wild* redeems him, Terhune repeatedly and approvingly highlights Lad's aristocratic status.[21] Like Woolf's Flush, who is delighted to discover that he is "a dog of birth and breeding," Lad views himself as "an aristocrat among inferiors" (27).[22] Yet while Woolf wryly critiques Victorian class structures through Flush's transformation from "an aristocrat considering his points" to a "democratic" mongrel—his shorn coat implicitly caricaturing "the pomposity of those who claim that they are something"—Terhune endeavors to justify Lad's snobbery and the social hierarchies in which it is grounded.[23] Exhibiting the markers of good breeding, Lad carries himself with "the benign dignity that was a heritage from endless generations of high-strain ancestors" (1). His polite but aloof attitude toward guests reflects his highbred status: "Civilly, he would endure the pettings of these visiting outlanders. Gravely, he would shake hands with them, on request" (27). Lad's refusal to grant outsiders anything more than the courtesy that "becomes a thoroughbred" (26–27) only increases the value of his absolute devotion to the Master and Mistress; "calmly unapproachable" to all other humans, he reinforces their status through his own refinement and fidelity (27).

Terhune emphasizes the aristocratic connotations of the word "thoroughbred" by applying it to the Mistress, the fictional counterpart to his wife, Anice Stockton Terhune. Anice, Litvag notes, was "always very conscious of her distinguished family lineage," and her perceived vanity and stubbornness earned her the nickname "The Duchess." Christened Anna and nicknamed Annie, she later adopted the more formal-sounding Anice, probably to signify her "notable breeding." As mistress of Sunnybank, Anice "occupied the role of a sort of grande dame, a dowager of Victorian times," adopting manners and dress considerably more formal than contemporary custom and fashion required.[24] The idealized Mistress of the Lad stories is the proud, well-bred, and unfailingly wise complement to the well-meaning but sometimes bumbling Master. The good breeding she shares with Lad is most evident in "The Gold Hat," in which she and the Master are duped into entering Lad in a rigged contest at a charity event. The Mistress, refusing to withdraw, leads Lad into the ring (and, of course, to his improbable but inevitable victory) with the pride and dignity that she, too, has inherited from "high-strain ancestors": "She was very pale, but her thoroughbred nerves were rocklike in their steadiness. She, like Lad, was of the breed that goes down fighting." The image of the collie "walk[ing] majestically beside" his well-bred mistress encapsulates the link between Terhune's vision of the thoroughbred dog and his aristocratic sensibilities (204).

The connection between Lad and the idealized Mistress emphasizes the moral dimension of Terhune's thoroughbred ideal. Terhune dedicates *Lad: A Dog* to the protagonist's namesake, calling him "thoroughbred in body and soul," and the fictional Lad performs a host of heroic acts that Terhune attributes to his thoroughbred nature (vii). His love for the Mistress itself proves that he is "strong of soul and chivalric" (26); he possesses "the natural impulse of the thoroughbred . . . to guard the helpless" (2). In "A Miracle or Two," an acquaintance brings her physically impaired child to The Place in the hope of improving her health. The usually aloof Lad takes the child under his protection, not only enduring her clumsy handling but "positively revel[ing] in the pain the tugging fingers were inflicting on his sensitive throat" (52). Unsurprisingly, both of the titular miracles are performed by Lad. First, his constant companionship awakens the child's "dormant interest in life" (56), culminating in a scene in which her love for Lad prompts her to walk despite doctors' declarations that she is "hopelessly paralyzed" (69). Second, Lad risks his own life to protect the child from one of the rare things "of which the best type of thoroughbred collie is abjectly afraid": "a poisonous snake" (64). Though initially overwhelmed by a powerful instinct that "warn[s] him violently away" from this threat, Lad transcends a merely animal state and summons the courage that Terhune portrays as a marker of the thoroughbred (64).

The characteristic that, for Terhune, most powerfully illustrates the moral character of the thoroughbred dog is fidelity, as demonstrated through absolute obedience. A recurring theme in the Lad stories is "the Law," a set of rules established by the Master that Lad and his mate, Lady, unquestioningly and unerringly obey (4). Raised under the Law, both dogs regard the Master's house as "sacrosanct. It was a place for perfect behavior. No rug must be scratched, nothing gnawed or played with" (4). Lad, with his "uncannily human brain" (85), not only understands "every spoken wish of the Master's" but possesses a supercanine ability to suppress his animal impulses in response to a command (7). In several stories, Terhune illustrates the depth of Lad's obedience by having him charge aggressively at a perceived intruder but, at a word from the Master, arrest "his onset—coming to earth bristling, furious and yet with no thought but to obey" (7). Lad's mate, Lady, and their son Wolf also demonstrate the fidelity of the thoroughbred. Lady models absolute obedience by accepting a thrashing from the unwitting Master for a crime she did not commit: "Being a thoroughbred, she did not try to run, nor did she roll for mercy. She cowered, moveless, nose to floor, awaiting her doom" (15).[25] Wolf, though he lacks his father's superior physical conformation, proves himself equally thoroughbred in character by protecting The Place from an intruder who has poisoned him: "He was dizzy and nauseated . . . but as he was just a thoroughbred dog and not a wise human, he did not stop to think up good reasons why he should shirk his duty because he did not feel like performing it" (315).

Significantly, Terhune stresses that the breed dog does not automatically possess the moral character of the thoroughbred. The stories introduce a series of canine foils who serve to distinguish the thoroughbred Lad from the purebreds of the show world. One such dog is Knave, Lad's nemesis in the first Lad story, "His Mate." A canine emblem of the seductions of modern decadence, Knave is a "showy, magnificent collie" who arrives by train for a sojourn at The Place while his owner travels abroad (5). Knave's "flashy" personality and appearance contrast sharply with Lad's "benign dignity," and the newcomer quickly becomes an object of the Master's admiration and Lady's affections (9). The Master eagerly welcomes "so beautiful an ornament to The Place," proudly receiving Knave at the train station before "an admiring crowd of commuters" (5). Lady, for her part, regards the alluring visitor with a reverence far removed from her impertinent behavior toward Lad: "She never presumed to boss [Knave] as she had always bossed Lad. He fascinated her. Without seeming to follow him about, she was forever at his heels" (8). Yet Knave, though "splendid-looking," soon reveals his lowbred character (5). While Lad exemplifies the principled dignity of a rapidly receding social order, Knave destroys the Master's prized stuffed eagle and lets Lady take the fall for his misdeed. Lad, of course, uncovers the truth and avenges Lady in a fight with his rival. Pinned and defeated, Knave proves all show and no substance when he cries out "as might any gutter cur whose tail is stepped upon" (24).

While Knave's physical beauty might seem to belie his despicable character, Terhune presents the two as causally linked in order to contrast the thoroughbred with the purebred. The first hint that Knave is not a true thoroughbred comes with Terhune's description of his coat. The collie standard declares coat color to be "immaterial," leaving this point especially subject to those "idiosyncrasies of fashion" that Compton urges his readers to accept as the collie transitions from working dog to pet or ornament.[26] For Terhune, Lad's coloring—"orange-flecked mahogany . . . set off by the snowy ruff and chest" (1)—marks him as a more authentic representative of his breed. As Dalgliesh explains, collie fanciers favored a "rich sable coat with long flowing white mane" when the breed first rose to popularity in the Victorian era.[27] However, subsequent "improvements in [the collie's] style and appearance" produced the "black and tan colouring" (which later gave way to the next craze, a "mingling of black, white, and tan") that Knave's coat more closely approximates. By giving Knave a "red-gold" coat and "black 'saddle,'" Terhune insinuates that the dog's appearance is an achievement of modern fashion rather than of generations of good breeding (5).

Knave's coat also provides the first of several hints that he is a product of crossbreeding—the practice of introducing genes from other breeds in order to enhance desired traits and prevent, according to one of Compton's contributors, the "unsoundness [that] follows on too much in-breeding."[28] Both Compton and Dalgliesh discuss the theory that the black-and-tan coat pattern was achieved by crossing the collie with the Gordon setter (though Dalgliesh views this theory with skepticism), so Knave's coat coloration might signal mixed ancestry. His pedigree is further called into question by a perceptive baggage man who scoffs, "I never yet saw a yellow-eyed, prick-eared dog I'd give hell-room to" (6). The baggage man seems a credible judge, given that the collie standard calls for dark eyes and tulip ears, counting light eyes and prick ears among "the main faults to be avoided."[29] Knave's critic also points out "them streaks of pinkish-yeller on the roof of his mouth" (6), alluding to the folk wisdom that the roof of a purebred dog's mouth is "full black."[30] This observation foreshadows Knave's undoing; his cowardly yelps for mercy after Lad's drumming justify "those yellowish streaks in his mouth-roof whereof the baggage man had spoken" (23). While crossbreeding may have created in Knave a strikingly beautiful dog, it has also left telltale signs that he is not a true thoroughbred in Terhune's sense of the word.

Terhune's portrait of Knave echoes the rhetoric of Victorian gentry fanciers who sought to distance themselves from the increasingly middle-class world of dog fancy. The rural aristocracy, Ritvo explains, grew resentful "when their favorite breeds began to appear as urban pets and in the show ring," and the Kennel Club introduced competitive field trials in part to preserve the class divide that middle-class fanciers aspired to cross.³¹ As C. J. Davies writes in a 1905 handbook, "it is significant that the sportsman will as a rule have nothing to do with the fancier's production. The fancier sacrifices every utility point to purely fancy ones, and it stands to reason that the sportsman will not be contented with an animal which although it may be a 'thing of beauty,' yet is entirely wanting in those characteristics, both mental and physical, which are essential to the successful performance of the particular class of work for which the variety is employed."³² In defending "the utility of their animals," Ritvo argues, "gentry fanciers were defending their turf" against the social aspirations of middle-class fanciers.³³ Similarly, in contrasting the flashy but cowardly Knave with the more authentic and functional Lad, Terhune aligns Lad with the aristocratic lineage to which he and Anice laid claim.

Lad's defeat of Knave is one of several narratives Terhune employs to affirm the superior utility of the thoroughbred dog. This is no easy task, given that the collie's natural aptitude for herding has become useless even in the rural environs of The Place. Lad is not "a 'working' sheep-dog" (196), and we learn in a story called "The Throwback" that "in Northern New Jersey a live sheep is well nigh as rare as a pterodactyl" (157). Nevertheless, the small flock that visits The Place in this story stirs "myriad half-memories" in Lad's thoroughbred mind (160), just as the sight of a fleeing rabbit in *The Call of the Wild* awakens "parts of [Buck's] nature that were deeper than he."³⁴ The same cannot be said for Melisande, an expensive, imported "Prussian sheep-dog" (164) whose pretentious owner intends "to train her for shepherding" despite the fact that "she hates the sheep" (167). A "fuzzy monstrosity" (164), Melisande epitomizes what Davies regards as dog fancy's preference for "exaggerated peculiarities" (114) over "working abilities" (113). When Melisande tries to kill the sheep in a perverse inversion of her purpose, Lad expertly herds the flock into a tight ring, all the while holding their "would-be killer" at bay (176). Terhune attributes this "atavistic task" to "the throwback of a great collie's instinct" (177). The thoroughbred Lad has inherited his ancestors' "almost supernatural skill at herding flocks," enabling him to perform a novel task that the purebred Melisande—a sheepdog in name only—cannot even be trained to do (176–77).

As the unlikely plot of "The Throwback" suggests, though, Terhune often must strain credulity in order to demonstrate the thoroughbred's utility in the modern world. Lad's most implausible exploits tend to involve

Melisande's owner, Hamilcar Q. Glure, a nouveau-riche urbanite called almost invariably by his apt nickname, the Wall Street Farmer. First introduced in "The Throwback," Glure appears in two other stories in the middle of the Lad series and increasingly embodies the encroachment of urban modernity into Terhune's "North Jersey hinterland" (180). While earlier stories represent Lad's world as "bounded by The Place" (26) and far removed from the modern city, the opening lines of "The Gold Hat," the story that features Glure most prominently, reveal that only a lake separates The Place "from the village and the railroad and the other new-made smears which had been daubed upon Mother Nature's smiling face in the holy name of Civilization" (180). This description serves as the backdrop against which Terhune reintroduces Glure, now explicitly characterized as an urban upstart bent on beautifying the wilderness and reproducing "the story-book glories of the life supposedly led by mid-Victorian country gentlemen" (181). A "financial giantlet" (181), he purchases "a rambling old wilderness farm" near The Place (180), transforms it into a "hideously expensive estate" (235), and populates it with "pricelessly imported" livestock and employees (181). The area's longtime residents—"Jersey mountaineers of Revolutionary stock" (181)—have scant patience for his gentlemanly charade, and their equally authentic livestock continually frustrate him by defeating his expensive imports at local shows.[35]

Terhune uses Glure not only to contrast the simplicity and authenticity of rural life with urban materialism but also as a straw man representing the view that dogs, under the conditions of modernity, have outlasted their utility. Glure makes his final appearance in "Speaking of Utility," visiting The Place with the goal of persuading the Master to contribute to the war effort by destroying his dogs. Calling dogs "a useless, senseless, costly luxury," Glure argues that they "eat food that belongs to soldiers" (227).[36] The Master angrily refutes Glure's "antidog" position (228), insisting that his own dogs more than make up for the "bare fifty dollars a year" required for their maintenance (229). While he claims that "the dogs bring in cash income" in "several" ways—presumably through stud fees, show prizes, and the sale of puppies—his counterargument relies most heavily on their role as The Place's protectors: "mine is the only house—and mine is the only stable—on this side of the lake that has never been looted. Mine is the only orchard—and mine is the only garden—that is never robbed. . . . The women of my family are as safe here, day and night, as if I had a machine-gun company on guard" (230). Framing this exchange and supporting the

Master's claims are two encounters between Lad and a would-be burglar. The story opens with Lad treeing the intruder and standing guard below until a distant call from the Master compels him to abandon his watch. The intruder escapes and, in an improbable turn of events, meets Glure and joins his staff of animal handlers. In the end, Lad recognizes and exposes the trespasser—though not before saving him from Glure's expensive and "homicidal" bull, Tenebris (241).

That Terhune needs a plot as farfetched as this and a character as unlikeable as Glure to refute the argument that dogs have become a frivolous luxury warranting extermination signals the tenuousness of Lad's position in the modern world. As the Master's argument for his dogs' utility indicates, The Place functions not merely as the setting for the Lad stories but as the primary justification for Lad's existence. Beyond serving as watchdogs, Lad and his fellow collies are simply "companionable chums, and ... an ornament to The Place" (231). The size and "lonely situation of The Place," coupled with the legions of "hobo[s] and less harmless intruder[s]" evidently intent on invading it, make "Lad's self-appointed guardianship of its acres" essential (180). Yet even a thoroughbred collie cannot ward off the urban sprawl, modern transportation, and other "new-made smears" that threaten to transform Terhune's rural paradise into an extension of the modern city. These threats to The Place are also threats to Lad himself, as the heroic collie needs The Place in order to maintain a foothold in the modern world. The Place is not simply Lad's home but his "universe," a world to which he is perfectly adapted and beyond which he has no desire to venture: "It was an ideal home for such a dog as Lad, even as Lad was an ideal dog for such a home" (97). Lad and The Place exist in fragile interdependence, their perfect compatibility implying that changes to one would require changes to the other. Thus the expansion of urban modernity threatens to transform not only The Place but also its occupants—both human and canine—and the antiquated lifestyle and values they embody.

Ultimately, it is Terhune's desire to preserve this precarious interdependence that fuels his ambivalence toward the purebred dog world. Leighton inadvertently pinpoints the contradictory aims of modern dog fancy when he observes that, in the case of his deerhound, "the true type is being steadily preserved and ... in many respects decided improvements are reached."[37] The goal of preserving canine types through selective breeding no doubt appealed to Terhune, whose own breeding program was born of a desire to produce "successors" to his aging collies and thus to perpetuate life at

Sunnybank as he had idealized it since childhood, even as the surrounding area was "dissolving from countryside to suburb."[38] Breed standards and kennel club oversight, Terhune surely recognized, were essential to ensuring the preservation of a breed's defining characteristics at a time when modern transport enabled the mating of specimens from different coasts—even different continents—and the fame achieved by a single stud dog in the show ring could lead him to father the bulk of the next generation. Yet the concurrent goal of "improving" or "perfecting" a breed undermines dog fancy's preservationist rhetoric; as Compton boasts of the state of dog breeding at the dawn of the twentieth century, "the fancier has evolved what is, in most cases, practically a new species of dog."[39] Knave and Melisande are products of this goal, their exaggerated forms and unsavory characters reflecting the arbitrary tastes of a purebred dog world that promotes beauty and novelty at the expense of preserving the mental and physical characteristics proper to each breed.

That Terhune associates the excesses of the purebred dog world with urban modernity itself—a link already hinted at by Knave's celebrated arrival "on the train from town"—becomes evident when the Master and Mistress enter Lad in the Westminster Kennel Club show in "For a Bit of Ribbon" (5). Before this show, "Lad had never been in a city or in a crowd" (97) and has been perfectly content to remain ignorant of the world beyond The Place and the "foolish and strange folk" who inhabit it (26). The idea of entering him in his first dog show comes, tellingly, from this outside world, in the form of a visitor to The Place "who loved dogs far better than he understood them" (97). And just as this guest invades Lad's rural domain, "the most virulent type of the Show Germ" infects the minds of the Master and Mistress, who eagerly enter "Sunnybank Lad" into the novice class (99). The Mistress undertakes a daily regimen of brushing and "soap-infested scrubbings," and while this meticulous grooming leaves Lad "miserable" (100), he is infinitely more dismayed to be "taken away from the sweet Place he loved" by a "car whizzing him along toward some dreaded fate" (103). As the car enters Manhattan and nears Madison Square Garden, the city and the dog show blend into a hideous cacophony of odor and noise. The "million new and troublous odors" that bombard Lad's nostrils merge with "an all-pervasive scent of dog," and the "plangent roar of the city" (104) commingles with "the chorused barks and howls of many of his own kind" (105). For Lad, the "unremitting torture" that awaits him at the dog show is part and parcel of the city itself (101).

Terhune's description of the scene inside Madison Square Garden portrays the dog show as a microcosm of the modern city. Lad, accustomed to roaming freely about The Place, is "bewildered" by the overcrowded, restrictive conditions to which Westminster subjects its entrants: "Dogs—dogs—DOGS! . . . Lad had never known there were so many dogs on earth." The Master and Mistress lead him through a series of narrow "alleys" to the cramped cage in which show rules demand he must be chained "for the next four days and nights." That these stressful and congested conditions breed disease is implied when a "yawning" veterinarian paid "to bar out sick entrants" allows Lad to pass without "so much as touch[ing] him." In contrast to The Place, to which Terhune attributes mysterious healing properties in "A Miracle or Two," conditions at this and other dog shows result in "scores of kennels [being] swept by distemper and by other canine maladies" (106–7).

In addition to replicating on a smaller scale the overcrowded, unhealthy conditions of city life, the dog show exemplifies the vices Terhune associates with the modern city. The painful grooming procedures that the Master and Mistress witness reveal a culture of excess and artifice: coats are "plucked," "whitened" (101), brushed backward, and fluffed with "talcum powder" (112); ears are "sandpapered" (101) and "scrunched . . . to impart the perfect tulip-shape; ordained by fashion for collies" (102); and the Master and Mistress, having naively prepared Lad for the show ring with baths and brushing alone, watch in dismay as handlers put "finishing touches on the poor beasts' make-up" (113). This account appears largely accurate, as a 1922 article in the *Dog Fancier* recommends similar methods for preparing collies for the show ring: "Brush the coat . . . in the direction from tail to head. . . . Trim the hair a little on the back hocks. Then lift up each foot and trim the hair even with the pads of each toe. This will make many a heavy coated Collie with feet that look rabbit-footed, have nice balled feet. . . . Vaseline the tip of the nose to give good contrast with the sable face. Whiten all white parts of the coat with whitening. Chalk up the blaze of the face, breast, collar, and whites of feet and tip of tail."[40] The same article recommends "training [puppies'] ears to proper carriage" by taping "splints of wood or card-board" inside drooping ears to prop them up and pouring "melted grease from a candle" onto the tips of prick ears to weigh them down (18).

By bringing Lad to Westminster, Terhune stages a contest between the thoroughbred and the purebred—as well as between the gentry fancier, represented by the Master and Mistress, and the upstart fancier, represented by an acquaintance dubbed the "collie man" (108). Much like Compton, who not only acknowledges but praises the dramatic morphological changes achieved through modern breeding, the collie man recognizes Lad as "the true type" but dismisses him as "too old-fashioned for such fast company as he's in" (110–11). When the Master derides several of Lad's coiffed competitors as "freaks," the collie man explains that they represent "the up-to-date collie—this year's style, at least" (109). This description uncannily anticipates General Motors executive Alfred P. Sloan's successful efforts to cultivate an aesthetic of "continuous, eternal change" in the automotive industry—most notably by introducing the concept of the annual model in the 1920s. Like the continually updated models of automobiles, which Terhune disdained as emblems of "suburban sprawl," the modern fancier's collie embodies Sloan's ingenious marketing technique of "creating a bigger and better package each year."[41] Fanciers in pursuit of an ever-changing model of perfection, Terhune intimates, mongrelize the very breed they purport to preserve by selecting for a "borzoi . . . head" (109), "terrier expression" (110), and "greyhoundlike" body (118). The superficiality of these "improvements" is confirmed by the Master's observation that "the span of their heads . . . isn't as wide as my palm," as well as by the collie man's retort (which echoes Compton's defense of modern breeding practices): "What's the use of [the collie's] having brain and scenting-power? He's used for exhibition or kept as a pet nowadays—not to herd sheep" (98). In the absence of demand for the intelligence and behavioral repertoire required for herding, the breed is subject to the careless whims of fanciers and pet owners, and Lad's "truer" points go unappreciated.

Lad wins the novice class at Westminster, but only because the "old-fashioned" collie encounters an equally old-fashioned judge: "Angus McGilead, Esq. (late of Linlithgow, Scotland)" (117). A native of the country in which the collie is widely believed to have developed, McGilead sees in Lad "a dog that brought back to him the murk and magic of the Highland moors," a welcome departure from "the ultramodern, inbred, and greyhoundlike collies which had so utterly departed from their ancestral standards" (118). Yet even McGilead is temporarily taken in by the fancier's artifice. After selecting Lad as the winner of the novice class, he nearly awards the blue ribbon for the winners' class to Champion Coldstream Guard, "a grand dog, gold-and-white of hue, perfect of coat and line, combining all that was best in the old and new styles of collies" (121). Coldstream Guard fleetingly signals the possibility of uniting Terhune's thoroughbred ideal with dog fancy's purebred ideal, but the dog is exposed as a fraud. Laying a hand on the champion's head to signal his victory, McGilead discovers "a most clever bit of surgical bandaging" used to mold his faulty "prick-ears" into the preferred tulip shape (122). McGilead thus transfers his hand to "Lad's great honest head," awarding him the blue ribbon and affirming the superiority of the genuine thoroughbred over the superficially beautiful purebred (123).[42]

While Lad's victory at Westminster symbolically aligns the purebred dog with the excesses and materialism of urban modernity, his subsequent experiences on the streets of Manhattan demonstrate the incompatibility of the thoroughbred dog with the material conditions of the city itself. In "Lost!" (the sequel to "For a Bit of Ribbon"), Lad discovers that the city imposes constraints just as unwelcome as those of the show ring. Before leaving Madison Square Garden, the Master and Mistress are compelled to purchase a muzzle because, as an attendant informs them, "the law demands that all dogs in New York City streets shall be muzzled" (129). This passage refers to a 1914 New York City ordinance banning unmuzzled dogs from public spaces in an effort to prevent the spread of rabies. Terhune, though opposed to the spirit of such a law, found himself in unexpected agreement with some of its proponents, who argued that "dogs have no proper place in a great city." While such proponents advocated banning dogs "from all parts of the greater city" in order to protect the human public, Terhune—who refused to sell puppies "to anyone living in an apartment"—sought to protect his thoroughbred dogs from the miseries and dangers of urban life.[43] Chief among these dangers are automobiles, which killed or crippled at least three Sunnybank collies.[44] Lad narrowly escapes the same fate in "Lost!" when he is flung from the car into traffic as the Master swerves to navigate the congested city streets. Equally dangerous is the "fool cry of 'Mad dog!'" (144) that prompts a crowd of "howling New Yorkers" to chase Lad into the Hudson River (145). Deftly evading this mob and a series of other threats, Lad eventually makes his way back to The Place, "where there were no clang and reek and peril as here in New York" and where, for Terhune, the thoroughbred belongs (139).

As Lad's urban misadventure demonstrates, Terhune's thoroughbred dog is the antithesis of the purebred dog envisioned by modern dog fanciers. Whereas dog fancy is eager to "perfect" breeds to accommodate the constraints of urban spaces and the preferences of the dog-owning public,

Terhune opposes the modification of the collie to suit the conditions of modernity. While he raises important questions about the extent to which human desires should shape canine bodies, Terhune ultimately clings to an imagined past in which human and dog coexisted harmoniously, both in their proper place. Moreover, like the Victorian gentry fanciers who grew to resent the middle-class upstarts who so radically transformed their sport and their dogs, Terhune uses the thoroughbred collie to affirm, in Ritvo's words, "a stratified order which sorted animals and, by implication, people into snug and appropriate niches."[45] As long as The Place exists, Terhune's image of the human/dog relationship remains coherent, yet the Lad stories increasingly portray both Lad and The Place as relics of a social order threatened by urban modernity. By refusing to reimagine the human/dog relationship in light of rapidly changing material conditions, Terhune tacitly accepts the idea that the dog has no legitimate place in the modern world, making his vision of canine futures no less problematic than that of modern dog fancy. Terhune thus fails to reconcile his nostalgic love of the collie breed with his desire to justify that breed's continued existence in a historical and spatial context so far removed from the misty Highland moors that shaped Lad's ancestors.

Ackerley's "New Dog"

Like Terhune's collie, Ackerley's Alsatian inhabits a precarious place in the modern world. The Alsatian, or German shepherd dog, was developed quite deliberately as a working breed in the 1890s by a group of fanciers led by German breeder and retired cavalry captain Max von Stephanitz. A former student of the Berlin Veterinary College, Stephanitz observed the rise of Britain's collie to its position as "the outstanding international luxury dog of the day" and sought similar recognition for the sheepdogs of western Germany. Together with a network of fellow fanciers, he formed the Verein für Deutsche Schäferhunde (Society for the German Shepherd Dog) and developed a standard that merged what the group regarded as "the best traits of a number of regional varieties of sheepdog." Stephanitz vigorously promoted the result, according to historian Edward Tenner, "as a distinctively German alternative to the frivolous and superficial ways of foreign breeders"; he endeavored to elevate the German shepherd to the collie's status while rejecting collie fanciers' willingness to sacrifice working ability for "mere looks." Though he was aware of the rapidly declining need in fin-de-siècle Europe for sheep-herding dogs, Stephanitz insisted upon the importance of working ability and intelligence, and his organization succeeded in establishing the breed as the military and police dog of choice in the United States and Europe. Yet Stephanitz's tireless promotion of his breed's "loyal and protective character" proved almost too effective, as the breed's resulting popularity transformed it, like the collie, into a "luxury import item" desired by fanciers and pet owners who showed little regard for its "working virtues."[46]

Ackerley's work, drawing on his experience as an Alsatian owner and recent entrant into "the dog world," illuminates how these effects of Stephanitz's marketing campaign were compounded by the conditions of urban modernity.[47] Mr. Plum in *My Dog Tulip*, typical of the Alsatian owners and admirers Ackerley encounters in his London neighborhood, "specially wanted an Alsatian" precisely because "they're said to be so devoted" (78). Mr. Plum's dog, Chum, whose name underscores how breed stereotypes shape people's expectations of individual dogs, is no longer the "pal" he once was and has taken to "jump[ing] the garden wall and run[ning] away" (77). Though Mr. Plum is dumbfounded by his loyal pet's treachery, Ackerley intimates that Chum's behavior is a predictable result of being banished to the garage after his owner's marriage. "I've a feeling I let him down," Mr. Plum admits sheepishly, but he nevertheless resents Chum's disobedience and indiscriminate friendliness to strangers—neither of which he bargained for when he "paid quite a bit" for a devoted Alsatian (84). Ackerley's own dog, Queenie, likewise suffered the consequences of ignoring the human demand for canine fidelity, as we see when she appears in the guise of Evie in *We Think the World of You*. Johnny, the fictional stand-in for Ackerley's former lover and Queenie's original owner, declares himself "mad on them dogs" and envisions a faithful Alsatian ever at his heels: "I'd 'ave took 'er up to the pub and she'd 'ave sat there quiet beside me while I 'ad a few pints and a game of darts. Then she'd 'ave walked 'ome be'ind me afterwards."[48] Johnny's arrest and imprisonment for burglary at the beginning of the novel, though, quash this vision and force him to place the puppy in the care of his mother and stepfather, Millie and Tom Winder. Tom, though only boarding Evie in Johnny's absence, relishes occupying the role of master to the loyal Alsatian. Having worked with the breed during his army years, he boasts, "I knows about them dogs. They 'as to be trained. . . . But as soon as they've learned oo's their master, they're yours till closing time. One man dogs they are, and they foller be'ind you like a shadder" (42). Tom's violent training methods, however, coupled with his failure to exercise the dog, succeed only in turning Evie into a neurotic adolescent.

Acquired for egocentric reasons rather than for the work she was bred to perform, Ackerley intimates, the Alsatian becomes superfluous. Her intelligence and stamina, denied an outlet in productive work, morph into nervousness and hyperactivity. That Evie signifies excess is evident both in the plot of *We Think the World of You* and in the physical spaces in which it unfolds. Evie is introduced as an unwanted addition to the love triangle that drives the plot. The protagonist, Frank (a fictionalized Ackerley), remembers the puppy "vaguely" as something upon which he "had inadvertently trodden" during a past visit to Johnny (6). Though eager to maintain his relationship with Johnny by offering financial assistance—even to Johnny's detested wife, Megan—he adamantly refuses to take Evie in. There is no question of Megan's keeping the puppy, as the already incompetent mother of three is penniless and pregnant with a fourth child. Millie, who dislikes Megan and is more than willing to unburden her of baby Dickie in Johnny's absence, grudgingly agrees to look after Evie when no one else will. At the Winders' house in the working-class borough of Newham in London, Evie leads "a lonely and frustrating life in captivity" (83), spending most of her time alone in the small backyard or locked in the scullery, only to be admitted to the main living space when the family want her to form "a pretty tableau with baby on the hearthrug" (59). Her confinement mirrors not only Johnny's imprisonment—in one scene, Millie bemoans the plight of "poor old Johnny" while ironically ignoring the desperate sounds of Evie hurling herself against the scullery door—but also Frank's frustration at being denied access to Johnny by the jealous Megan (76). Initially, Frank visits the Winders in order to maintain ties to Johnny via Millie, and when Evie first emerges from behind the scullery door, he realizes, "I had forgotten all about Johnny's dog" (22).

Yet Evie refuses to remain confined to the marginal place she occupies in Frank's mind or to the physical spaces the Winders deem her proper place. On Frank's second visit, the now "immense" Evie is relegated to the backyard but, seeing Frank through the kitchen window, "vault[s] lightly over the sill into our midst, capsizing some tea-cups with her long bushy tail" (32) and causing "an immediate outcry" (33). Far from completing the "pretty tableau" of domesticity that Millie desires, Evie unsettles the domestic space, prompting Frank to marvel later at "her incongruity in this tiny working-class kitchen" (54). Evie's awkwardness is reinforced when Frank, pitying the "wild creature" with her pent-up energy, takes her for a walk: "Throttling herself in her collar and wrenching my arm out of its socket, she lugged me after her" (38). Her displays of affection toward Frank when he unleashes her in an empty alley are equally excessive. Following each call of her name, "she came bounding back and, planting her forepaws on my chest so as almost to knock me over, licked my nose"; during a later visit, she greets Frank with a "wild demonstration of joy" that overturns still more kitchenware (38). Frank, for his part, is enchanted "by her beauty . . . and the feeling she gave of boundless energy and vitality" (39)—qualities that make her just as incongruous in "the small gritty playground" where he takes her as she is in the Winders' kitchen (32).

As the peculiar image of this "sort of wolf" on the streets of London suggests, Evie is as out of place in the modern city as Terhune's Lad, and much of the novel narrates Frank's efforts to accommodate and transport her large, energetic presence (32). Several months into Evie's stay at the Winders', Frank takes her for another walk and discovers that she has developed a debilitating fear of the city streets: "As she tore along, almost on her stomach . . . she hugged the walls, keeping as far as possible from the curb. She was terrified. The racket of the road drove her against the shops; people suddenly emerging from these startled her out again towards the traffic, and she kept up a constant high-pitched barking at everyone and everything. . . . It was as though the whole outside world, to which she was so little used, had thrown her into a state of nervous confusion and, totally unstrung, she tore panting through it like a demented creature" (80–81). The woefully undersocialized Evie is ill equipped to cope with the chaos of the urban landscape and thus only exacerbates the chaos, first by darting into traffic and barking and later by biting a child—an act that causes Frank to share her panic as he hurries "to remove her as quickly as possible from the scene of the crime" (81). Resolving to undo some of the damage caused by Tom's cruelty and neglect, he takes Evie home for a weekend of companionship and exercise, but this well-meaning venture presents its own difficulties. Transporting her to Frank's neighborhood by taxi or bus is "out of the question," drivers being "as likely to accept Evie for a passenger as to accept a tigress" (85). When Frank ultimately succeeds in boarding a train with the dog, the noise of the "great monster . . . clanking and belching" into the station reduces her to a "quaking heap" (86), and once on board she becomes "excited and irrepressible," disrupting other passengers with her erratic movements and incessant barking (87).

But a determined Frank soon discovers spaces within the city better equipped to accommodate a large and energetic Alsatian. In Hyde Park, for example, Evie merges harmoniously with her environment: "Across the open spaces of the park the rough wind blew with its full strength, and she became a part of the dancing day, leaping and flying among the torn trees, wild in her delight" (88–89). Of course, Frank, a middle-class bachelor with a flexible work schedule, has the resources and time not only to care for Evie but to take her for "long, countrified walks" that allow her to release pent-up energy (184). His dismay at seeing "so large and active a beast . . . condemned to [the Winders'] poky house in this dismal district" (39–40) conveys the class dimension of Ackerley's vision of the human/dog relationship, and in *My Dog Tulip* he acknowledges that the "working-class people" from whom he acquired Tulip were "fond of her in their way" but unable to care for her properly owing to their long work hours (7). But Frank's modest flat is hardly better equipped to accommodate Evie than the Winders' "poky house"—a description of her "fly[ing] into the kitchen and hurl[ing] about the vegetables" recalls her disorderly conduct in the Winders' kitchen—so he, too, must negotiate the constraints of urban life in order to meet her needs. While Frank, like Terhune, initially reasons that a dog of Evie's size and power "ought to be in the country," circumstances force him to reconcile her body and behavior to the space of the city.[49] By the time we encounter Evie in her mature form as Tulip, she has become a bona fide "town dog" (45) who trots confidently down the city streets, uses public transportation, and, like Woolf's Flush in Florence, hobnobs with a network of neighborhood dogs.

As an urban dog freed from the scullery, though, Tulip finds herself subject to constraints that the city imposes on canine bodies. Ackerley discovers that even a well-behaved dog's use of buses hinges on the arbitrary preferences of their drivers. Members of this "powerful and capricious race . . . can refuse to carry dogs and often do, even when their buses are empty and likely to remain so." Tulip's size and breed make her access to public transport particularly uncertain: "'Sorry, no dogs,' they say. Or, 'Only little dogs.' Or, less subtly, 'Too big'. . . . Or (more frequently and crushingly), 'Not them dogs! Any dogs but them!'" (152). As a female dog, moreover, she undergoes biannual heats that make transporting her by bus both more necessary and more difficult. Unlike owners with "the resolution and the facilities . . . to shut [their bitches] away out of sight and sound" during estrus (103)—thus sparing themselves the inconvenience and embarrassment of cohabiting with a "burning creature burning with desire" (158)—Ackerley has neither garden nor cellar and thus must devise ways of making Tulip's heats endurable for them both: "Why exercise her at all at such a time? it may be asked—but only by those people who have never had my problem to contend with, the problem of confining an active, eager and importunate young bitch to a small London flat for three weeks" (102). An early morning bus ride to Wimbledon Common enables Ackerley to exercise Tulip while avoiding the "quantities of Putney mongrels" who hound her whenever she leaves the flat, yet this solution depends entirely upon his finding a cooperative bus driver (101). Even when he succeeds, he must carefully conceal the "small bead[s] of blood" that, if spotted, might get them banished from the bus (151).

Tulip's heats also heighten Ackerley's awareness of how severely cities and their human inhabitants restrict canine sexual behavior. "Opportunities for privacy are rare" in the city, and while discretion may be a matter of indifference in the canine world, this lack of privacy means that the sexual activities of urban dogs are continually policed by a squeamish human public (45). As an openly gay man living in London at a time when homosexuality was criminalized, Ackerley empathizes with the urban dog, whose "expectation of sex is slender in the extreme. He is equipped for it, but the equipment is not used" (175) thanks to "human intervention . . . in the shape of a bucket of water" (177). Such prudishness, moreover, is not restricted to a particular gender or social class. While Ackerley reserves special contempt for "those nervous women who, far from being sympathetic to intimate canine relationships," continually jerk their beloved pets "away from all communication with other dogs" in order to prevent "'nasty' behavior," men, too, "frequently exhibit the deepest aversion to such poor sexual satisfactions as are left to their beasts" (178–79). These puritanical sensibilities, Ackerley observes, are most pronounced among the middle and upper classes, yet even in working-class neighborhoods, "where greater laxity and muddlement prevail," a dog is "singularly fortunate" if he encounters a receptive bitch "unanointed with 'Keepaway,' irridated chlorophyll, eucalyptus oil, or some similarly repellent preparation" (176). Ackerley's refusal to confine Tulip during estrus leads him to witness continually humans' "intolerant reaction to the natural conduct of a dog and a bitch" (179).

Resolving to provide Tulip with the genuinely doggy life that prudish urbanites deny their infantilized pets, Ackerley sets about "finding a husband for her." "A full life," he reasons, "naturally included the pleasures of sex and maternity," yet his foray into the London breeding world only unearths more disturbing ways in which humans regulate canine sexuality (63). Initially, Ackerley operates on the assumption, common in the purebred dog world, that dogs should be mated according to breed. Though he is determined to give Tulip a fulfilling life, he cannot countenance her preference for mongrels. Tulip is particularly drawn to Watney, "a very small and rather wooden terrier, with a mean little face streaked black-and-white like a badger," and Ackerley is dumbfounded by his beautiful bitch's flirtation with this ugly little mutt: "Tulip would greet him with all her prettiest demonstrations of pleasure, curtsying down to him on her elbows in her play attitude, with her rump and its waving tail up in the air.... What she saw, or smelt, in this dreary little dog I never could understand" (91–92). Unlike Terhune, Ackerley evinces no profound investment in the breed dog; he confesses that all "pedigree Alsatians... look to my inexpert eye pretty much the same" (90). However, in deciding that "so beautiful a creature as Tulip should certainly have children as pretty as herself" (64), he tacitly accepts dog fancy's naturalization and aestheticization of the purebred, "conveniently forgetting," Susan McHugh points out, "that breed dogs are human inventions that require interspecific social interventions."[50] Though not motivated by any "profit-making interest in the matter," he steers Tulip away from "undesirable suitors" like Watney and toward the more appropriate choice of another purebred Alsatian (64). He thus becomes complicit, as he later realizes, in the systematic and sometimes violent control of canine bodies required to genetically isolate and perpetuate recognized breeds—a set of practices the geographer Krithika Srinivasan identifies as a particularly potent manifestation of "the power-knowledge nexus": "Biopower involves normalisation of populations, and breeding is an activity aimed at such normalisation."[51]

Initially, the purebred dog world's interference in canine sexual lives seems innocuous enough, as "the availability of a stud system of dogs for the hiring" merely simplifies the matter of choosing "a suitable mate—the question, in fact, that confronts us all" (64). Yet in his efforts to mate Tulip to another Alsatian, McHugh observes, Ackerley discovers that his "role in selecting canine mates structures the scene of canine copulation" in ways that precipitate other, more problematic interventions.[52] He thereby becomes complicit in what Shun Yin Kiang describes as "the production of normative sexual desires, and the imposition of normal sexual knowledge onto human and animal bodies alike."[53] Tulip's unreceptive behavior toward her first Alsatian suitor prompts Ackerley to consult a veterinarian, who informs him that it is "often necessary to hold the bitch's head and guide the dog into position," and to apply "a little Vaseline to the bitch ... to excite and define the interest" (77). Ackerley follows these instructions during a subsequent attempt but stops when he realizes "that our efforts to please had turned into cruelty" (82). His growing suspicion that there is "something unnatural about bringing two dogs, total strangers, together for an hour or so for the purpose of copulation, not to mention having to stimulate them into taking an interest in each other," is confirmed by his discovery of a passage in Major R. C. G. Hancock's book *The Right Way to Keep Dogs* (91). Insisting on the need for "a process of strenuous wooing" to stimulate the bitch before she "allows mating to take place," Hancock criticizes "the breeding technique of the present-day pedigree breeder," who confines the bitch during the critical wooing period and then restrains her while the stud dog penetrates her "with no love-making precedent to the act" (99). An acquaintance Ackerley meets in the course of his dealings with "the breeding world" confirms that such practices are routine at reputable kennels: "Breeding was a profitable business, so bitches had to be bred from whether they liked it or not; if they weren't willing they were helped, if they wouldn't be helped they were forced, and many a time he'd seen them muzzled and put into a sling to prevent them resisting" (95).[54]

The seemingly straightforward project of allowing Tulip to enjoy "the pleasures of sex and maternity" thus exposes a "human ignorance of and insensitivity to canine sexual agency" that proves just as harmful as those priggish owners who "impose their own standards of conduct upon their dogs" (46–47).[55] And while Hancock's discussion of canine wooing solves the mystery of Tulip's resistance to her purebred suitors, it suggests that the goal of facilitating intrabreed sex for Tulip without stripping her of agency can be achieved only by recruiting "a large pack of pedigree Alsatians to pursue and fight for her during the first week of her heat"—"a splendid idea," Ackerley grants, "but difficult to arrange" (100). In the streets of Putney, the closest approximation is the "miscellaneous crew" of mongrels who thwart Ackerley's attempts to exercise Tulip during her heats (105). Ackerley recognizes that these dogs, "snarling and squabbling among themselves" in pursuit of their goal, perfectly demonstrate "what Major

Hancock calls the 'primacy of approach,'" yet he remains determined to prevent a mésalliance (105). He makes a final unsuccessful attempt to mate Tulip with another Alsatian in Sussex, where his cousin rents a bungalow for the winter. Although Tulip initially benefits from the "sea air" and from "walks . . . superior to anything that Putney had to offer" (109), within days the bungalow—ironically called "Mon Repos"—is surrounded by a throng of local dogs whose frenzied attempts to access the "siren" within leave it (and Ackerley's cousin) "practically wrecked" (116). Following two more fruitless rendezvous with Alsatian suitors, Ackerley finally permits Tulip to mate with "a disreputable, dirty mongrel," not unlike Watney, "with whom it had always amused [her] to play" (120).

Ackerley's observation of the dogs' intercourse—and his assistance with its completion when the mutt's "too small" stature turns their "charming" embrace into awkward flailing—recalls Émile Zola's frank description of human-assisted bovine mating in the opening pages of *La Terre*, which Max Nordau, in his 1892 polemic *Degeneration*, cites as strong evidence of the author's "sexual psychopathy."[56] Rather than repudiate Nordau's implied equation of homosexual and bestial desire, Ackerley positions gay man and desiring bitch as what McHugh calls "queer comrades" allied against "a sexually repressive heterosexual culture" that polices both human and canine sexual behavior. McHugh builds on Michael Warner and Lauren Berlant's notion of a "queer counterpublic" to argue that Ackerley's rejection of heteronormative pairing and family structures in favor of what she terms "pack sexualities" underscores "how heterosexuality's juridical, economic, and aesthetic structures extend beyond sex acts and . . . into nonhuman animal bodies and behaviors." Whereas Terhune enlists Lad to defend these structures against modern decadence, Ackerley subverts them by staging scenes, like Tulip's union with the mongrel, in which "a third agent" (here, Ackerley's fictional self) "triangulates" desire, undermining the heteronormative mandate of breed coupling by "witness[ing] sex acts" and "help[ing] to construct their significance in relation to packs that traverse deeply mixed communities and contexts."[57] In observing and facilitating Tulip's mongrel intercourse, he brings an end to his active "intervention" (120) in her sexual life and thus dissociates himself from the heteronormative structures that underwrite the breeding world's project of controlling canine bodies.

But Ackerley's experience raising Tulip's puppies and preventing subsequent litters demonstrates the impossibility of noninterference in canine lives, particularly for the urban dog owner. When Tulip whelps a large litter in his small flat, Ackerley, envisioning "a future that contained eight extra dogs," contemplates the ultimate interference: culling "the female part of Tulip's progeny" (132) to spare himself the difficult task of finding homes for bitches, whose "sexual trouble" renders them less desirable as pets (182).[58] Unable to betray Tulip's trust, Ackerley elects not to carry out this "dark deed," but, reflecting years later on the puppies' eventual fates, speculates that "it might have been better if they had been [drowned]" (133–34). The decision to keep the puppies only leads him to contemplate more fully his power to affect their future well-being: "Much as I longed to be rid of the puppies ... as I watched upon my terrace the unfolding of these affectionate, helpless lives, and saw them adventuring, in ever-widening circles, into a life which they clearly thought positively smashing, my sense of responsibility towards them increased and became a discomfort to me. To 'find them homes,' as I had phrased it to myself, began to seem a totally inadequate description of my duty. I perceived that their whole future, their health and happiness, depended entirely upon me" (139–40).

In foregoing intervention in Tulip's sexual life, Ackerley facilitates the creation of beings in whose lives he has no choice but to intervene, with profound consequences. The decisions he makes in "finding them homes," he is painfully aware, will powerfully shape and delimit their future lives. He sets out to locate potential owners with the "money, time, [and] physical energy" that, though not "in themselves a guarantee of canine happiness ... might be thought to lay a hopeful foundation for it," yet this plan fails to account for the challenges of housing eight growing puppies in a small London flat, which his landlord soon compounds with threats of eviction (140). The pups' mongrel status further exacerbates his predicament. In heteronormative culture, progeny typically serve, in Monica Flegel's words, "to publicly display that the right kind of sex has taken place."[59] The puppies' nonconforming bodies, by contrast, signify impurity and deviancy, limiting their desirability as companions in a breed-centric world. These pressures ultimately prove too much; Ackerley abandons his "conditions" and gives the pups hastily "to whomsoever would take them" (140). While one of Tulip's daughters becomes "a proper street dog" and enjoys, thanks to her owners' laissez-faire approach to pet-keeping, a life of relative freedom, several of her siblings end up in conditions similar to those from which Ackerley rescued their mother (147). Others are given away yet again "by applicants who had begged most earnestly for them" (145), and one succumbs to "fits"—for Ackerley, a suspiciously vague diagnosis—and is destroyed (144). Clearly haunted by his role in determining the pups' "small destinies," Ackerley concludes that "the only way to avoid the onus of responsibility for the lives of animals is never to traffic in them at all" (143).

Avoiding this responsibility means interfering once again in Tulip's life by preventing her from reproducing. The final chapter of *My Dog Tulip* describes an outing on Wimbledon Common, part of Ackerley's campaign to allow Tulip to enjoy a fulfilling life even during her heats. While he goes to great lengths to give Tulip "just as happy a time as she normally has"—"developing an elaborate plan" to convey her to the park without encountering anything or anyone that might upset her "physically or emotionally" (153)—ultimately, he acknowledges, his actions are calculated to "frustrate her" (160). Unwilling to accept responsibility for additional canine lives, Ackerley must instead join the "human conspiracy" (175) against sex-seeking dogs and witness at regular intervals the "physical torment" of a bitch in heat denied access to "the thing she needs" (160). "Notably absent" from Ackerley's deliberations, McHugh observes, is what seems to twenty-first-century readers "the simplest conclusion, that is, spaying the bitch."[60] Yet in the days before elective spay/neuter surgery was commonplace for companion dogs, Ackerley probably would have regarded such a procedure as anthropocentric meddling of the worst kind—particularly given his view of sexuality as an integral part of both human and nonhuman life. Even when Queenie developed chronic pyometra, a medical condition for which a veterinarian recommended a hysterectomy, Ackerley elected to treat her instead with "a course of injections" and only opted for a permanent surgical solution when "her womb turned septic for the third time [and] therapy failed to control it" (189).[61]

As pet-keeping historian Katherine C. Grier notes, sterilization, even if justified today as a means of reducing the number of companion animals destroyed in shelters, constitutes "a profound surgical intervention on [animals'] behavior and natural life courses."[62] Though he never explicitly discusses sterilization as a possible solution to his (and arguably Tulip's) dilemma in *My Dog Tulip*, Ackerley preempts the question with a rhetorical one: "And how can I tamper with so beautiful a beast?" But his subsequent reflections demonstrate, in McHugh's words, "his self-consciousness about how his control over her access to sexual partners already alters his bitch": "Yet I *am* tampering with her. I am frustrating her" (163).[63] Ackerley is forced to accept, as Grier does, that the "power to control or at least partly direct animal behavior is an inevitable part of choosing to share space with creatures whose wishes and natural behaviors are not always compatible with [human] routines."[64]

While the aftermath of Tulip's first and only successful mating underscores how humans cannot avoid intervening in their canine companions' lives, the bodily functions detailed in a chapter called "Liquids and Solids" reveal the limits of that control. Ackerley's attempts to prevent the fecund Tulip from copulating with local dogs are continually thwarted by her ability "to spread the news of her condition by sprinkling the doorstep on her way in and out," thus establishing herself as a canine celebrity whose daily walks are "as harassed as are the attempts of film stars . . . to leave the Savoy Hotel undetected by reporters." Hordes of neighborhood dogs, drawn by the scent of her urine, "hang hopefully about" Ackerley's flat and take "no hint . . . from the symbolic use of the lead" he attaches to Tulip in a feeble display of authority (103, 102).

That canine urine and feces undermine human control on a broader scale is evident in the ineffectual signs posted by the Wandsworth Borough Council that read: "To dog owners. Please assist in maintaining PUBLIC HEALTH by restraining your dog from fouling footpaths. It is an offense to allow them to do so. The penalty being 40/-" (38). Spotting this sign in the course of his daily walk with Tulip, Ackerley pauses to deconstruct it:

> Overlooking the peculiar grammar and punctuation of this piece of literature, what does it mean? Here is an alley way stretching ahead of me for two or three hundred yards. It is enclosed by high walls. There is no escape from it except forwards or back. Dogs do not hold up their paws and say 'May I?' They simply squat and begin. What do I do if Tulip suddenly squats in the middle of it? . . . Anxious as I am to assist in maintaining PUBLIC HEALTH, I should be interested to know what method the Town Clerk would have me employ. (39)

The town clerk, Ackerley insinuates, dooms his project to failure, first by assuming that owners possess any control over their dogs' bowel movements, and second by failing to account for any autonomous agency on the part of dogs. As Ackerley points out, the legal mandate forbidding dogs from fouling walkways applies "only if they are on the lead and therefore (as it is quaintly phrased) under control" (34), a qualification that already begins to expose the "weakness of [the town clerk's] position" (39). Further undermining municipal authority over canine bodies are "the notice itself, which starts with a request and ends with a threat," and "the fact that these alley ways are dotted with offenses from end to end" (39). By scattering "offenses" throughout the borough, the dogs whose bowel movements the notice is intended to police deconstruct it even more effectively than Ackerley does.

The Wandsworth Borough Council's failed attempt to restrict the distribution of canine "solids" demonstrates the excess that canine bodies signify in urban spaces. Defecating in public, Ackerley observes, is classed among the behaviors "commonly regarded as the insanitary habits of dogs" (44), yet all of Tulip's attempts to shit "in seclusion" meet with objections from outraged humans (45). She earns rebukes both for turning "through an open gate into someone's front garden" and for "using a public lavatory, and not on the grounds that it was a Gentlemen's" (45). The only places where Tulip can "unburden herself" without offending public decency are spaces reserved for collecting the waste products of urban life (37). One is a muddy embankment littered with trash: "Here, amid the flotsam and jetsam of wood, cork, bottles, old tin cans, french letters, and the swollen bodies of drowned cats, dogs and birds left by the tide, she is often moved to open her bowels" and can do so without penalty to herself or Ackerley (36). A second haven is "another species of refuse dump": a "secluded" cemetery where Tulip is not only tolerated by but aligned with the dead when she ingests the "medicinal grasses . . . springing from their long-forgotten bones" (36). The cemetery further signifies a repository of that which mainstream Londoners forget or disavow, as we see when Ackerley discovers evidence that "the poor fleeting living, who have nowhere of their own, have been there to make love among the dead" (37). The final space reserved for Tulip's needs is "the gutter," where "pedestrians and shopkeepers" (not to mention the town clerk) would have her "squat" (34) at her peril while "vehicles whizz by within a foot or so of the curb" (35). Legal and social mandates thus forbid urban dogs to leave their trace in all but the most marginal spaces. In a time before designated dog-waste bags and so-called poop-scoop laws, the efforts to confine dog feces to such spaces constitute a refusal to accept dogs as legitimate inhabitants of urban environments.

The offenses littering the alleyway and making a mockery of the posted warning, though, remind us that dogs cannot be confined to the marginalia of urban modernity. They inevitably interact with and shape the spaces they inhabit. Like other urban animals, in sociologist Tora Holmberg's words, they prove "difficult to discipline; they often transgress legal as well as cultural ordering systems, while roaming the city in what appear uncontrolled ways" that give the lie to anthropocentric understandings of urban spaces. Unlike the modern dog envisioned by dog fancy—the purebred pet molded to fit aesthetically and unobtrusively into the homes and lives of modern urbanites—Ackerley's New Dog actively participates in constructing the space of the city, and thus urban modernity itself. Moreover, as coevolutionary partner to the human, she implicitly challenges the separation between "'wild' and 'domestic,' 'pet' and 'vermin,'" pushing the "boundaries of what may be considered proper living."[65] As Ackerley points out, "Multitudes of urban dogs roam the streets by themselves, lifting their legs or tails upon the man-made world as necessity or fancy takes them, and can hardly be brought to court" (34).

This anarchic leg lifting, besides undermining official efforts to control canine bodies, sprinkles the city with messages inaccessible to humans but readily decipherable by its canine inhabitants. As Kiang claims, Ackerley depicts urine as "a viable way for some beings to apprehend and navigate the world they inhabit, and to record lived experience through means other than the written word," thus affording insight into more-than-human ways of moving through and interpreting urban space.[66] "Dogs read the world through their noses and write their history in urine," Ackerley observes, and he assumes the role of urban ethologist in recording Tulip's different modes of urination (47). In a letter to the publisher of *My Dog Tulip*, he even boasts of outdoing "that chap Konrad Lorenz" by producing previously unpublished "findings about [canine] anal glands" based on careful study of Queenie.[67] Most of his contemporaries would have accepted Lorenz's still-popular view that canine urine marking is strictly territorial. But, as ethologist Alexandra Horowitz explains in *Inside of a Dog: What Dogs See, Smell, and Know*, "research in the fifty years since [Lorenz] proposed that theory has failed to bear that out as the exclusive, or even predominant, use of urine marking."[68] Ackerley, eager to understand Tulip's marking behavior, likewise dismisses the idea that she is "staking a personal claim," noting that "nothing in her subsequent behavior suggested appropriation" (49).

Compared to Lorenz's territorial theory of canine urine marking, Ackerley's insistence that urine is a "highly complex source of social information" appears much closer to the truth (47). Urine marking, according to Horowitz, "seems to leave information about who the urinator is, how often he walks by this spot in the neighborhood, his recent victories, and his interest in mating."[69] Ackerley similarly hypothesizes that "it is a language, a code, by means of which [dogs] not only express their feelings and emotions, but communicate with and appraise each other" (47). Thus even when Tulip's heats oblige him to restrict her access to other dogs, she "reads" the "marks of attention" left at the front door by her "numerous callers," studying the "superimposed stains" so "meticulous[ly] that she gives the impression of actually identifying her acquaintances and friends" (47). Urine marking, particularly in a populous area like Ackerley's London neighborhood, constructs an "invisible pile of scents" that Horowitz likens to "a community center bulletin board, with old, deteriorating announcements and requests peeking out from underneath more recent posts of activities and successes."[70] The messages conveyed through urine thus enable Tulip to remain connected to and active in Wandsworth's canine community even when her physical contact is restricted. Canine urine, in other words, inscribes the space of the city with meanings unavailable to, and uncontrollable by, human inhabitants.

Urine marking, Ackerley suggests, also grants humans partial access to the canine *Umwelt*—the term coined by German biologist Jakob von Uexküll to signify, in Horowitz's words, "the salient elements in an animal's world."[71] Tulip's marking behavior reveals which objects in the city are salient to her: "the droppings, both liquid and solid, of other animals ... buns, bones, fish, bread, vomit ... dead and decaying animals" (48). In addition to these organic objects, Tulip directs her attention toward human-made objects: "drains, disinfectants and detergents ... pieces of newspaper ... a heap of socks and shoes" (49). Urine marking indicates not only that these items are salient to Tulip but also their relative degrees of salience. While she "attends socially to a wide range of objects," some appear to have "a special attraction for her" (48). "Fresh horse dung ... is always liberally sprayed," and dead animals in "advanced stages of decay ... affect her so deeply" that she circles them "in a swooning way," unable even to lift her leg (48). Walking down a residential street, she inspects each doorstep and seems deliberately to mark "the one most recently scoured" (49). Ackerley observes Tulip's urine marking with an ethologist's "curiosity": "I saw that ... all these objects had a quality in common, smell; even so, why did she pee on them? It could not be because other dogs had done so before her, for that only pushed the question further back: who began, and why?" (49). Though unable to discern Tulip's exact motives, he speculates "that she was simply expressing an appreciative interest; she was endorsing these delectable things with her signature, much as we underline a book we are reading" (49–50). Ackerley does not claim direct access to Tulip's mind, but her urine marking demonstrates that she *has* an *Umwelt*—a point of view regarding her urban environment—and offers some clues as to its makeup. By observing Tulip's behavior, Ackerley catches a whiff of London as she perceives it. Further, he becomes aware of—if unable to read—the larger network of canine "signatures" that record dogs' experiences and evaluations. This awareness, Kiang argues, "opens Ackerley to a different mode of perception and a different way of registering the world in which we live that rely more on material contact and interaction than on abstract positionality or special relations originating from and apprehended by the subject's eye/I."[72] The human perspective thus becomes just one of many ways to apprehend urban modernity—and a limited one at that.

As Ackerley's attention to Tulip's urination implies, sharing urban spaces with dogs also changes the human experience of those spaces— indeed, it changes the human *Umwelt*. Horowitz, reflecting on her relationship with her own dog, explains, "Pump changed my own umwelt. Walking through the world with her, watching her reactions, I began to imagine her experience." As an urban dog owner, she came to "see city blocks, and their sidewalks and buildings, with their investigatory sniffing possibilities in mind: a sidewalk along an uninterrupted wall without fences, trees, or variation, is a block I'd never want to walk down."[73] Ackerley's *Umwelt* likewise began to expand via Queenie; in *We Think the World of You*, when Frank first takes Evie for a weekend, he has "the pleasure of setting her free upon grass. . . . Gay though she was, it was a shared gaiety always; to caper about was not enough, I must caper too; and who could have resisted such ebullience of spirit, which caught one up into itself and the buffeting wind?" Evie's boundless energy pushes a usually self-absorbed Frank to experience and interact with his environment in new ways. In fact, Frank's most profound realization is that there are "other realities besides my own." While this epiphany is primarily an acknowledgment of the "iniquity" with which he has treated Johnny's working-class family, he arrives at it via Evie; her alternately "charming" and "regret[table]" behavior defamiliarizes his surroundings, inviting (and often forcing) him to imagine them from a radically different point of view.[74] Praising Ackerley's "unswerving dedication to his dog's significant otherness," Donna Haraway reads his account of the human/dog relationship as a story "not about unconditional love, but about seeking to inhabit an inter-subjective world that is about meeting the other in all the fleshly detail of a mortal relationship."[75] That Frank's triangulated affections for Evie and Johnny lead him to the "profound truth" of other realities points to the role of companion species relations in teaching humans to meet each other, and other animals, in the pluralistic spaces of urban modernity.[76]

This expansion of human *Umwelt*, moreover, reveals to Ackerley the more broadly interspecies nature of urban modernity. An ostensibly unnatural environment, the city is home to countless nonhuman species whose members actively and continuously participate in its construction. Dogs, besides demanding to be recognized as agents whose actions and desires inflect the space of the city, draw humans' attention to other nonhuman participants in urban life. Entering Wimbledon Common with Tulip, Ackerley contemplates how the park "must reek of its small denizens," and, though he is unable to detect "the scent of the recent passage of rabbits and squirrels, or the sound of the nervous beating of their nearby hidden hearts" (155), he becomes aware of their presence by observing Tulip. Her "tall ears pricked and focused" and her silent stalking indicate that she has detected the "tiny, furtive movement" of an unseen rabbit in a nearby bush (155). By attending to Tulip's attentiveness, Ackerley becomes mindful of the whereabouts and habits of other nonhuman inhabitants of London. This mindfulness extends beyond the relatively "remote" space of the park (155). In the 1964 essay "I Am a Beast," Ackerley credits Queenie not only with teaching him "all about herself and her species" but also with revealing to him the biodiversity of the modern city: "no dog, cat, or horse in our urban streets passes me unnoticed, and above the clatter and chatter of traffic and human voices I hear every note of a bird." Queenie thus seems "to contain within herself a diversity and community of beasts," not because she functions as an abstract representation of the homogenous category "the animal" but because her specific, embodied interactions with the urban landscape and its human and nonhuman occupants emphasize the more-than-human nature of that landscape.[77] Ackerley does not idealize the city as a space constructed equally by and for humans and nonhumans, but he uses his New Dog to underscore how urban spaces are shaped by all of the many species to which they are home.

Conclusion

The expansion of urban modernity in the late nineteenth and early twentieth centuries had profound implications for the human/dog relationship. No longer primarily a working partnership, this relationship faced either dissolution or inevitable and dramatic change. Modern dog fancy offered one solution to this dilemma: the modification of canine bodies to suit human preferences and urban environments. For Terhune, however, the thoroughbred dog is physically and psychologically irreconcilable to the space of the city, as Lad's misadventure in Manhattan demonstrates: "He was a dog of forest and lake and hill, this giant collie with his mighty shoulders and tiny white feet and shaggy burnished coat and mournful eyes. Never before had he been in a city. The myriad blended noises confused and deafened him. The myriad blended smells assailed his keen nostrils. The swirl of countless multicolored lights stung and blurred his vision. Noises, smells and lights were all jarringly new to him. So were the jostling masses of people on the sidewalk and the tangle and hustle of vehicular traffic" (131–32). Terhune's inclusion of a seemingly irrelevant catalog of Lad's conformation points—shoulders, feet, coat, and eyes—indicates that it is precisely Lad's fidelity to the "true" collie type, and not simply his unfamiliarity with the city, that renders him incompatible with urban life. His acute senses, precisely calibrated over generations of selection to aid in the guarding and herding of sheep, are overwhelmed by the chaotic sights, sounds, smells, crowds, and technologies that pervade the modern city. Acclimating to this environment, Terhune suggests, would require that Lad depart, like his "ultramodern" competitors at Westminster, from his breed's "ancestral standards" (118). This departure, in turn, would render Lad incapable of guarding The Place and preserving Terhune's fictional haven from the spread of urban modernity. Yet *Lad: A Dog* concludes with a story billed as "the true tale of Lad's last great adventure" and tellingly titled "In the Day of Battle" (321). While the aging Lad manages to win the battle referenced in the title, his "silvered muzzle" and the deterioration of his formerly "clean lines" signal modernity's inevitable victory over Terhune's outmoded vision of the human/dog relationship (321–22).

While Ackerley ultimately joins Terhune in rejecting modern dog fancy's project of unprecedented human control over canine bodies, by emphasizing how dogs both adapt to and shape urban modernity, he grants them a mode of agency that Terhune denies them. Initially, Evie's encounter with the modern city is as disastrous as Lad's, and her/Tulip's subsequent experiences underscore the ways in which urban environments restrict dogs' bodies and behaviors. Ackerley, too, cannot avoid tampering with Tulip, and in a moment of frustration, he confesses, "Situated as I am, I see that I never should have taken her at all; I cannot mend that now. . . . Years of devotion, years of habit, bind us together" (163). His acquisition of Tulip cannot be undone, and in this way it is a microcosm of the human/dog relationship itself. The evolutionary and historical forces that have shaped this relationship are irreversible, and life with dogs can be reconfigured only in the diverse and ever-changing spaces that humans share with them. Ackerley does not present the city as an ideal environment for dogs, nor does he pretend that humans can avoid intervening in their lives. Yet his accounts of life with Queenie demonstrate what Terhune ignores: the complexity and resilience of a long-standing interspecies relationship that already has adapted to countless contexts and environments. And while the constraints of urban spaces leave Ackerley with little choice but to interfere in his bitch's affairs more than she does in his, they also force him to become more mindful of her habits and desires—indeed, of her *Umwelt*—and of the limits of human control. Thus, while dog fancy offers a model of the human/dog relationship in which canine bodies and behaviors are wholly subject to human preference, and while Terhune counters with a rejection of any changes in this relationship that would enable it to adapt to the conditions of modernity, Ackerley posits a New Dog, and consequently a new human/dog relationship. For Ackerley, a modern articulation of this relationship challenges each party to become attuned to the other's *Umwelt*, and thus to experience urban modernity as the interspecies phenomenon it is.

CHAPTER 4

DOGGING THE SUBJECT
Samuel Beckett and Emmanuel Levinas

The late modernist fiction of Samuel Beckett figures the human as having a tenuous grasp on its species identity—as "[clinging] on to . . . the human," in the words of one narrator.[1] This theme, visible in Beckett's early work, comes to the forefront in his novels written in the wake of the radically dehumanizing atrocities of World War II. The eponymous protagonist of *Watt* is "troubled . . . by this indefinable thing that prevented him from saying, with conviction, and to his relief, of the object that was so like a pot, that it was a pot, and of the creature that still in spite of everything presented a large number of exclusively human characteristics, that it was a man."[2] As the pun on Watt/What suggests, the ontological status of the human is a central concern in this and subsequent novels—especially the trilogy of *Molloy*, *Malone Dies*, and *The Unnamable*, whose narrators, Paul Sheehan notes, share a "relationship with their species [that] is provisional and under constant renegotiation."[3] Molloy, for instance, abandons the "erect motion . . . of man" in the course of his narrative and makes only qualified assertions about his species identity: "I am human, I fancy."[4]

Beckett's work has thus been invoked in recent debates concerning the demise or persistence of humanism in late modernity. Critics have long debated whether Beckett's work supports or opposes humanism in its various forms. Richard Begam reads *Three Novels* as mapping a "shift from a humanist discourse, centred on man, to an antihumanist discourse, centred on language . . . as an end in itself."[5] Interpretations of Beckett's work as antihumanist frequently focus on the debased circumstances of his protagonists, which highlight the human's ontological subordination to language and other interpellating structures. Eric P. Levy describes the Beckettian human's tendency to move toward "primordial non-being" as "a *parody* of the humanist ontology" that elevates the human above the creaturely and material world in both the classical and Christian traditions.[6] By thus critiquing "human pretensions to knowledge and preeminence over other living beings," Angela Moorjani argues, Beckett "announces the poststructuralist antihumanism of subsequent decades."[7] Conversely, Gilbert Yeoh insists that Beckett's work affirms humanism by conveying "the very genuine despair of human subjects overwhelmed by the growing darkness, obscurity and impenetrability that result from the proliferating negative textuality."[8] By this account, Beckett's degraded human figures, far from confirming his misanthropy, reveal his deeply humanist sensibilities.

Further complicating matters is the question of Beckett's relationship to *post*humanism. Jonathan Boulter deems Beckett's stance posthumanist insofar as it probes "the very limits of the human," yet he adds that Beckett's insistence on "the persistence of the human even in its most denuded form . . . essentially collapses the opposition 'human-posthuman.'"[9] The slippage between "posthumanist" and "posthuman" in Boulter's analysis warrants attention, as theorists like Cary Wolfe insist on a distinction between the two. Posthumanism, Wolfe explains, "isn't posthuman at all—in the sense of being 'after' our embodiment has been transcended—but is only posthumanist, in the sense that it opposes [humanist] fantasies of disembodiment and autonomy."[10] Indeed, particularly perplexing for Beckett's human is the fact that he remains recognizable as such.[11] Despite his "loss of species," he exhibits reason, free will, and language—defining characteristics of the subject in the Western humanist tradition—and thus remains "all too human" in the words of Moran (107), the detective who narrates the second half of *Molloy*.[12] Sheehan thus characterizes Beckett's stance as an "apostasised humanism" that "reopens the possibility of value renewal" within the category of the human while simultaneously denouncing the "overconfident critical orthodoxy" of the humanist tradition.[13]

Until recently, despite rigorously examining Beckett's relationship to humanism, scholars have paid scant attention to the presence of animals in Beckett's oeuvre—a notable omission considering the centrality of the human/animal binary to humanist delineations of the subject by thinkers as varied as Aristotle, Descartes, Kant, Heidegger, Lacan, and Levinas. Early studies tended to read Beckett's animals as metaphors for the dehumanized modern subject, but a number of critics have begun to take seriously Beckett's interest in animals as such.[14] Steven Connor, for example, argues that Beckett treats animals as "subjects of interest in their own right rather than merely providing a vocabulary of defamation" to denigrate the human.[15] Shane Weller, building on Connor's claim that Beckett's animals resist "both emblematization and anthropomorphism," notes that Beckett presents animals "as suffering beings" and repeatedly challenges "the strict Cartesian distinction between human and animal."[16] Martin Puchner similarly contends that Beckett blurs the human/animal boundary through a "decentering of the human."[17] Puchner, though, situates Beckett's animals within debates about animal rights, a perspective that Wolfe critiques as "essentially humanist" in its goal of extending a more or less Kantian subjectivity to animals, "thus effacing the very difference of the animal other that it sought to respect."[18] Weller, by contrast, argues that Beckett's insistence on animals' radical alterity—even as he troubles the Cartesian binary—precludes a simplistic response to animal suffering. Beckett's stance, he proposes, is best understood as "anethical": "a double movement both toward and away from any ethical position."[19]

We can start to make sense of this apparent ambivalence by examining how Beckett complicates not just the human/animal distinction but the very idea of "the animal." Derrida takes this concept to task in *The Animal That Therefore I Am*, denouncing the "asinanity"—translator David Willis's approximation of Derrida's *bêtise*—of grouping "every living thing that is held not to be human" into a single category without regard for "the infinite space that separates the lizard from the dog, the protozoon from the dolphin, the shark from the lamb," and so on.[20] Unsurprisingly, given dogs' unique role in modernist reconfigurations of the human, Beckett's resistance to the homogenizing gesture inherent in the concept of "the animal" is particularly evident in his representations of dogs. Of the nonhuman inhabitants of the Beckettian landscape, dogs are the most conspicuous and, arguably, the most resistant to being reduced to mere emblems. While their mangy bodies and grotesque sexuality have led critics to regard them as symbols of degraded humanity, they rarely elicit feelings of disapproval or even pity from Beckett's protagonists; more often, they inspire envy or fascination.[21] As Connor notes of two scenes in *Molloy*, the canine encounter "arouses a powerful sense of *otherness*" that prompts Molloy and Moran "to suspend the fractious scepticism of their narratives and forget themselves in consoling reverie."[22] Further, Beckett's humans and dogs are inextricably linked by an interspecies legacy that, Donna Haraway reminds us, "is not especially nice; it is full of waste, cruelty, indifference, ignorance, and loss, as well as of joy, invention, labor, intelligence, and play."[23] Perhaps counterintuitively, it is via the familiar and often darkly comic figure of the dog that Beckett expresses most forcefully the problem of animal alterity for humanist ethics.

Dogs' capacity to perforate the borders of the human is also evident in the work of Jewish philosopher Emmanuel Levinas, whose ethics of alterity shares a complex relationship with the humanist/antihumanist debate in which Beckett's work engages. By positing alterity as the basis for ethical subjectivity, Derrida notes, Levinas breaks with "a certain traditional humanism" that regards rationality and autonomy as essential attributes of the subject. His rejection of such criteria would seem to remove the obstacles that have barred animals from ethical subjectivity, yet Levinas maintains that the other who calls the subject into ethical relations can only be another human. Derrida thus dubs Levinasian ethics a "profound humanism" that excludes animals from moral consideration by drawing the boundaries of subjectivity at the borders of the human.[24] A canine encounter, though, famously tempted Levinas to extend ethics beyond the species divide. In "The Name of a Dog, or Natural Rights," he describes a dog who wandered into the Nazi concentration camp where he was imprisoned during World War II. Bobby, Levinas recalls, "would appear at morning assembly and was waiting for us as we returned, jumping up and down and barking in delight. For him—it was incontestable—we were men." Bobby's welcome is so compelling that Levinas dubs him "the last Kantian in Nazi Germany."[25] Despite the implicit ironic disavowal, Levinas's attribution of something like subjectivity to Bobby indicates just how powerfully dogs confound humanist subject formation.

In what follows, I examine the destabilizing presence of dogs in Beckett's late modernist fiction—especially *Watt* and *Molloy*—and Levinas's neo-humanist philosophy in order to outline the ontological and ethical challenge posed by animal alterity in the aftermath of World War II. Beckett and Levinas both locate the dog in a paradoxical position within what Derrida deems the "sacrificial structure" of Western humanism, wherein the animal is excluded from subjectivity through discursive and literal sacrifice.[26] The dog, as animal, belongs to a realm of abjection that defines through negation the humanist subject; yet, as Beckett and Levinas insinuate, dogs occupy a quasi-subjective status by virtue of their coevolutionary relationship with humans. As humans' longtime hunting and herding partners whose labor facilitated the rise of hunter-gatherer and agricultural societies, dogs are implicated in the subjugation and sacrifice of other animals, complicating the ethical quandary in which Western humanism finds itself vis-à-vis the animal. While the human's loss of species in Beckett's fiction evokes both the unspeakable horrors of World War II and the destructive and alienating forces of modernity, the canine encounter, as Beckett and (more reluctantly) Levinas demonstrate, precipitates a more radical, primary confrontation with the sacrificial logic of post-Enlightenment humanism.

In order to illuminate dogs' privileged role in Beckett's reconfiguration of the human/animal relationship, I first examine how the simultaneously subjugated and privileged status of the Beckettian dog complicates the problem of animal suffering for humanist ethics. I then turn to Levinas's essay on Bobby to demonstrate how humanist formulations of the subject persistently falter in the canine encounter. Next, I link the desire for connection that Beckett's narrators experience in the presence of dogs to Beckett's broader antihumanist critique of the subject's claim to language and rational autonomy. Finally, I argue that dogs' disruptive power stems from their vital role in facilitating human violence against other animals, illustrating how Beckett and Levinas implicate dogs in the crimes against animality epitomized by the modern slaughterhouse. The interconnected motifs of human/dog relations and slaughter in the Beckettian landscape thus signal dogs' special capacity to undermine humanist configurations of the subject. Throughout, as the chapter title suggests, I build on Carrie Rohman's formulation of "stalking the subject," replacing "stalking" with "dogging" to evoke the doubly signifying image of a dog at heel. The dog following the human seems to promise ontological reassurance via her anthropocentrically prized fidelity, yet her intimate proximity also signals coevolutionary entanglements that persistently undermine the human's autonomy and ethical primacy. Ultimately, I reveal how Beckett's dogs, like Levinas's Bobby, mutely articulate the need for a posthumanist ethics that recovers and respects the radical alterity subsumed under the category of "the animal."

A Dog's Life

The persistence with which Beckett portrays animals in states of suffering makes it difficult to dismiss them as mere symbols of human futility or degradation. As Weller observes, one of the primary ways in which Beckett undermines the human/animal divide is by depicting animals suffering and "human beings expressing sympathy for that suffering" (although Beckett's refusal to efface their alterity means that he remains skeptical as to "whether or not the attempt to alleviate the suffering of an animal is in fact an unambiguously ethical action"—a question to which I will return).[27] In Beckett's early story "Dante and the Lobster," the protagonist Belacqua is troubled by the routine suffering of animals. He spots a downed horse with a man sitting on its head and acknowledges "that that is considered the right thing to do. But why?" Later, he watches in horror as his aunt prepares to boil the eponymous lobster, who "tremble[s]" before "going alive into scalding water." In admonishing him to "have sense" and insisting that lobsters "feel nothing," Belacqua's aunt echoes the Cartesian view of animals as automata.[28] For Descartes, "pain exists only in the understanding," so animals, although they may exhibit "the external movements which accompany this feeling in us," cannot experience "pain in the strict sense" because they lack reason.[29] Belacqua tries to reassure himself that "it's a quick death," but the narrator's retort—"It is not"—bluntly undercuts the Cartesian distinction between the human as rational subject and the animal as living machine.[30] To the extent that Beckett represents animals as suffering beings, and insofar as his characters' sympathy for their suffering indicates that it warrants ethical consideration, Beckett (like Derrida) appears to endorse Jeremy Bentham's oft-quoted formulation: "The question is not, Can they *reason?* nor, Can they *talk?* but, Can they *suffer?*"[31]

Yet Beckett's blurring of the Cartesian divide neither negates alterity nor translates into a straightforward call to eliminate suffering in the name of animal rights or a utilitarian maximization of happiness. An autobiographical fragment from his late novella *Company* illustrates the danger of naive attempts to assign rights or alleviate suffering.

> You take pity on a hedgehog out in the cold and put it in an old hatbox with some worms. This box with the hog inside you then place in a disused hutch wedging the door open for the poor creature to come and go at will. To go in search of food and having

eaten to regain the warmth and security of its box in the hutch. ... Kneeling at your bedside you included it the hedgehog in your detailed prayer to God to bless all you loved. And tossing in your warm bed waiting for sleep to come you were still faintly glowing at the thought of what a fortunate hedgehog it was to have crossed your path as it did.... Now the next morning not only was the glow spent but a great uneasiness had taken its place. A suspicion that all was perhaps not as it should be. That rather than do as you did you had perhaps better let good alone and the hedgehog pursue its way. Days if not weeks passed before you could bring yourself to return to the hutch. You have never forgotten what you found then. You are on your back in the dark and have never forgotten what you found then. The mush. The stench.[32]

Weller uses this passage to demonstrate that, for Beckett, "the alterity of the animal means that any human intervention [in cases of apparent suffering] is liable to be catastrophic."[33] Yet as Belacqua's response to the downed horse suggests, animal suffering assumes multiple forms, complicating the questions of whether and how the human should respond. In the case of a nondomesticated animal like the hedgehog, intervention seems ill advised, especially when the animal's perceived distress is an anthropomorphic projection. By contrast, Beckett presents the suffering of equines as unjust when it results from their use as means to human ends. Lambert in *Malone Dies*, for example, rescues an old mule "at the gates of the slaughterhouse," but only because he hopes to "screw" more labor out of him (212). Moreover, the sight of equines enduring abuse at human hands typically elicits genuine sympathy from Beckett's protagonists, as when Molloy sees a man whipping a team of donkeys: "My eyes caught a donkey's eyes, they fell to his little feet, their brave fastidious tread" (26).[34]

Even among domesticated animals, suffering—and consequently its ethical import—is not a uniform phenomenon. Whereas equines suffer in their function as draft animals, Beckett's dogs suffer in their seemingly elevated status as humans' companions. The most obvious figures of canine suffering in Beckett's oeuvre are the famished dogs of *Watt*. While employed as a servant to the mysterious Mr. Knott, Watt is instructed to give leftover food "to the dog"—a puzzling order because "there was no dog in the house, that is to say, no house-dog, to which this food could be given." So begins a more than thirty-page exposition of the absurdly complex system for uniting Mr. Knott's leftovers with a dog hungry enough to ensure that "not an atom remained." The resulting arrangement involves the employment of the five-generation, twenty-eight-member Lynch family to breed and maintain a "colony of famished dogs set up by Mr Knott in order that there should never be wanting a famished dog to eat his food on those days that he did not eat it himself." The famished dog arrangement is typically regarded as a satire of preestablished harmony, Leibniz's attempt to reconcile Cartesian dualism with the apparent interaction of mind and body by proposing that each entity is programmed at creation to act independently but in harmony with the other; Watt thus ponders "the manner in which this problem had been solved . . . in that far distant past, when Mr Knott set up his establishment."[35] Watt's exhaustive reasoning, obsessively organized into numbered lists and tables detailing each possible system and its imperfections, also mocks Descartes's method of making "enumerations so complete, and reviews so comprehensive, that I could be sure of leaving nothing out."[36]

Beckett's emphasis on the suffering of the famished dogs reveals the ethical dimension of his satire of Cartesian rationalism. Even Watt, who has "no love for dogs," is preoccupied with the canine participants in Mr. Knott's arrangement: "But much more than with the Lynches, or with Mr Knott's remains, Watt's concern, while it lasted, was with the dog." That he is most disturbed by their suffering is evident in his longing to know "which the sufferer, and what the sufferer, and what the suffering."[37] And suffer they do.

> The dogs employed to eat Mr Knott's occasional remains were not long-lived, as a rule. This was very natural. For besides what the dog got to eat, every now and then, on Mr Knott's backdoorstep, it got so to speak nothing to eat. For if it had been given food other than the food that Mr Knott gave it, from time to time, then its appetite might have been spoilt, for the food that Mr Knott gave it. . . . Add to this that the dog was seldom off the chain, and so got no exercise worth mentioning. This was inevitable. For if the dog had been set free, to run about, as it pleased, then it would have eaten the horsedung, on the road, and all the other nasty things that abound, on the ground, and so ruined its appetite, perhaps for ever, or worse still would have run away, and never come back.[38]

That the famished dogs suffer from perpetual emaciation and confinement extends Beckett's critique of Enlightenment rationalism to the problem of animal suffering. Caught up in a Cartesian "mecanism [sic]" that rationalizes their condition as "natural" and "inevitable," the famished dogs offer a mute critique of the absurdity of a philosophical tradition that strips animals of feeling and agency in order to legitimize their exploitation. If the idea of maintaining a colony of dogs on the brink of starvation "for the sole purpose of eating Mr Knott's food" seems too comically absurd to be read as a commentary on actual canine suffering, Watt's reference to "the large numbers of hungry and even starving dogs with which the neighbourhood abounded, and doubtless had always abounded, for miles around, in every direction," underscores the extent to which real dogs suffer by virtue of their dependence on humans. The Lynch family, too, is one of the "immense impoverished families [that] abounded for miles around in every conceivable direction." Beckett pushes the comparison between the Lynches and the dogs further in his notebooks, in which he outlines a breeding program whereby Irish setters and Palestine retrievers are crossed to produce the optimal variety of "well-bred well-trained famished dog" found in the novel.[39] The congenital defects that plague the incestuous Lynch family thus evoke the grotesque consequences of a practice euphemistically termed "line-breeding" in the purebred dog world—a world with which Beckett no doubt came into contact via his mother, May, who owned and exhibited a number of Kerry Blue terriers. Taken together, the hunchbacked, rheumatic Lynches and the emaciated dogs satirize the material ways in which human whims shape canine bodies via modern breeding practices.

In Beckett's *Three Novels*, the use of dogs to satisfy human desires is most visible in Teddy, the pet dog Molloy accidentally runs over with his bicycle. Teddy's death, rather than causing him pain, serves to "put [him] out of his misery" as his owner, Lousse, is taking him to be destroyed. Teddy is "old, blind, deaf, crippled with rheumatism and perpetually incontinent," yet the real misery from which Molloy unwittingly frees him is his degraded life as a woman's pet (33). As his name suggests, Teddy is little more than a comforting object, like the "woolly bear" Moran's son must "hug" in order to fall asleep (122). He belongs to that category of animals so disparaged by Deleuze and Guattari: "individuated animals, family pets, sentimental, Oedipal animals each with its own petty history."[40] Far from embodying a radical alterity that dissolves human fantasies of identity and autonomy,

Teddy merely "take[s] the place of a child" (47). This logic of surrogacy negates his alterity so that he becomes, like Miss Dew's dachshund in *Murphy*, a "so-called dog." When Murphy first meets Miss Dew, she is holding "a lead whereby her personality was extended to a Dachshund so low and so long that Murphy had no means of telling whether it was a dog or a bitch," indicating the literal and figurative neutering of the pet dog.[41] Teddy, too, is an infantilized and desexed surrogate. Molloy easily replaces him in turn, atoning for his misdeed by leading "a dog's life"—a phrase Beckett uses elsewhere to describe the situation of a henpecked man—while detained by the oppressively maternal Lousse.[42] Molloy even evinces a willingness to be neutered, remarking that "if they had removed a few testicles into the bargain I wouldn't have objected" (35). Lousse, whose name is a homophone for the singular form of "lice," buries Teddy with "ticks in his ears," confirming that his existence is delimited by parasitic human desires (37).

Lousse's smothering affection for dogs and men alike evokes Beckett's vexed relationship with his mother, whose well-documented fondness for dogs and donkeys no doubt informs their prominence in the Beckettian bestiary. Piecing together biographical accounts revealing that Beckett ran over one of May's Kerry Blue terriers in 1926, Daniel Katz proposes that "Teddy's fatal accident is itself a re-elaboration of [this] traumatic event."[43] Yet Beckett's critique of the profoundly humanist sentimentalizing of the pet extends beyond his maternal characters. A masculine form of pet love is satirized in the story of Ernest Louit, told by the servant Arthur in *Watt*. Louit, a university student, embarks with his bull terrier O'Connor on a research expedition to County Clare. His pastoral vision of traversing the countryside with his faithful dog at his heels and sleeping "in the sweet-smelling hay ... of the local barns" soon gives way to a harsh reality punctuated by his discovery of "the skeleton of a goat" in one of only three barns to be found. Starving and stranded in a bog, Louit is "reluctantly obliged ... to hold O'Connor head downward in the morass, until his faithful heart ... ceased to beat, and then roast him." Man's best friend to the end, O'Connor makes the ultimate sacrifice for the human pursuit of knowledge represented by Louit's research findings, which "could not be of the smallest value to any person other than himself and, eventually, humanity." O'Connor's sentimentalized fidelity, moreover, ironically allows Louit to ennoble the squeamishness that prevents him from skinning his beloved pet: "He took no credit for this, O'Connor in his place would have done the same for him."[44]

The paradoxically elevated and subordinated status of the dog as pet is also evident in Levinas's essay on Bobby, the dog who visited the concentration camp where Levinas was imprisoned during the war. Just as canine companionship bolsters Lousse's maternal identity and Louit's pastoral fantasy, Bobby serves the (albeit worthier) purpose of affirming the humanity of the prisoners of camp 1492. Bobby's welcoming behavior echoes that of the ultimate figure of canine fidelity and pathos: Argos, the ancient dog who "recognized Ulysses beneath his disguise" and, "though he had no strength to drag himself an inch toward his master," managed to drop his ears and thump his tail in an unmistakably canine greeting.[45] Bobby likewise recognizes the prisoners as "men" despite the fact that the Nazi guards have "stripped us of our human skin. We were a quasi-humanity, a gang of apes."[46] The central irony of Levinas's essay is that the dog emerges as the camp's most human inhabitant. The Nazi guards, though "called free," are brute enforcers of "Hitlerian violence," while the prisoners are "beings entrapped in their species; despite all their vocabulary, beings without language." Bobby, with his Kantian gesture, is able to do what the prisoners cannot: "deliver a message about our humanity which . . . will come across as anything other than monkey talk."[47] In sniffing out the prisoners' violently suppressed humanity, the dog seems poised to transcend the subhumanity that has been deemed his (and their) proper place.

Ultimately, though, Bobby's value for Levinas lies in his role as a vehicle for human transcendence. As Richard Nash observes, Levinas's account of the dog's welcome echoes "the sentimental logic of the pet—those special 'domesticated' animals who function to confer upon us a greater humanity by actions and articulations that simultaneously transcend their 'animal' status and accept the logic of domination and domestication in which such transcendence is recontained."[48] This paradoxical status of the pet is evident in the act of naming invoked by the essay's title: "The Name of a Dog." Bobby appears quite literally in name only, for Levinas offers no description of the dog as inhabiting a physical body of a given type, size, shape, age, or color. Derrida articulates the implications of naming an animal when he describes the experience of standing naked before a cat:

> If I say "it is a real cat" that sees me naked, this is in order to mark its unsubstitutable singularity. When it responds in its name . . . it doesn't do so as the exemplar of a species called "cat," even less so of an "animal" genus or kingdom. It is true that I identify it as

a male or female cat. But even before that identification, it comes to me as *this* irreplaceable living being that one day enters my space, into this place where it can encounter me, see me, even see me naked. Nothing can ever rob me of the certainty that what we have here is an existence that refuses to be conceptualized. And a mortal existence, for from the moment that it has a name, its name survives it. It signs its potential disappearance. Mine also, and that disappearance, from this moment to that, *fort/da*, is announced each time that, with or without nakedness, one of us leaves the room.[49]

Bobby's name clearly survives him, appearing as it does in an essay written decades after his obscure death. Insofar as it marks his "unsubstitutable singularity" and the mortality he shares with the prisoners, his name seems at least to constitute a move toward literalizing him, especially as Levinas's essay turns on a transition from the nameless (and therefore, he implies, "figurative") dogs in the verse from Exodus that serves as his epigraph to the named ("literal") dog of camp 1492.[50]

But Levinas's investment in affirming the prisoners' humanity via Bobby competes with the need to silence the dog and thus secure the borders of the subject. Bobby's name, though it seemingly elevates him by marking his individuality, also relegates him to the subordinate position he shares with Beckett's Teddy and O'Connor. Further, it echoes Adam's naming of the animals in Genesis, which establishes their status as his companions but also confirms his dominion over them. In "The Name of a Dog," Levinas presents the act of naming sentimentally, as something "one does with a cherished dog." Elsewhere, though, he characterizes naming as "a violence and a negation [that] denies the independence of a being: it belongs to me." By this account, naming is a fundamentally appropriative act that seeks to incorporate the other, who by definition "escapes comprehension," into "my comprehension and possession."[51] Bobby's name, as I have argued elsewhere, thus neutralizes the challenge he presents to humanist ethics by casting him in the familiar role of man's best friend: "At the supreme hour of humanity's inception—and without ethics and without *logos*—the dog will attest to the dignity of the person. This is what the friend of man means."[52] As we will see, though, Beckett insists (and Levinas intimates) that canine alterity is not so easily effaced, and its doggedness poses a grave threat to the intelligibility of humanist ethics.

The Face of a Dog

Levinas famously dubbed his ethics a "humanism of the other man," marking both his affinity and his dissatisfaction with Enlightenment humanism.[53] Levinasian ethics remains resolutely humanist in asserting the ethical primacy of the human subject, yet his conceptualization of this subject marks a radical break with a Cartesian or Kantian model that posits rationality as a prerequisite for ethical relations. For Levinas, the Western philosophical tradition is dominated by "the concept of totality," which reduces individuals "to being bearers of forces that command them unbeknown to themselves."[54] To define the subject based on its possession of a given attribute is to impose such a totality, delimiting the subject ontologically and reducing human being to a collection of capabilities that the human is thus compelled to perform. Levinas opposes totality to the infinite exteriority and alterity of the other. In the encounter with the other, the self seeks impulsively to "nullify separation" and possess the other as an object of knowledge.[55] The face—Levinas's term for the unassimilable alterity of the other—prohibits this totalizing gesture by silently voicing the commandment "Thou shalt not kill." In Levinas's configuration, I emerge as a subject in my encounter with the other precisely because I become *subject to* the commandment enacted by the face. My realization of the other-as-subject precedes and enables my own becoming-subject, making Levinas's ethical exchange first and foremost a humanism—and humanization—of the other.

Levinas's concept of the face thus constitutes a significant departure from traditional humanist subject formation. The face-to-face encounter, far from confirming the subjectivity of "a being endowed with certain qualities called moral, which it would bear as attributes," subjects the self to "an infinite passivity."[56] In this formulation, as Levinas readily notes, "Man is an unreasonable animal" in that he is compelled to suspend his self-interest for the sake of the other.[57] This refusal to ground subjectivity in rational autonomy leads Levinas to align his project partially with the antihumanism he associates with thinkers like Nietzsche, Heidegger, Lacan, and Lévi-Strauss: "Modern antihumanism, which denies the primacy that the human person, a free end in itself, has for the signification of being, is true over and above the reasons it gives itself. It makes a place for subjectivity positing itself in abnegation, in sacrifice, and in substitution. Its great intuition is to have abandoned the idea of [the] person as an end in itself. The Other is the end, and me, I am a hostage."[58] The antihumanist deconstruction of the a priori subject, far from bringing an end to ethical subjectivity, reveals (in spite of itself) that traditional humanism "is not sufficiently human"—particularly in light of the atrocities of World War II, which have "render[ed] tragicomic the concern for oneself and illusory the pretension of the rational animal to have a privileged place in the cosmos."[59] For Levinas, modern antihumanism exposes the need for an ethics that theorizes the radical exteriority of being and acknowledges the finitude and vulnerability of the human. Levinas's reconfiguration of ethical subjectivity thus frees the human from the constraints of a rationalist tradition even as it renders the self hostage to the other.

The antihumanist bent of Levinas's formulation might appear to dismantle barriers that have limited ethical consideration of nonhuman animals within humanism. Given its emphasis on alterity and its rejection of ontological delineations of the subject, Peter Atterton argues, Levinasian ethics seems ideally suited "to accommodate the inclusion of the other animal, and thereby go beyond the very humanism—and human chauvinism—that has served as a philosophical justification for the mistreatment of animals for over two millennia."[60] Indeed, Rohman reads Derrida's reflections on his encounter with the cat as "a formal meditation on what many of us have felt while reading Levinas's description of the face: that the qualities of this ethical relation are not only descriptive of our experience of the animal other, but are sometimes *more* true of the ethical call that issues from animals."[61] What, after all, does the human discover in the face of an animal if not an alterity even more radical than that of the other human? Something rather less compelling to Levinas, who explains, "The Other is not other with a relative alterity as are, in a comparison, even ultimate species, which mutually exclude one another but still have their place within the community of a genus—excluding one another by their definition, but calling for one another by this exclusion, across the community of their genus. The alterity of the Other does not depend on any quality that would distinguish him from me, for a distinction of this nature would precisely imply between us that community of genus which already nullifies alterity."[62] Counterintuitively, Levinas proposes that animals cannot call humans into ethical relations because our evolutionary kinship negates the alterity of species difference; in Derrida's words, the animal is simultaneously "too other to be our brother or neighbor [and] not enough other to be the wholly other."[63] Levinas's comments in a 1986 interview indicate that ethical relations between "ultimate species" thus emerge through means quite different from the epiphany of the face: "Clearly, one [approach to] ethics is the transference of the idea of suffering to an animal, certainly. The animal suffers. It is because we as men know what suffering is that we can have this obligation."[64] The ethical treatment of animals stems not from an encounter with radical alterity but from a transference of "the idea of suffering" across axes of genetic continuity. Lacking the absolute alterity required to be considered a face in the ethical sense, an animal cannot command of (or be commanded by) the other, "Thou shalt not kill." Despite his concession that "we do not want to make an animal suffer needlessly, etcetera," Levinas reserves this commandment for the human alone.

Levinas's essay on Bobby is especially puzzling given his evident desire to dismiss the possibility of animal alterity. "I am thinking of Bobby," he announces near the outset, yet despite this declaration and the title, Bobby does not appear until the final two paragraphs. Thus it is difficult to determine the nature and degree of Bobby's significance even in the context of this essay, let alone in relation to Levinas's entire philosophy. Several critics have argued that Bobby presents an especially potent challenge to Levinas's concept of the face. David Clark, for example, notes that "Bobby doubles for the human, yet he is not human, and this indeterminacy about his ontological and moral status at once triggers Levinas's most dogmatic claims about nonhuman life and tests the limits of their coherence."[65] No sooner has Levinas called Bobby "the last Kantian in Nazi Germany" than he retracts this statement, insisting that the dog lacks "the brain needed to universalize the maxims of its drives" (and perhaps revealing a residual Cartesianism in his understanding of the subject).[66] Derrida thus reads the many exclamation marks in this short essay as "disavowal marks" that preempt any serious consideration of Bobby's moral standing by signifying Levinas's "allegorical incredulity."[67] These disavowals certainly confound any literal reading of the passage, yet Levinas ultimately seems unwilling to either affirm or deny the validity of Bobby's apparent recognition of humanity—which, in turn, would necessitate the attribution of something like humanity to the dog—and his playful ambiguity facilitates this avoidance. Even if we read Bobby's Kantianism in a purely figurative sense, Levinas's near-total silence on the ethical status of animals lends significance to his decision to write an essay that implicitly raises the question of animal subjectivity and never explicitly answers it.

Why does Levinas refuse (forgive me) to let sleeping dogs lie? The invocation of Bobby opens up questions that Levinas strenuously avoids throughout most of his oeuvre. Even in "The Name of a Dog," Levinas is heavily invested in "policing the species border," as Nash puts it, and he labors elsewhere to maintain a categorical distinction between humans and animals, relegating the latter to a secondary moral status when he is willing to consider them at all.[68] In the 1986 interview, when asked what is required for a being to have a face in the ethical sense, he explains:

> I do not know at what moment the human appears, but what I am going to underline is that the human breaks with pure being, which is always a persistence in being. That is my principal thesis. A being is something that is attached to being, to its being. That is the idea of Darwin. The animal being is a struggle for life, a struggle for life without ethics. Is that not true? It is a question of might, no? Darwinian morality.... The living being struggles for life. The aim of life is life itself. However, with the appearance of the human—here is my entire philosophy—that is, with man, there is something more important than my life, and that is the life of the other.[69]

Here, Levinas takes pains to uphold the uniqueness of the human face in spite of an awareness of Darwinian continuity implied in his uncertainty about the "moment the human appears." In *The Descent of Man* and *The Expression of the Emotions in Man and Animals*, Darwin refuses to draw an absolute boundary between humans and other animals, instead demonstrating the impossibility of such a distinction by citing numerous examples of animals' exhibiting rudimentary forms of "higher" faculties like language, ethics, and reason.[70] Thus Levinas's attempt to mobilize "Darwin's idea" in support of his ethics is deeply problematic given his insistence that "in relation to the animal, humanity is a new phenomenon."[71]

In the same interview, though, Levinas implies a continuum of what we might call "faciality" even while attempting to maintain his categorical distinction. His interviewers ask whether "the face of an animal [can] be considered also as the other who must be welcomed" and whether ethical relations require "the possibility of speech"; Levinas replies, "I cannot tell you at what moment you have the right to be called 'face.'" Although he ultimately reaffirms the primacy of the human face—"The human face is an altogether different thing, and we rediscover [only] afterward the face in the animal"—his response opens up possibilities that were foreclosed in, for example, the essay "Is Ontology Fundamental?," in which he insists, "A being is a human being" and "the relation with a *being* is the invocation of a face and already speech."[72] By contrast, his answer to his interviewers leaves room for the possibility not only of an animal face but of a face in the absence of speech. Moreover, he offers an astonishingly inclusive response to the question of whether humans have ethical obligations to other animals: "I also think that quite clearly, even if it is not as simple as that, even if animals are not considered as human beings, the ethical extends to living beings."[73] Exactly why this is clear, and how such a potentially far-reaching declaration is reconcilable to his resolutely humanist ethics, remains unexplained.

In contemplating the extension of ethics to all living beings and thus threatening to muddle his "entire philosophy," it appears that Levinas is once again thinking of Bobby. That the dog poses a particularly compelling challenge to the humanist discourse of the face is evident in the regularity with which Levinas returns to it as a test case when pressed on the possibility of the animal face. When asked what differentiates the face of the human other from that of an animal, he replies:

> One cannot entirely refuse a dog the face. It is in terms of the face [that one understands] the dog. . . . It is not in the dog that the phenomenon of the face is in its purity. . . . The parentage of this phenomenon of the face is not at all in the dog. . . . On the contrary, in the dog, in the animal, there are other phenomena. For example, that force of nature—it is pure vitality. That which characterizes above all the dog [is] its vitality—yet there is also a face. . . . But . . . there is [something] in our attraction, in a complex regard, in regard to an animal, an animal that is beautiful—myself, I don't have much to do with animals—but, there are those who love the dog, for example, and what they love in the dog is perhaps its childlike character. As though it were strong, cheerful, powerful, full of life, but [also] because it doesn't know everything. . . . A child is often loved for its animality, no? It is not suspicious of anything; it jumps, walks, runs, bites. It's delightful.[74]

Although his interviewers use the generic "animal" in posing their question—bringing to mind Derrida's critique of that category—Levinas specifically refers to the dog in his reply. It is perhaps not surprising that a philosopher would look to man's proverbial best friend when trying to articulate the relationship between the human and "the animal," and to some extent Levinas posits the dog as representative of that category: "in the dog, in the animal" suggests a conflation of the two. Yet his anthropomorphic musings on the dog as child recall both the surrogate status of the pet and the memorable image of Bobby "jumping up and down and barking in delight," indicating that Levinas's choice of species when asked to contemplate "the animal" is far from arbitrary. He is willing to grant a face (albeit an impure one) specifically to the dog. His unprompted consideration of the possibility of other, more alien species' possessing a face is notably more dismissive: "I do not know whether one finds it in the snake! [*laughter*] I do not know how to answer that question, since more specific analyses are needed. Not in the flea, for example. The flea! It's an insect, which jumps, eh? [*laughter*]."[75]

While the face of a dog pushes Levinas to the brink of abandoning the human/animal distinction that underwrites his neohumanist ethics, Beckett uses the canine encounter as a point of departure for his more radical reconfiguration of the human. Just as Watt becomes preoccupied with Mr. Knott's famished dogs, Molloy and Moran are irresistibly drawn to dogs. Significantly, these attractions do not necessarily evince or inspire fondness; rather, they underscore the ontological precariousness of the human—serving, in Chris Ackerley's words, "as a constant reminder of our 'loss of species'"—and intensify the characters' desire to escape the humanist subject position via a primary encounter with animality.[76] This desire is evident in Moran's interactions with the neighbors' dog, whom he takes perverse delight in teasing:

> They had an aberdeen called Zulu. People called it Zulu. Sometimes, when I was in a good humour, I called, Zulu! Little Zulu! and he would come and talk to me, through the railings. But I had to be feeling gay. I don't like animals. It's a strange thing, I don't like men and I don't like animals. As for God, he is beginning to disgust me. Crouching down I would stroke his ears, through the railings, and utter wheedling words. He did not realize he disgusted me. He reared up on his hind legs and pressed his chest against the

bars. Then I could see his little black penis ending in a thin wisp of wetted hair. He felt insecure, his hams trembled, his little paws fumbled for purchase, one after the other. I too wobbled, squatting on my heels. With my free hand I held on to the railings. Perhaps I disgusted him too. I found it hard to tear myself away from these vain thoughts. (105)

This exchange seems initially to affirm the dog's function as a symbol of degraded humanity; in one of the earliest studies of the Beckettian dog, Philip Howard Solomon reads the implicit "comparison between man and dog" as offering an unflattering commentary on "the human condition": "In *Molloy*, human beings are condemned to lead a dog's life and to die like a dog."[77] That both parties "fumble" and "wobble" indeed suggests a comparison, and their likeness is reinforced by the image of Moran squatting to assume "a posture closely resembling that of the dog" while Zulu "rears up" in the erect posture of a human (86). Moreover, Moran's disgust with humans, animals, and God alike collapses not just the human/canine distinction but the entire Judeo-Christian chain of being. (That "dog" is "God" spelled backward would hardly have escaped Beckett.)

Yet while Moran's encounter with Zulu serves in part to blur the species boundary signified by the railings separating his yard from the Elsner sisters', it also underscores the alterity of the canine neighbor that in turn challenges the ontological status of the human. The physical instability of human and dog recalls the calling into question of the self in the Levinasian encounter with the other, while Moran's musings attest to the dog's unassimilable alterity. His clarification that "people called it Zulu" alludes to the appropriative act of naming, and his observation of the dog's penis conjures the negated sexual agency of the pet. Zulu's unknowability, however, does not prevent Moran from contemplating the dog's perspective; he speculates that Zulu "felt insecure" and wonders whether the dog reciprocates his disgust. His recollections later in the novel confirm that Moran does indeed have difficulty tearing himself away from thoughts of Zulu (122, 168). His awareness of being looked at by the dog parallels Derrida's realization in his encounter with the cat that "it can allow itself to be looked at, no doubt, but also—something that philosophy perhaps forgets, perhaps being this calculated forgetting itself—it can look at me. It has its point of view regarding me. The point of view of the absolute other, and nothing will have ever given me more food for thinking through this absolute alterity of the neighbor . . . than these moments when I see myself seen naked under the gaze of a cat."[78] Like Derrida, Moran sees himself *seen by* an animal and avoids both anthropomorphic projections that efface alterity and the anthropocentric refusal to acknowledge the animal's point of view. That Moran resists the impulse to appropriate the other is all the more significant given his tendency to define himself through possessions. Unlike Molloy, who intends but never manages "to draw up the inventory of my goods and possessions" (14), Moran peppers his narrative with references to "my lamp," "my bees," "my house," "my grounds," etc.; he even adds his son to this inventory, first by naming young Jacques after himself and then—as if to retract the nod to individuality implicit in the act of naming—by referring to him almost invariably as "my son" (92–93). By contrast, Moran's interaction with Zulu indicates dogs' resistance to such appropriative gestures, signaling the potential of the canine encounter to draw the human out of the confines of its conventional subject position.

Beckett's Antihumanism

As Moran's attraction to Zulu suggests, human/dog encounters in *Molloy* reveal the human's pitiable isolation within the subject position delineated by the humanist tradition. Molloy expresses frustration with this condition at the outset of his journey when he observes a "face to face" meeting between two men he calls A and C (9). After they part, Molloy continues to watch one of them—"A or C, I don't remember"—but, "in spite of my soul's leap out to him," sees him "only darkly" (11). The anonymity of this encounter and its interchangeable participants, coupled with Molloy's ineffectual desire to connect with the human other, stands in sharp contrast to A's or C's subsequent interaction with a Pomeranian who appears at his heels: "At a given moment, preestablished if you like, I don't much mind, the gentleman turned back, took the little creature in his arms, drew the cigar from his lips and buried his face in the orange fleece" (12). Another jab at Leibniz's preestablished harmony, this passage portrays humans and dogs as always-already joined by an interspecies intimacy that permeates their encounters. Molloy thus wonders:

> What prevented the dog from being one of those stray dogs that you pick up and take in your arms, from compassion or because

you have long been straying with no other company than the endless roads, sands, shingle, bogs and heather, than this nature answerable to another court, than at long intervals the fellow convict you long to stop, embrace, suck, suckle and whom you pass by, with hostile eyes, for fear of his familiarities? Until the day when, your endurance gone, in this world for you without arms, you catch up in yours the first mangy cur you meet, carry it the time needed for it to love you and you it, then throw it away. (12)

To some extent, this passage positions the stray dog, like the pet dog, as a disposable surrogate for the human other; unable to embrace his "fellow convict," the wanderer desperately grasps "the first mangy cur" to cross his path. Yet Molloy also expresses the loneliness peculiar to a being trapped within a "nature answerable to another court"—that is, human nature as circumscribed by the humanist tradition. Longing to transgress the borders of a subject position premised on the subjugation of embodiment and animality, he finds himself "up against [A or C], up against the dog, gasping" (12). Alarmed, A or C soon departs, leaving Molloy "alone, no . . . restored to myself, no, I never left myself" (13).

As Molloy's longing for embodied connection within and across species suggests, Beckett's fiction is antihumanist insofar as it critiques the humanist predication of subjectivity on transcendence of animality. Beckett repeatedly disparages the Judeo-Christian strand of this dogma through ironic references to the Great Chain of Being, the hierarchy alluded to in Moran's encounter with Zulu. Suspended between the divine and animal realms, the human strives to ascend to the former by disavowing the latter; thus Moran tries to instill in his son "that most fruitful of dispositions, horror of the body and its functions" (118). Conversely, Pozzo in *Waiting for Godot* ridicules the human's aspirations to divinity: "You are human beings none the less. . . . As far as one can see. . . . Of the same species as myself. (*He bursts into an enormous laugh.*) Of the same species as Pozzo! Made in God's image."[79] The human's precarious position within the chain of being is evidenced by anxiety surrounding the collision of the divine and animal realms, a possibility introduced in *Watt*: "A rat, or other small animal, eats of a consecrated wafer. 1) Does he ingest the Real Body, or does he not? 2) If he does not, what has become of it? 3) If he does, what is to be done with him?"[80] The Catholic doctrine of transubstantiation renders Christ's physical body vulnerable to ingestion by unintended recipients, creating the possibility that a rat might usurp the human's intermediate position in the cosmos by consuming the Eucharist. Similarly, the collapse of the chain of being in *Molloy* displaces the humanist subject by merging the two realms between which it has traditionally hovered. While the human is ostensibly "made in God's image," animals appear more frequently in close proximity to the divine. Teddy is buried "like a Carthusian monk" (36), and even Moran's priest, Father Ambrose, upsets the divine-human-animal hierarchy when he notes that laughter "is peculiar to man. . . . Animals never laugh. . . . Christ never laughed either" (101).

In addition to wresting the human from its privileged position in the chain of being, Beckett satirizes the rational thought whereby, in Descartes's view, the human can theoretically achieve knowledge of God. The impasse to which this pursuit inevitably leads is confirmed by Watt's fruitless attempts to understand the workings of Mr. Knott, whose name recalls Aquinas's claim that "we cannot know in what God's essence exists, but solely in what it does not."[81] Despite his exhaustive cogitations on the famished dogs and their caretakers, Watt fails to comprehend "the forces at play" in the arrangement and remains "in particular ignorance" of "the nature of Mr Knott himself."[82] His rigorous application of rational principles ironically produces irrationality, ultimately landing him in an insane asylum. Molloy, too, pursues reason to its absurd end when he attempts to resolve the problem of rotating his collection of sucking stones from pocket to pocket without abandoning the "principle" of "equal distribution" (74). His determination to suck the stones "not haphazard[ly], but with method" invokes Descartes's *Méthode*, and he acknowledges the futility of the enterprise by admitting that "deep down it was all the same to me whether I sucked a different stone each time or always the same stone, until the end of time" (74). Moran similarly values reason for its inexhaustibility, delighting in his discovery of the intricate system of movements through which his bees communicate: "I said, with rapture, Here is something I can study all my life, and never understand" (169). The sucking stones and the bee dance, like the famished dog arrangement, undercut the Cartesian aspiration to achieve knowledge of divine (or even earthly) phenomena through the application of reason. Rational thought instead becomes a closed circuit that produces not definite knowledge but only its own continuation.

This pursuit of rationality for its own sake confines Beckett's human to the radical interiority of the Cartesian subject. As Steven Connor observes, the "obsessive consciousness" of Beckett's characters "re-enact[s] in narrative terms the regime of systematic doubt prescribed by Descartes, in which everything potentially deceptive, the external world, memory, the senses themselves, is ruled inadmissible for philosophical enquiry, until all the philosopher is left with is the flicker of doubt itself, the self-reflexive 'cogito' which is the ground and guarantee of being."[83] Descartes's determination to accept as true only "what presented itself to my mind so clearly and so distinctly that I had no occasion to doubt it" leaves consciousness of being—the *cogito, ergo sum*—as the only certainty.[84] Molloy thus finds himself confined to "that sealed jar to which I owed my being so well preserved" (49)—that is, the cogito that preserves the self by shutting out the uncertainty of exteriority. Yet Molloy's need to continually remind himself "not only who I was, but that I was" (49) competes with his persistent longing to connect with the exterior world, as evidenced by his desire "to see the dog, see the man, at close quarters" after witnessing the embrace between A or C and the Pomeranian (12).

Molloy's desire for the other signals his attraction to the radical openness of being that underlies Levinas's neohumanist revision of the subject. Levinas's subject, like Descartes's, is a "thinking being" who breaks with the persistence in being that ostensibly defines animal life. Neither Descartes nor Levinas denies animals the capacity for sensation; Levinas even locates "the eternal truth of the Cartesian thesis" in the distinction between the sensation without thought that defines the consciousness of the purely "living being" and the consciousness "illuminated by thought" that marks the human subject. In both formulations, the human as "reasonable animal" transcends a merely animal consciousness. Yet whereas Descartes's subject is constituted through the self-reflexivity of the cogito, Levinas's subject emerges through its exposure to exteriority: "Thought begins the very moment consciousness becomes consciousness of its particularity, that is to say, when it conceives of the exteriority, beyond its nature as a living being, that encloses it; when thought becomes conscious of itself and at the same time conscious of the exteriority that goes beyond its nature, when it becomes metaphysical. Thought establishes a relationship with an unassumed exteriority. As thinking being, man is the one for whom the exterior world exists. From now on, his so-called biological life, his strictly interior life, is illuminated by thought." Levinas reverses the Cartesian formulation wherein self-consciousness precedes and enables the subject's relationship to the other. Instead, consciousness of exteriority gives rise to the thought that transforms "biological consciousness" into "consciousness of self."[85]

For Levinas as for Descartes, however, self-consciousness remains the exclusive purview of the human. Consciousness of self, in Levinas's analysis, cannot exist without access to exteriority. The merely living being, though "not without consciousness," is "without exteriority" and consequently lacks the "interiority that, to [the] thinking being, is opposed to exteriority." Without consciousness of exteriority as such, the living being cannot enter into the relationship with the other that in turn produces self-consciousness. In opposing the thinking (human) being to the living (animal) being on the basis of an "absence of exteriority" in the latter, Levinas's thought perpetuates a humanist tradition that Derrida accuses of defining the animal in terms of "a lack, defect, or general deficit."[86] Gesturing toward recent discoveries in ethology and other sciences that undermine any absolute distinction between human and animal, Derrida questions not only "whether one has the right to refuse the animal such and such a power" but "whether what calls itself human has the right rigorously to attribute to man, which means therefore to attribute to himself, what he refuses the animal, and whether he can ever possess the *pure, rigorous, indivisible* concept, as such, of that attribution."[87] Indeed, any uncertainty about whether the human has access to exteriority as such would undermine the encounter with absolute alterity that calls Levinas's subject into being.

Beckett, for his part, is less concerned with demonstrating that animals possess attributes traditionally deemed proper to the human than with questioning whether the human actually possesses those attributes. Whereas Levinas singles out the human as "the one for whom the exterior world exists," the unlocatable quality of the voice in Beckett's *Three Novels* challenges this attribution. Molloy repeatedly hears a voice that seems to issue from "far away inside me," a place both within and beyond the self: "Somewhere someone laughed. Inside me too someone was laughing" (26). The voice is simultaneously interior and exterior, irremediably blurring the boundary between self and other. Molloy thus finds himself "compelled to attribute to others intelligible words, or hear my own voice uttering to others more or less articulate sounds," in order to comply "with the convention" of a self separable from exteriority (88). He experiences not the self-consciousness that secures the boundaries of the Cartesian or Levinasian subject, but only "a kind of consciousness" that "arose within me, confusedly" (88). Molloy's inability to distinguish inside from outside, augmented by the ambiguity as to whether he and Moran are separate selves or simply divergent expressions of the same ego, prefigures the radical dissolution of self in *The Unnamable*: "If I could only shut myself up, quick, I'll shut myself up, it won't be I, quick, I'll make a place, it won't be mine, it doesn't matter, I don't feel any place for me, perhaps that will come, I'll make it mine, I'll put myself in it, I'll put someone in it, I'll find someone in it, I'll put myself in him, I'll say he's I, perhaps he'll keep me, perhaps the place will keep us, me inside the other, the place all round us" (400). Like Molloy, the Unnamable is unable either to shut himself up in the totality of the cogito or to affirm the capacity of Levinas's thinking being to "situat[e] itself in relation to an exteriority."[88] The image of "me inside the other" undercuts the separability that gives rise to the self-consciousness of the Cartesian and Levinasian subjects.

Further, the impossibility of locating the voice in *Molloy, Malone Dies*, and *The Unnamable* undermines the human's claim to language, which Levinas posits as constituting the relationship between self and other. Levinas's view of naming as an appropriative act might suggest that language itself seeks to negate alterity by bringing the other into the totalizing comprehension of the self. But the other-directedness that Levinas ascribes to language prevents such a conclusion:

> Language is a relation between separated terms. To the one the other can indeed present himself as a theme, but his presence is not reabsorbed in his status as a theme. The word that bears on the Other as a theme seems to contain the Other. But already it is said to the Other who, as interlocutor, has quit the theme that encompassed him, and upsurges inevitably behind the said.... In discourse the divergence that inevitably opens between the Other as my theme and the Other as my interlocutor, emancipated from the theme that seemed a moment to hold him, forthwith contests the meaning I ascribe to my interlocutor. The formal structure of language thereby announces the ethical inviolability of the Other.[89]

Because language is always directed toward an interlocutor (or at least the possibility of one), it inevitably exposes consciousness to the exteriority that transforms it into a coherent self. Thus language does not just facilitate the relation with the other; it *is* the relation. While it entails the possibility of injustice in the form of reducing the other to a theme, language remains, for Levinas, the foundation for the self's response-ability toward the other. Paradoxically, Levinas privileges language for its inadequacy; in failing to assimilate the other as an object of knowledge, it confirms the absolute exteriority that renders self and other intelligible as discrete subjects.

This failure prompts Derrida in "Violence and Metaphysics" to question the infinitude Levinas ascribes to language when he insists that "language is justice."[90] Levinas maintains that the exteriority that produces self-consciousness is not spatial, yet his continual reliance upon the word "exteriority" to describe the nonspatial location of the other, Derrida argues, indicates the impossibility of "think[ing] *true* exteriority" without recourse to a "spatial metaphor," revealing in turn language's inseparability from space. The inherent spatiality of language undermines its capacity to state the infinite relation between self and other: "To say that the infinite exteriority of the other *is not* spatial, is *non*-exteriority and *non*-interiority, to be unable to designate it otherwise than negatively—is this not to acknowledge that the infinite (also designated negatively in its current positivity: in-finite) cannot be stated? Does this not amount to acknowledging that the structure 'inside-outside,' which is language itself, marks the original finitude of speech and of whatever befalls it?" Levinas's equation of language with justice hinges on language's capacity to respond to the other's infinite demand for justice without negating alterity. If language's inability to state the infinite relation between self and other reveals its finitude, though, language becomes inseparable from the totality that Levinas opposes to the infinite alterity of the other. There can be no nonviolent language—no language that does not seek to nullify alterity and establish a totality—because there is no language without "the verb *to be* and the predicative act . . . implied in every other verb, and in every common noun."[91]

The theme of language as violence runs throughout Beckett's *Three Novels*. As Anthony Uhlmann argues in his reading of *The Unnamable*, Beckett reverses the trajectory of injustice proposed by Levinas: "rather than injustice arising from the efforts of the same to reappropriate the other into its totality, it appears in inverted form with the other moving to appropriate the I (or the same) by plying it with its language and hauling it into the light of its day." The Unnamable hears voices of unidentified others commanding him to speak: "I say what I am told to say, in the hope that some day they will weary of talking at me" (345). Language becomes not the capacity of the self to respond to the other but an external power to which the self is subject. Uhlmann thus concludes that language for Beckett is not justice but injustice—"the infinite non-relation, or failure to relate, between a shadowy same and an equally shadowy other."[92] Molloy and Moran share the Unnamable's resentment of being hauled into exteriority by language. Consequently, their encounters with human others produce not justice but violence. Molloy reacts aggressively to the verbal overtures of a human other: "Either I didn't understand a word he said, or he didn't understand a word he said, or he knew nothing, or he wanted to keep me near him.... So I smartly freed a crutch and dealt him a good dint on the skull" (84). Moran's reaction to a stranger's approach is even more violent. He "start[s] violently" and, like the self in the Levinasian encounter, becomes conscious of an exteriority calling him into relations: "I heard myself hailed" (149). While he harbors "obscure feelings of love and pity" (150) for trees, the human voice "infuriates" him, prompting him to beat the stranger's head to "a pulp" (151). Moran's description of the man's face as "resembl[ing] my own" foreshadows this violence by signaling the totalizing nature of language, while the image of his victim's mouth as "raw from trying to shit its tongue" suggests a desire to obliterate language, freeing the self from the compulsion to speak—here equated with the necessity of excreting bodily waste (151).

Unfortunately for their human interlocutors, Molloy and Moran frequently resent the Levinasian call to ethics, preferring to remain in the sealed jar of the cogito. Yet even Moran's murder of the human other fails to free the self from language. Watt longs to have the world around him "wrapp[ed] up safe in words," but just as rationality's failure to eliminate all doubt fuels its own perpetuation, language's inability to correspond to and contain exteriority compels the human to continue speaking.[93] Hence Molloy's diagnosis of the human condition: "Not to want to say, not to know what you want to say, not to be able to say what you think you want to say, and never to stop saying, or hardly ever" (28). Beckett's human, rather than being in possession of language, is immobilized by it; even attempts to "eliminate language" in pursuit of what Beckett calls "a literature of the unword" must be expressed through language.[94] Molloy and Moran evince a desire to shed human language in their attraction to nonhuman signs and vocalizations. Molloy prefers "sounds unencumbered by precise meaning" (49) to orders issued by the human voice, and he feels "divided between the murmurs of my little world ... and those so different (so different?) of all that between two suns abides and passes away. Never once a human voice. But the cows ... crying in vain to be milked" (15). Moran is fascinated by the untranslatable language of his bees and feels acutely "exiled in his manhood" as he contemplates "the complexity of [their] innumerable dance" (169). The "system of signals by means of which the incoming bees, satisfied or dissatisfied with their plunder, informed the outgoing bees in what direction to go, and in what not to go," enables the bees to accomplish precisely what he and Molloy cannot: reach their destination and return home (168). The allure of animal sounds and gestures for Beckett's narrators is a product of what Joela Jacobs calls a "modernist language crisis" brought on by an acute awareness of both "the inability of language to represent anyone's perceived reality accurately" and "the arbitrariness of signs and their referents."[95] Like the German modernist texts Jacobs examines, *Molloy* goes even further to present language not just as inadequate but "as a central obstacle to the perception of the world and the self" (67).

To return to the question of Beckett's relationship to humanism, the world of *Three Novels* is antihumanist in its eschewal of the humanist aggrandizement of rationality, autonomy, and language, but it remains all too human*ist*—to recast Moran's insight—in representing the human as paradoxically immobilized by the very attributes upon which its transcendence of animality is premised. Given the privileged role of language even in Levinas's antirationalist humanism, the voice that commands Beckett's narrators can be read not just as language itself but as the voice of humanism compelling the human to repudiate animality and perform its alleged attributes. Both Molloy and Moran are unable finally to relinquish their subject position, however fraught it may be. Molloy's narrative closes with the speaker in a ditch at the edge of the forest, suggesting the theoretical gulf separating the human from the animal. He "long[s] to go back into the forest"—to abandon humanist subjectivity at last—but hears "a voice telling me not to fret, that help was coming" (91). The voice of humanism dispels his longing, causing him to "[lapse] down to the bottom of the ditch," where he passively awaits the resurgence or demise of the humanist enterprise (91). Moran, like Molloy, wishes to abdicate his subject position: "I have been a man long enough, I shall not put up with it any more, I shall not try any more" (175). While Molloy longs to return to the forest, Moran resolves (tellingly dropping his customary "my") to "go into the garden"—another liminal space between the human and nonhuman realms (175). Like Molloy, though, he hears "a voice telling me things," the voice of his species, and goes "back into the house" (175–76). Obligated to respond to the voice of humanity, Molloy and Moran are left paralyzed, clinging to the remains of humanist subjectivity.

In contrast to Beckett's constrained and debilitated narrators, the dogs of *Molloy* are remarkably mobile, refusing to remain confined to their position in the humanist species hierarchy. An anonymous dog who strays into the grove where Moran has set up camp confirms just how thoroughly Moran is "exiled in his manhood." Having suspended his search for Molloy, Moran wanders aimlessly around his camp for three days before this passing dog "relieve[s] the monotony" (153). Whereas Moran's search never progresses beyond the campsite, the dog exits the grove almost as soon as he has entered, "having simply as it were gone straight through" (153). Even Teddy outpaces Molloy, who is every bit as captive as Lousse's pet parrot as he "sweep[s], with the clipped wings of necessity," to his mother's house (27). Teddy, despite his similarly decrepit condition, achieves Molloy's elusive objective: to "finish dying" (7). Molloy thus resents the dead dog, reasoning, "His death must have hurt him less than my fall me. And he at least was dead" (35). Teddy is buried "like a Carthusian monk, but with his collar and lead," his interment ironically signifying both spiritual ascension in death and degrading captivity in life (36). Ultimately, though, Molloy is the one who remains captive, compelled to "take the place of the dog I had killed" (47). While death frees Teddy from his decrepit body, with its collar and lead, Molloy is left, like the narrator of *Malone Dies*, to "pant on" in captivity (91). He eventually escapes Lousse's clutches but ends up falling into a ditch, where his narrative ends in resignation: "Molloy could stay, where he happened to be" (91).

Dogs' relative mobility makes them objects of fascination for Molloy and Moran, whose respective encounters with a flock of sheep driven by a shepherd and his dog offer a welcome respite from an all-too-human mode of being. Molloy experiences a rare moment of "tranquil assurance" (28), while the usually overbearing Moran finds himself "incapable of speech" (159). Molloy watches the shepherd and his dog and becomes interested in the latter, wondering, "Did he take me for a black sheep entangled in the brambles and was he waiting for an order from his master to drag me out? I don't think so. I don't smell like a sheep, I wish I smelt like a sheep, or a buck-goat" (28). While the dog is preoccupied with "gnaw[ing] at his flesh ... where the ticks were in him," Molloy seems eager to be "dragged out" of his interiority by the canine other (28). He also wants to meet the dog not in the Levinasian realm of language but on the dog's terms, in an olfactory exchange. Moran, for his part, identifies with the dog. He "long[s] to say" to the shepherd, "Take me with you, I will serve you faithfully, just for a place to lie and a little food," but in lieu of his typically possessive prose, he can utter only nonsensical sounds (159). As with Zulu, he speculates about the dog's point of view without claiming access to it, noting that the dog departs "jauntily, waving his long black plumy tail, though there was no one to witness his contentment, if that is what it was" (160). Both encounters breed a powerful desire to transcend human form without negating canine alterity, pointing to dogs' special significance for Beckett's posthumanism.

Facing Other Animals

The reverent awe Molloy and Moran exhibit in the presence of the human-dog-sheep assemblage, besides signaling the attraction of dogs for Beckett's human, ushers in Beckett's critique of the most potent instantiation of humanism's sacrificial structure—the modern slaughterhouse—and its devastating impact on humanity and animality alike. This critique emerges almost surreptitiously, through ironic invocations of the British pastoral tradition, whose usual representative in Beckett's work is William Wordsworth. Molloy alludes to Wordsworth's notion of "emotion recollected in tranquillity" when he notes, "It is in the tranquillity of decomposition that I remember the long confused emotion which was my life" (25).[96] That Molloy awakens to the sight of the shepherd and his flock evokes a misreading of a line from Wordsworth's "Immortality Ode" whereby "fields of sleep" becomes "fields of sheep"—a "compositor's error" referenced in *Murphy* when Miss Dew tries vainly to feed lettuce to a "miserable-looking lot" of sheep.[97] Moran's description of the shepherd further conjures (in Murphy's words) "that most excellent man" (100): "He was sitting on the ground stroking his dog. A flock of black shorn sheep strayed about them, unafraid. What a pastoral land, my God. . . . The silence was absolute. Profound in any case. All things considered it was a solemn moment. The weather was divine. It was the close of day. . . . How I would love to dwell upon him. His dog loved him, his sheep did not fear him" (158). In the presence of animals, Moran ironically assumes the role of the Wordsworthian speaker, his reflections painting an idealized portrait of rural life.

Yet Beckett's pastoral landscape, far from being a pristine retreat from the human world, is filled with signs of humanity's devastating presence; as Clov in *Endgame* asserts, "There's no more nature . . . in the vicinity."[98] In "Tintern Abbey," Wordsworth himself describes the pastoral landscape as a composite of "what [human senses] half create, / And what perceive" (lines 107–8). As a cultivated landscape, the pastoral conveys both the sublime and the grotesque effects of humans' interactions with the nonhuman world. Wordsworth's speaker regards a countryside transformed by agriculture as part of the "nature" in which he finds "The anchor of my purest thoughts, the nurse, / The guide, the guardian of my heart, and soul / Of all my moral being" (lines 110–12). By contrast, Arsene in *Watt* describes the cyclical process whereby "the poor old lousy old earth" becomes "an excrement": "the pastures red with uneaten sheep's placentas and the long summer days and the newmown hay . . . and the children walking in the dead leaves and the larch turning brown . . . and of course the snow and to be sure the sleet and bless your heart the slush . . . and then the whole bloody business starting all over again. A turd."[99] Animal presence in romantic pastoralism typically signals the peaceful coexistence of humans and nonhumans in a landscape where "every Beast keep[s] holiday,"[100] but in Beckett's fiction it reveals the grotesque and violent underside of the agricultural economy. Molloy's encounter with the sheep leads him to wonder whether the flock is bound for pasture or slaughter, and Moran interrupts his own reverie with the disturbing thought that the sheep might perceive him as "the butcher come to make his choice" (159). Inhabiting a landscape that manufactures death, Beckett's human cannot achieve the spiritual transcendence associated with the contemplation of nature in the pastoral tradition.

Dogs' complicity in the violence of slaughter in *Molloy* brings us again to Levinas's essay on Bobby, which alludes to the sacrifice of other animals by opening with a verse from Exodus: "You shall be men consecrated to me; therefore you shall not eat any flesh that is torn by beasts in the field; you shall cast it to the dogs." He postpones discussion of the dogs in this verse, though the reader might well expect them to be of primary interest in an essay titled "The Name of a Dog." His thoughts turn instead to the animals most humans encounter "at the family table, as you plunge your fork into your roast. There is enough, there, to make you a vegetarian again. If we are to believe Genesis, Adam, the father of us all, was one! There is, at least, enough to make us want to limit, through various interdictions, the butchery that every day claims our 'consecrated' mouths!"[101] Here, it is not Bobby but other domesticated animals—those destined for slaughter—who seem on the verge of making moral claims on Levinas. And unlike Bobby, whose name denotes his individuality and mortality and whose memory the essay preserves, these animals have become what Carol J. Adams calls "absent referents": "Behind every meal of meat is an absence: the death of the animal whose place the meat takes." Culinary language further divorces the act of consuming animals from the act of killing them; as Adams observes, "Animals in name and body are made absent *as animals* for meat to exist."[102] So, too, are they absent from Levinas's description, effaced both literally and figuratively through their transformation into "roast." Tellingly, Levinas elsewhere uses food as a metaphor for that which the merely "living being" experiences as "co-substantial with it[self]"—"a 'something' stripped of its independence"—in contrast to the absolute other whose face compels an ethical response from the "thinking being."[103] Here, he links humans' consumption of animals as food to the violent appropriation of the other.

By alluding to butchered animals and thus to their material and rhetorical erasure at the start of his essay, Levinas foregrounds the unpalatable matter of animal suffering. Although he preserves the primacy of the human in merely suggesting that we might "want to limit" the suffering our appetites routinely inflict on nonhuman animals, his allusion to industrialized slaughter in the context of what is, among other things, a "Holocaust testimony" intensifies what might otherwise seem like a facetious critique of the inherent animality of human carnivorism.[104] Through these reflections, John Llewelyn observes, Levinas "all but proposes an analogy between the unspeakable human Holocaust and the unspoken animal one."[105] The subtlety with which Levinas posits this analogy is, in part, a response to Heidegger's infamous declaration that "as for its essence, [the mechanized food industry] is the same thing as the manufacture of corpses in the gas chambers and the death camps"—a cursory comparison Levinas summarily deems "beyond commentary."[106] Yet, as Clark argues, the comparative subtlety of Levinas's rhetoric makes the analogy all the more powerful: "The fact that the question of our obligations to animals is raised in such a maximally important context, indeed, as the opening move in the evocation of that context, puts to us that the thought of the human, no matter how profound . . . can never be wholly divorced from the thought of the animal."[107] By implicitly linking the institutionalized sacrifice of humans to that of other animals without simply equating the two qua Heidegger, Levinas compels his reader to entertain thoughts that "make one lose one's appetite" for animal flesh.[108]

Levinas's analogy—like Molloy's and Moran's concerns about the fate of the flock of sheep—underscores the paradox of slaughter, which demonstrates powerfully both the violence that the human-as-subject permits itself to inflict on animals and the tenuousness of the humanity that serves as its justification. This paradox has only intensified, Derrida argues, with the "unprecedented transformation" of the human/animal relationship under the conditions of modernity. The most potent sign of this transformation is industrialized animal agriculture, the perverse cruelties of which Derrida also likens to genocide: "As if, for example, instead of throwing a people into ovens and gas chambers (let's say Nazi) doctors and geneticists had decided to organize the overproduction and overgeneration of Jews, gypsies, and homosexuals by means of artificial insemination, so that, being continually more numerous and better fed, they could be destined in always increasing numbers for the same hell."[109] Molloy, too, notes the dizzying magnitude of animal life and death in modern agribusiness: "Good God, what a land of breeders, you see quadrupeds everywhere" (29). The grim fate of many of these animals is confirmed by Molloy's observation that "slaughter-houses are not confined to towns, no, they are everywhere, the country is full of them, every butcher has his slaughter-house and the right to slaughter, according to his lights" (29). So omnipresent is the slaughterhouse that several characters in *Three Novels* live near one: the "violent raucous tremulous bellowing" of cattle can be heard from Molloy's mother's room (22), Moran suspects his son of sneaking off to a nearby slaughterhouse to avoid going to church, and the Unnamable lives on "a quiet street near the shambles" (327).[110]

The unprecedented scale of slaughter in late modernity, a result of increasingly efficient technologies for producing and processing animal bodies, generated equally unprecedented concerns about its implications for humanity. As Heidegger's remarks on industrialized meat production suggests, debates surrounding the conflicting values of ethics and efficiency in animal slaughter intensified during and after World War II. In his study of changes in slaughtering methods over a period that spans the first several decades of Beckett's and Levinas's lives (both were born in 1906), Jonathan Burt notes that these debates typically "focused on the killing alone" rather than on broader animal welfare concerns.[111] Molloy, too, fixates on the scene of animal death; "left . . . with persisting doubts, as to the destination of those sheep," he envisions them falling, "their skulls shattered, their thin legs crumpling, first to their knees, then over on their fleecy sides, under the pole-axe, though that is not the way they slaughter sheep, but with a knife, so that they bleed to death" (29). The act of killing, imagined so vividly by Molloy, is precisely what interested a committee appointed by the British

Admiralty in 1904 to evaluate methods of slaughter—including shechitah, or ritual Jewish slaughter—for their efficacy and humanity. The committee concluded that shechitah "was not of 'equal humanity' with those methods in which a pole-axe was used" to stun animals prior to killing them. An industry handbook published several years later similarly advocated mandatory stunning "in all civilised communities," further signaling the fraught entanglement of the concepts of humanity and humanness that would reappear in the anti-Semitism of the animal welfare movement in 1930s Germany and in Hitler's 1933 ban on shechitah.[112] In pursuit of the elusive goal of humane slaughter, the method of killing became a litmus test for humanity in both senses of the word. But Molloy's blunt description of sheep crumpling under the poleaxe or bleeding to death—two methods deemed humane by their respective proponents—offers no assurance of a humane death.

For many, the key to making slaughter more humane lay in the development of increasingly sophisticated stunning tools, and technologies improving upon the poleaxe began to appear in the 1920s. Electrical stunning in particular promised to "further the cause of humanity," as one of its developers boasted in 1929.[113] This method had the particularly attractive effect of silencing animals, according to the author of a 1935 article in the *British Veterinary Journal*: "I have watched dozens of pigs being anaesthetised by the electro-lethaler in a most easy and perfect way. After each one was narcotized it was hoisted, stuck and bled without struggle or squeal; the slaughterhouse was thus made a place of peaceful quiet."[114] As this description indicates, the ethical impetus for humane slaughter is difficult to disentangle from the aesthetic. Burt argues that such efforts to make slaughter more humane disturbingly produce "slaughter at its most orderly and mechanistic. There are no sounds of pigs squealing in agony, nothing to indicate to a wider world, neighbors, or passersby the extent of the life-taking going on within the slaughterhouse."[115] The aestheticizing of slaughter supports Derrida's observation "that men do all they can in order to dissimulate this cruelty or to hide it from themselves; in order to organize on a global scale the forgetting or misunderstanding of this violence."[116] In Beckett's fiction, though, "the slaughter-house loom[s] larger and larger" (212), signaling the inevitable failure of attempts to silence dying animals in the name of humanity.

To some extent, Levinas positions Bobby as a proxy for these silenced animals. While the description of Bobby's welcome does not appear until the penultimate paragraph, Clark argues that the Kantian dog manifests himself in the opening paragraph by way of analogy: "For a scandalous instant, Levinas acts the part that Bobby will more or less play at the end of the essay, that is, as the one who, in the absence of others and in the absence of a respect for the other, *testifies* to the worthiness of the imprisoned and the murdered. Indeed, he reminds us that these others *are* murdered, butchered so that we may eat well."[117] This reading, though, overlooks the decidedly unsentimental essence of Levinas's connection to Bobby signaled by the verse from Exodus, which instructs humans to feed flesh torn from the field to dogs. By opening with this verse and his meditation on eating meat, Levinas presents humans and dogs not simply as victims of violence but first and foremost as beneficiaries of the institutionalized sacrifice of other animals. In the industrialized West, mass-produced meat has replaced the flesh once torn from the field, and its by-products—even the flesh of sick and euthanized animals—are funneled into commercial pet food, where, Susan McHugh notes, they are "legally allowed to be listed on packages under the innocuous-sounding ingredient names 'meat meal' and 'meat and bone meal.'"[118] Though their tastes might differ, humans and dogs are complicit in this system of flesh consumption, an act Levinas portrays as inherently animalistic. His positioning of "beasts in the field" alongside humans at the "family table," Clark argues, implies that "we are those beasts . . . sublimating our carnivorous desires."[119] This sublimation, moreover, has divorced the act of eating meat from the violence that produces it; as Levinas puts it, "the sight of flesh torn by beasts in the field seems meat too strong for the honest man who, even if he is a carnivore, still feels he is watched over by God." While the biblical verse commands humans to cast undesirable meat "to the dogs" (as the meat industry quite literally does), Levinas implies that the distinction between flesh and roast is entirely semantic—that perhaps the verse attaches "too much importance to what 'goes into man's mouth' and not enough to what comes out."[120]

In citing a verse that compels humans to cast undesirable flesh "to the dogs," Levinas, like Beckett, exposes the violent foundation of the human/dog relationship. By underscoring how dogs facilitate and benefit from the sacrifice of nonhuman, non*canine* animals, Beckett and Levinas suggest that dogs are best understood not as representatives of "the animal"—a homogenous category opposed to the human—but as what Haraway calls "partners in the crime of human evolution." Not only do dogs share humans' appetite for flesh, but this shared appetite enabled them to become accomplices in acts of violence (and, indeed, in the institutionalization of violence) against other nonhuman animals. On an evolutionary scale, Haraway explains, the opportunistic wolves who exploited "the calorie bonanzas provided by humans' waste dumps" eventually became the domesticated companions whose labor facilitated "the emergence of herding or agricultural societies."[121] Haraway thus characterizes humans and dogs as "messmates," noting that the "companion" in "companion species" comes from the Latin *cum panis*, "with bread." Humans and dogs have shaped each other's evolutionary and cultural histories precisely because each species enabled the other "to consume well."[122] On an evolutionary scale, the shared appetite for meat engendered a partnership premised on the subjugation of other animals—a legacy that haunts the canine encounter in Beckett's fiction and Levinas's essay.

Conclusion

While Levinas ultimately attempts to assimilate Bobby's alterity by sentimentalizing him as "the friend of man," Beckett's dogs invariably exceed their roles as emblems of degradation, as surrogates for the other human, and as representatives of "the animal." Beckett's insistence on dogs' dual status as victims of the humanist disavowal of animality and as vital participants in systematized violence against other animals indicates that any ethical thinking about "the animal" must begin by interrogating that very category and acknowledging the heterogeneous multiplicity of life-forms it purports to encompass. In this way, Beckett anticipates Derrida's critique not only of the *bêtise* whereby post-Enlightenment humanism condemns beings called animal to "a noncriminal putting to death," but also of the residual humanism in much of the postmodern and poststructuralist thought with which Beckett's work is frequently aligned.[123] It follows that any examination of the animal and its relationship to the human in Beckett's oeuvre must consider the ways in which Beckett complicates these very terms by deconstructing the sacrificial logic that underwrites the death camps and the slaughterhouse alike.

At the same time, Beckett's dogs offer the human a kind of hope via the interruptive power of the canine encounter. Molloy's need to shore up the self by confining himself to the "precarious calm" of his "sealed jar" competes with his persistent longing for connection—a longing both intensified and frustrated by the animal suffering that permeates the Beckettian landscape (49). Even from within the jar, he hears "other things calling me and towards which too one after the other my soul was straining, wildly. I mean of course the fields . . . and the animals . . . and my hand on my knee and above all the other wayfarer, A or C, I don't remember, going resignedly home" (11). The sealed jar of the humanist subject position estranges Molloy from his environment, its animal inhabitants, his fellow human wayfarers, and even his own body, but occasionally "a wall [gives] way" as he strains toward exteriority (49). Dogs' ability to interrupt the endless cogitations of Beckett's narrators offers the human a way out of its egoistic being—one that requires a rethinking of the self/other relation that extends beyond the narrow category of the human. Thus Beckett's apparently anethical stance toward animal suffering stems not from a refusal to acknowledge the animal face but from his cognizance of the immense but urgent task of learning, in Haraway's words, "how to see who [animals] are and hear what they are telling us, not in [the] bloodless abstraction" of sweeping pronouncements about "the animal," "but in one-on-one relationship, in otherness-in-connection."[124] Like Bobby and the dogs considered throughout this book, Beckett's dogs challenge the human to learn how to respond, not just to the human other in its relative alterity but to other animals in their radical alterity and heterogeneity.

CODA
Modernism and Literary Canine Studies

In an endnote to *Flush*, Virginia Woolf posits an intriguing hypothesis: "The whole question of dogs' relation to the spirit of the age, whether it is possible to call one dog Elizabethan, another Augustan, another Victorian, together with the influence upon dogs of the poetry and philosophy of their masters, deserves a fuller discussion than can here be given it."[1] By raising the possibility of historicizing not just dogs' role in human lives but canine experience itself, Woolf implicitly questions humanist dualisms that figure animal life as natural and therefore ahistorical. I have endeavored in the preceding chapters to show how the "influence" Woolf speculates about cuts both ways in the modernist period. Historical and cultural developments in late nineteenth- and early twentieth-century Britain and America dramatically altered canine bodies and experience, but dogs' co-constitutive relationship with the human means that they too played an important role in cultivating "the spirit of the age." Thus, while I follow Woolf's lead in postulating a distinctly modernist dog inflected by the period's characteristic ontological, formal, and aesthetic concerns, the human subject figured by modernism is likewise indelibly dogged—inscribed with traces of its coevolutionary partner.

Propelled by the pioneering work of scholars like Harriet Ritvo, Marjorie Garber, Donna Haraway, Alice Kuzniar, and Susan McHugh, animal studies has begun to account for the conspicuous presence of dogs in literature and other ostensibly human cultural formations, resulting in the emergence of a distinct subfield that we might call literary canine studies.[2] Much of this work has focused on the periods before and after modernism, with particular emphasis on the rise of modern breeding and pet-keeping in the eighteenth and nineteenth centuries and how these practices continue to inform postmodern representations of the human/dog relationship. A particular image of the dog emerges in such accounts—one that, while acknowledging limited forms of canine agency, primarily emphasizes dogs' absorption into human-authored and fundamentally anthropocentric worlds. In *Victorian Dogs, Victorian Men*, for example, Keridiana Chez shows how dogs in nineteenth-century British and American literature function "as emotional prostheses" whose purpose is "to enhance [humans'] affective capacities and to complete their humanity."[3] Ivan Kreilkamp has similarly read Victorian representations of dogs as particularly salient examples of "anthroprosthesis," "the process by which human beings use animals in order to define the non-animality of the human."[4] By serving as prostheses via which (some) humans could cultivate and demonstrate the right kind of affect, Victorian dogs helped define the fully human subject as bourgeois, white, heterosexual, and male. It is no coincidence, then, that the eighteenth and early nineteenth centuries—the period that saw the humanist subject assume "its recognizably modern form"—also produced the modern "technology" of the breed dog, as Martin Wallen demonstrates in *Whose Dog Are You?* As "responsiveness to animals" came to be regarded as a marker of the properly human(e) subject, the dog bred "to perform in predetermined fashion" its "love for 'us'" became the ideal "prosthesis of Western narcissism."[5]

Yet the humanity that dogs prosthetically affirm is tenuous precisely because it depends on the affective reciprocity of a canine other who is "eager to perform for us." While Wallen ascribes the power to disrupt humanist narcissism to "the cur," who eludes the "techno-aesthetic" interventions of breed, Kreilkamp and Chez propose that even the prosthetic dog is capable of exceeding or inverting its anthropocentric function.[6] As Kreilkamp explains in *Minor Creatures*, "The domesticated animal is creaturely precisely because domestication is always incomplete and provisional: no animal, however loved, fully enters the realm of the human and of culture, fully escapes its animal status."[7] The prosthetic dog thus serves as a reminder of the animality that threatens to erupt both beyond and within the human, especially following Darwin's revelation of humans' animal origins. Moreover, Chez argues, the prosthetic function itself has the potential to backfire, undermining rather than extending the subject's humanness:

> With a set of false teeth or a peg leg, the prosthesis was a mere object, with no hope for the independent agency, will, feelings, and so on that humanity considered its exclusive purview. . . . But in the case of an animal prosthesis, the nature of the assemblage was more dynamic and dangerous. What if a prosthesis became too useful, too essential? Dogs would continually challenge attempts to reduce them to mere tools. The greatest threat posed by the prosthesis was this potential for inversion: should the tool's agency significantly increase or its abilities surpass the human's, the user would become the prosthesis.[8]

The specters of the incompletely domesticated dog and the unruly prosthesis point to the canine agency that Victorian literature acknowledges but ultimately strives to contain. Kreilkamp describes Victorian realist fiction itself as "a cultural form of domestication, a means of bringing animals symbolically away from pure nature into culture." In doing so, the Victorian novel sometimes grants a "partial personhood" to dogs and other companion animals, yet its anthropocentric commitments mean that "nonhuman life ultimately remains to some degree formally marginalized and minor within it."[9]

As I have argued throughout this book, canine agency asserts itself much more forcefully in modernism, destabilizing the humanist subjectivity that Enlightenment and Victorian writers sought to define and defend. Indeed, Kreilkamp concludes his study of minor creatures in the Victorian novel by questioning whether "literary realism [can] truly accommodate animal personhood, let alone protagonicity, without turning into something else (such as children's or fantasy literature or perhaps the modernist novel)."[10] While I am not suggesting that the prosthetic dog vanishes entirely in the modernist period, or that modernist literature perfectly "accommodates animal personhood," the modernist novel's experimental approaches to narrative form, character, and temporality mean that it is better equipped than the Victorian realist novel to depict the subjective experiences of humans and other animals as they are shaped by species-being in its radical contingency. As Carrie Rohman notes, "the modernist eruption of literary convention parallels the perforation of the humanized subject by its evolutionary connection to animality."[11] The shift to modernism thus initiates a more radical linguistic and formal decentering of the human, irrevocably exposing the animality that Victorian anthroprosthesis endeavors to domesticate or conceal. This shift, moreover, coincides with a point of crisis in the human/dog relationship produced by the excesses of Victorian breeding practices and the modernizing forces that threatened to render dogs obsolete, with profound implications for modernist understandings of domestication, human evolution, and civilization. Thus, while Wallen "skip[s] over much of the nineteenth and twentieth centuries," reasoning that the trajectory of human/dog relations in the Victorian and modernist periods "unfolded with the necessity of a logic determined" in the eighteenth century, modernism marks a crucial transition for the human/dog relationship that Wallen's otherwise incisive account elides.[12] This makes literary canine studies a particularly useful framework for elucidating the crisis of the human in modernist literature, as I have argued, but it also indicates that further examination of modernist dogs will yield valuable insights for literary canine studies and produce a more comprehensive understanding of the human/dog relationship.

To date, despite significant critical attention to some of the individual works discussed in the preceding chapters (most notably Jack London's *Call of the Wild* and *White Fang* and Woolf's *Flush*), the broader significance of modernism for literary canine studies has not been sufficiently addressed. By analyzing a range of modernist representations of the human/dog relationship, I have endeavored to contribute to a more complete account of how this relationship develops in modernity. Although elements of the Victorian canine prosthesis persist, for example, in London's and Konrad Lorenz's masculine Überhunds, this modernist version facilitates the renewal, not the disavowal, of the human connection to animality. Woolf's feminist reappraisal of the woman/lapdog connection and J. R. Ackerley's narratives of queer interspecies comradeship further challenge the logic of anthroprosthesis by emphasizing the intersubjective nature of human and canine experience, while canine encounters in Samuel Beckett's novels prompt a radical revaluation of animal alterity and human ethical responsibility in more-than-human worlds. In short, modernist literature envisions new, less anthropocentric forms of human/dog relating that acknowledge polymorphous expressions of canine agency and, consequently, multiple ways of being human.

While this book thus represents an effort to contribute to a more nuanced understanding of the human/dog relationship, it is crucial to note that the picture I have sketched is far from complete. The texts I examine represent a heterogeneous but ultimately limited range of Euro-American and predominately male perspectives—a deliberate choice since the humanist subject under scrutiny in modernist literature is prototypically white, male, and imperial. Thus, while these texts explore ways of being with dogs that extend beyond and challenge the Victorian pet-prosthesis model, they represent only a small sample of the multifarious forms the human/dog relationship assumes globally. For example, Natasha Fijn's cross-cultural examination of human/canine relations in the Khangai Mountains of Mongolia and in Aboriginal Australia reveals "different ways of being *with* dogs that . . . shape dog bodies" in ways that challenge the Eurocentric "domesticated/wild binary." Australian dingoes, commonly viewed by non-Aboriginals as undomesticated thanks in part to their retention of "wild" traits such as erect ears and solid-color coats, engage in "*significant* relations with people" in which they are not mere dependents but part of an Aboriginal "'social ecology,' where everything and everyone is interlinked through an extended form of kinship and grounded by the land, or place." Mongolian Bankhar dogs, although they exhibit "domesticated" characteristics like floppy ears and black-and-tan coats, are loosely selected not for the "tameness and docility" associated with domestication but for "independence and loyalty to the encampment." "What is common among Mongolian and Yolngu ways of relating to canines," Fijn concludes, "is a sense of inherent *dog competency* and *agency*. Dependency, asymmetry, and control—notions at the heart of Euro-American ideas of domestication—make little sense in relation to canines in either location, where adults are seen as competent and independent beings."[13] Both modes of interspecies being remind us that the Eurocentric model of domestication (which I have sought to complicate even in the context of British and American cultures) is far from universal and, if accepted uncritically, impoverishes our understanding of human/dog relations.

Indeed, the domestication model and the pet-keeping practices it informs can lead to undesirable and even fatal outcomes for dogs, challenging the superior humanity of the white, imperialist subject that the pet-prosthesis ostensibly confirms. For instance, the choice Ackerley faces between destroying Tulip's puppies and finding them homes (as I discuss in chapter 3) is conditioned by a biopolitics that limits "possibilities for animal being" and ultimately reinforces imperialist racial hierarchies.[14] Geographer Krithika Srinivasan reminds us that strictures that disallow the very existence of free-roaming dogs are not universal or inevitable in "humane" societies. Rather, they are particular to nations like Britain and the United States, where "the legal conception of dogs as property reinforces prevailing ideals of animal wellbeing by which dogs that are unable to live up to high welfare standards are rendered killable," making unowned dogs categorically subject to what Derrida calls a "non-criminal putting to death."[15] British rule imposed this legal framework on human/canine relations in India and other colonized nations, but in postcolonial India, "the law recognizes the independent status of ownerless street dogs and so these animals are not confronted with the stark injunction to live well or die."[16] Within the United States and Britain, too, human/dog relations are discursively and literally policed along racial and socioeconomic divides, as is particularly evident in the case of the so-called pit bull—a breed designation whose categorical "fuzziness" Harlan Weaver has adeptly demonstrated.[17] Banned altogether in the United Kingdom and banned or restricted in municipalities across the United States, dogs affixed with this label are subject to biopolitical control in ways that intersect with the perceived race, gender, and class of their owners.[18] As Colin Dayan argues in *With Dogs at the Edge of Life*, the "preemptive violence" that targets pit bulls and their owners in the form of "seizures, detentions, and exterminations" reveals how "prejudice against the disenfranchised is made real in the fate of their dogs."[19]

Given that the pet-prosthesis model ideologically supports such efforts to police the borders of the human(e), literary canine studies is uniquely poised to help deconstruct what Bénédicte Boisseron describes in *Afro-Dog* as the "so-called humanity" of the white, imperialist subject—"and, in the process, redefine the meaning of existence beyond the human-animal divide."[20] The complex and often fraught ways in which discourses of domestication, race, breed, and species intersect in the early twentieth century make a focus on modernism vital to this undertaking. Dogs' co-constitutive relationship with the human means that they are implicated in much of the destruction carried out in the name of "so-called humanity"; thus canine figures in modernist literature of the black Atlantic—for example, the mad dog in Zora Neale Hurston's *Their Eyes Were Watching*

God and the Creole dog in in the Francophone poetry of Aimé Césaire—illuminate how dogs alternately reinforce and undercut racial hierarchies within the category of the human.[21] But, as I have argued throughout this book, dogs' coevolutionary proximity to the human means that they are also ideally positioned to undermine the normatively human subject and aid in efforts to identify, theorize, and practice what Alexander Weheliye calls "different modalities of the human"—modalities not premised on Eurocentric humanist hierarchies.[22] Modernist efforts to challenge the logic of anthroprosthesis and depict alternative modalities of the human/dog relationship make the period a rich source for literary canine studies as the field seeks to imagine more ethical ways of being with dogs in a more-than-human world.

NOTES

Introduction

1. Barnes, *Nightwood*, 169.
2. Quoted in Plumb, introduction to *Nightwood*, xv.
3. Philip Nel, for example, contends that "the concluding scene is—at the very least—suggestive of bestial desires" (*Avant-Garde and American Postmodernity*, 22). While Barnes's coy refusal to label the encounter in her letter to Coleman leaves ample room for this interpretation, in a 1970 conversation with Chester Page, she reportedly insisted, "The dog is *not* being romantic towards Robin. It is furious at the mystery of her drunkenness" (from Page's reminiscence of Barnes in Broe, *Silence and Power*, 362). Leaving aside the question of whether Robin's intention is "to play with her lover's dog or to mate with it," Susan Gubar reads her actions as "enacting and sanctifying the myth of herself as an invert who recaptures the physical, the bestial, that has been debased by culture." Pointing out that "the word 'dog' is the word 'god' inverted," she argues that "Robin bows down in a rite of inversion which consecrates the female, not the male, deity," thereby challenging the phallic power that seeks to repress "chaotic, primal forces" ("Blessings in Disguise," 500). Diane Warren, however, questions Gubar's interpretation of the encounter "as an enabling moment," suggesting instead that "Robin's treatment of the dog replicates the aggressive impulse which colours the narrator's account of the woman [Robin] who was 'eaten death returning,'" and which characterizes her various lovers' attempts to master her. Robin's threatening gestures toward the dog can thus be read, Warren argues, "not as an act of animal expression, but as an illustration of the violence that the narrator locates at the heart of culture" (*Djuna Barnes' Consuming Fictions*, 138).
4. Rohman, *Stalking the Subject*, 157, 23, 30, 100, 12.
5. Meedom, "Impersonal Love," 225, 228.
6. Quoted in Plumb, introduction to *Nightwood*, xii. In the letter to Emily Coleman from which this quotation is drawn, Barnes claims that *Night Beast* would have been the perfect title for *Nightwood* if not for the negative connotations attached to the word "beast."
7. Rohman, *Stalking the Subject*, 157, 26.
8. Kalaidjian, "Black Sheep," 80, 84 (emphasis added).
9. Derrida, *Animal That Therefore I Am*, 34. For an analysis that supports Derrida's assertion by tracing his more explicit engagement with "the question of the animal" in *The Animal That Therefore I Am* to earlier works like *Of Grammatology*, see Calarco, *Zoographies*, 103–49.
10. Derrida, *Animal That Therefore I Am*, 31.
11. Haraway, *Companion Species Manifesto*, 12.
12. Barnes, *Nightwood*, 168; Gerstenberger, "Modern (Post) Modern," 39.
13. Barnes, *Nightwood*, 170 (the following two quotations are also from 170). Affirmative readings of the scene are further undermined by an earlier passage that characterizes Robin's arrival in the woods as an "intrusion." The disturbing image of her "grasp[ing]" the animals she encounters in her wanderings, "straining their fur back until their

eyes were narrowed and their teeth bare," suggests not a becoming-animal but a desperate, almost violent desire for an ultimately impossible merging with animality (168).

14. Haraway, *Companion Species Manifesto*, 27.
15. Seitler, "Down on All Fours," 544.
16. Eliot, *Waste Land*, lines 74–75; Cowan, "Echoes of Donne, Herrick, and Southwell," 97.
17. Solomon, "Samuel Beckett's *Molloy*," 91.
18. Rohman, *Stalking the Subject*, 11–12.
19. Sheehan, *Modernism, Narrative, and Humanism*, 8.
20. Armstrong, *Modernism, Technology, and the Body*, 3.
21. Rohman, *Stalking the Subject*, 3.
22. Bowler, *Charles Darwin*, 179–80.
23. Grosz, *Nick of Time*, 21.
24. Darwin, *On the Origin of Species*, 61, 62.
25. Armstrong, *Modernism, Technology, and the Body*, 3.
26. Diamond, *Guns, Germs, and Steel*, 158–59.
27. Ibid., 170.
28. Haraway, *Companion Species Manifesto*, 29.
29. Groves, "Advantages and Disadvantages," 11.
30. For an overview of these studies, see Hare et al., "Domestication Hypothesis for Dogs' Skills."
31. Shipman, "Do the Eyes Have It," 198, 201.
32. Grandin, with Johnson, *Animals in Translation*, 305–6.
33. Haraway, *Companion Species Manifesto*, 31.
34. Berger, *About Looking*, 3, hereafter cited parenthetically in the text.
35. Deleuze and Guattari, *Thousand Plateaus*, 240.
36. Haraway, *When Species Meet*, 30, 28.
37. Rilke, "Meeting," 285, 283.
38. Rilke, "Black Cat," lines 13–16.
39. Rilke, "Meeting," 285.
40. Rilke, preface to *Mitsou*, 304.
41. Lewis, *Tarr: The 1918 Version*, 288, 103, 104.
42. Nordau, *Degeneration*, 503.
43. Freud, *Civilization and Its Discontents*, 88n1.
44. Worboys, "Inventing Dog Breeds," 53.
45. Ultimately, this culture came to have a global reach, but Britain and America remained its epicenters, and in the early twentieth century members of the purebred dog world tended to regard what they affectionately termed "the fancy" as a transatlantic community of dog lovers. Herbert Compton, for example, though he focused on the breeding and showing of dogs in his native Britain, called America "a sort of heaven for all good dogs" and praised "the canine kingdom over the Atlantic" for translating "to its sphere much that is best and most perfect on this side of the water." *Twentieth Century Dog*, 1:232.
46. Ibid., 1:119.
47. Hopwood, "Old English Sheepdog," 120–21.
48. Leighton, *New Book of the Dog*, v.
49. Ibid., 578. So great was some enthusiasts' investment in maintaining absolute distinctions between breeds that Leighton applauds the mass extermination of nonbreed strays by the so-called homes for lost dogs that emerged at around the same time as the national kennel clubs: "During the forty-five years which have elapsed since the Dogs' Home at Battersea was established, as many as 800,000 dogs have passed through the books, a few to be reclaimed or bought, the great majority to be put to death. A very large proportion of these have been veritable mongrels, not worth the value of their licenses.... And if as many as 500 undesirables are destroyed every week at one such institution, 'tis clear that the ill-bred mongrel must soon altogether disappear" (578).

50. Compton, *Twentieth Century Dog*, 1:1. The greyhound was particularly indicative of the association of breed dogs with modern fashion and technology. As Gwyneth Anne Thayer explains, the popularity of the new sport of greyhound racing in the 1920s and 1930s was largely thanks to the innovations of mechanical lures, night lighting, and sports broadcasting. The spectacle itself came to be associated with "modernity, tourism, and glamour," and "slow-motion footage" of the "canine athletes" helped to make the "sleek form of the greyhound" an icon of the era—a "popular motif in art deco drawings and paintings" that also appeared on magazine covers and in "jewelry, sculpture, and architectural ornamentation." *Going to the Dogs*, 2–3, 110.
51. Worboys, Strange, and Pemberton, *Invention of the Modern Dog*, 7.
52. Wallen, *Whose Dog Are You*, 2. One consequence of this shift is the near impossibility of describing dogs without invoking the concept of breed, as terms like "mutt," "mongrel," and the less pejorative "mixed-breed" or "non-breed dog" indicate. Wallen proposes "the cur" as a category that, "unlike the mutt, holds no relation to breed—except as contaminating excess," and thus holds the potential to undermine the mastery of the "techno-aesthetic subject" (17).
53. Worboys, Strange, and Pemberton, *Invention of the Modern Dog*, 7.
54. Rilke, "Meeting," 284–85.
55. Deleuze and Guattari, *Thousand Plateaus*, 241.
56. Fudge, *Pets*, 10.
57. Baker, *Postmodern Animal*, 20–21.
58. Lawrence, "Him with His Tail," 139; Baker, *Postmodern Animal*, 20. Indeed, to represent visually a subjectivity experienced primarily through, say, olfactory rather than ocular perception seems an impossible task, and this is perhaps why Marc ultimately "moved away from such exercises in proprioception" (21).
59. Rohman, *Stalking the Subject*, 27.
60. Wolfe, *Animal Rites*, 6.
61. Wolfe, *What Is Posthumanism*, xv–xvi.
62. Rohman, *Stalking the Subject*, 27.
63. Kermode, *Sense of an Ending*, 45, 44.
64. Sheehan, *Modernism, Narrative, and Humanism*, 10.
65. Lukács, *Theory of the Novel*, 66; McHugh, *Animal Stories*, 1. David Herman similarly underscores "narrative's power when it comes to modeling dynamic, emergent interrelations among organisms' environment-bound life histories." *Narratology Beyond the Human*, 170.
66. Kreilkamp, *Minor Creatures*, 179, 180. In the late Victorian work of Thomas Hardy and Olive Schreiner, Kreilkamp detects a "restlessly experimental approach to the form of the novel" that prefigures the "less human-centered, linear, or end-directed approach . . . that emerge[s] more fully in modernism" (20).
67. Herman, *Narratology Beyond the Human*, 160.
68. Hovanec, *Animal Subjects*, 4, 5.

Chapter 1

1. Snow, *Two Cultures*, 2.
2. Cooper, "Primordialism and Some Recent Books," 278.
3. Sandburg, "Jack London," 230.
4. Labor and Leitz, introduction to *Call of the Wild*, xiii.
5. Lundblad, "From Animal to Animality Studies," 496.
6. Lopez, *Of Wolves and Men*, 269–70.
7. Burroughs, "Real and Sham Natural History," 298.
8. Clark, "Roosevelt on the Nature Fakirs," 771. For a fuller discussion of London's response to the nature faker controversy, see Kendall-Morwick, "Jack London, Nature Fakery."

9. Coppinger and Coppinger, *Dogs*, 186. In fact, London's representations of sled dogs vying for dominance are probably based on a flawed understanding of *wolf* pack behavior. Comparative psychologist Alexandra Horowitz notes that hierarchical models of the social structure of wolf packs are based on studies that examined the behavior of unrelated wolves confined to small enclosures. Wild wolves, by contrast, "are *families*, not groups of peers vying for the top spot"; therefore, behaviors traditionally understood as "dominance" and "submission" are more properly understood as attempts "to maintain social unity" within a familial structure. Horowitz, *Inside of a Dog*, 58.
10. Coppinger and Coppinger, *Dogs*, 35. For existing scholarship on the London/Lorenz connection, see Peterson, "London and Lorenz."
11. Lorenz, foreword to *Wild Canids*, x.
12. Lorenz, *King Solomon's Ring*, 110; Lorenz, *Man Meets Dog*, 163. *King Solomon's Ring* is the English translation of the original German publication *Er redete mit dem Vieh, den Vögeln und den Fischen*. *Man Meets Dog* is the English translation of *So kam der Mensch auf den Hund*.
13. Lorenz, *Man Meets Dog*, 73, 25. Lorenz cites *White Fang* in support of his claims that predators display an "innocent" (94) expression immediately before killing their prey and that "intelligent dogs . . . know when they are cutting an undignified and, from a human point of view, comical figure," becoming "deeply depressed if they are laughed at" (163). In *King Solomon's Ring*, Lorenz uses London to demonstrate that "huskies and other primitive breeds" exhibit a unique social organization in which "it is only the leader himself who is, in a true sense, his master's dog," while "the others are, strictly speaking, the leader's dogs" (110), and that the "deposing of an ageing tyrant is always a highly dramatic and usually tragic event, especially in the case of wolves and sledge dogs" (140). In *On Aggression* (the English translation of *Das sogenannte Böse: Zur Naturgeschichte der Aggression*), he again cites *White Fang*, this time when describing a "sideways catapulting with the hind-quarters" (126) that is the male dog's only defense against the attack of a female, whom "ritual demands" he must not harm (126, 125).
14. McHugh, *Animal Stories*, 215, 19, 1.
15. Lorenz, *Man Meets Dog*, 94.
16. London, *Before Adam*, 100, 99, hereafter cited parenthetically in the text.
17. Freud, *Civilization and Its Discontents*, 87n1.
18. London, *Call of the Wild*, 41, hereafter cited parenthetically in the text.
19. London, *White Fang*, 248, hereafter cited parenthetically in the text.
20. Lorenz, *Man Meets Dog*, 1, 3–4, hereafter cited parenthetically in the text; in cases where the source may be unclear, I've included the abbreviation *MMD*.
21. Coppinger and Coppinger, *Dogs*, 41.
22. Darwin, *On the Origin of Species*, 10, 16, 12, 32.
23. Ibid., 32.
24. Coppinger and Coppinger, *Dogs*, 60, 58, 59. The Coppingers propose that the theory that dogs evolved through natural selection for traits that enabled them to be efficient dump feeders helps to explain some of the morphological differences between dogs and wolves. Genetic variation, coupled with the selective pressures of this new niche, resulted in "a size and shape that were specialized for scavenging—a smallish size, with a proportionally small head, smaller teeth, and just enough brain to point it in the right direction" without requiring the additional calories needed to support the significantly larger wolf brain (61). Other morphological

differences, such as floppy ears, variations in coat color, and a propensity to bark were probably not selected for but rather developed spontaneously as a result of intense selection for specific traits, which often results in spontaneous development of other, seemingly unrelated traits, as demonstrated in Russian geneticist Dmitri Belyaev's famous experiment with Russian silver foxes. Intentionally bred for tameness alone, in just eighteen generations the foxes had developed the "doglike traits of floppy ears, diestrous [menstrual] cycling, and piebald coats" (63).
25. Lorenz, *King Solomon's Ring*, 109, hereafter cited parenthetically in the text; in cases where the source may be unclear, I've included the abbreviation *KSR*.
26. Auerbach, *Male Call*, 88.
27. Lundblad, "From Animal to Animality Studies," 496.
28. Chez, *Victorian Dogs, Victorian Men*, 130, 131. Like Lundblad, Chez underscores the homoeroticism of passages describing love between London's dogs and their masters, yet her interpretation indicates that the interspecies nature of these encounters is not merely a veil but a vital feature: "Figuratively, there is a kind of equality in this vision: in these moments, masculinity transcends all species boundaries. This new interspecies bond enabled the merger of eternal, masculine—and animal—essences, mutually penetrating through civilization's shells, infusing and reawakening virility, in a tightly intimate circle" (146).
29. Quoted in Labor and Leitz, introduction to *Call of the Wild*, xv.
30. Kuzniar, *Melancholia's Dog*. 9.
31. Chez, *Victorian Dogs, Victorian Men*, 136.
32. Anthropologist Elizabeth Marshall Thomas's account of canine social dynamics in *The Hidden Life of Dogs* undermines London's anthropocentric vision of dog love. After years of observing what her dogs did when granted as much autonomy as she could legally and practically allow, Thomas concludes, "What do dogs want? They want each other. Human beings are merely a cynomorphic substitute, as we all know" (134).
33. Lorenz, "Companions as Factors," 114, 115, 138.
34. For a discussion of the relationship between Lorenz's scientific views and his wartime activities, see Burkhardt, *Patterns of Behavior*, 231–80.
35. Deichmann, *Biologists Under Hitler*, 183.
36. See Burkhardt, *Patterns of Behavior*, 242–45.
37. As Burkhardt points out, "politics alone would not have been sufficient to secure [Lorenz] the appointment at Königsberg." Yet following the politically and racially motivated rejection of his funding application to the German Research Organization, Lorenz "had worked hard to demonstrate his commitment to the Reich," removing any similar obstacles that might have prevented his later appointment. Ibid., 263.
38. Ibid., 277.
39. Konrad Lorenz, "Biographical," The Nobel Prize, 2018, https://www.nobelprize.org/prizes/medicine/1973/lorenz/biographical.
40. Lorenz, foreword to *Wild Canids*, x.
41. Graham, *Graham System of Living*, 9, 24.
42. Darwin, *On the Origin of Species*, 15, 25.
43. Lorenz, "Companions as Factors," 187.
44. Sax, *Animals in the Third Reich*, 135, 74.
45. Lorenz, *On Aggression*, 129–30.
46. Chez, *Victorian Dogs, Victorian Men*, 134.
47. Freud, *Civilization and Its Discontents*, 88n1.
48. Rohman, *Stalking the Subject*, 23.
49. Hovanec, *Animal Subjects*, 8.

Chapter 2

1. *Diary of Virginia Woolf*, 4:181.
2. Scott, *In the Hollow of the Wave*, 155.
3. This specifically feminized stigma persists, as Alice Kuzniar observes in a chapter that examines female-authored dog narratives spanning the twentieth century: "Endearment to the pet will perhaps always be susceptible to the charge of sentimentality, but disparagement over this *'unspeakable'* attachment is especially a risk women artists face." *Melancholia's Dog*, 111.
4. *Letters of Virginia Woolf*, 5:140; *Diary of Virginia Woolf*, 4:123.
5. Quoted in *Diary of Virginia Woolf*, 4:186n.
6. Smith, "Across the Widest Gulf," 348 ("trivial potboiler"), 349 ("not really about a dog").
7. Wendy Faris, for example, regards Flush as "very un-beastlike" except when indulging his sexual appetites in Florence—a plot device she reads as "a parody of English clichés about the sexual freedom enjoyed in Italy" ("Bloomsbury's Beasts," 124). In one of the earliest sustained interpretations of *Flush*, Susan Squier reads the novel as an allegory of the struggles of the woman writer, as I discuss below (*Virginia Woolf and London*, 122–37). Alternatively, Pamela Caughie argues that "*Flush* can be read as an allegory of canon-formation" ("*Flush* and the Literary Canon," 49). Yet despite noting that the novel thus raises questions about "what experience is worthy of representation" (48), Caughie similarly interprets Flush as a stand-in for "the lives that have never been narrated" (61). That she has specifically human lives in mind is suggested by her observation, in response to Squier's reading, that "Flush resembles less the woman writer than the writer's servant, Wilson" (60). Finally, Anna Snaith argues that "the comedy and 'lightheartedness' of *Flush* has prevented critics from fully appreciating the politics of this work" and reads the novel as expressing Woolf's "fears about the growth of fascism in Britain and Europe" ("Of Fanciers, Footnotes, and Fascism," 615).
8. Smith, "Across the Widest Gulf," 359.
9. Ibid.
10. Garber, *Dog Love*, 45.
11. Smith, "Across the Widest Gulf," 349.
12. Woolf, "Character in Fiction," 421.
13. McHugh, *Animal Stories*, 15.
14. *Diary of Virginia Woolf*, 4:153. The other quotations in this paragraph are also from vol. 4 of Woolf's diary, 181, 37, 139, 123, 144, 181–82, 184.
15. Ryan, *Virginia Woolf*, 132.
16. *Diary of Virginia Woolf*, 4:153.
17. *Letters of Virginia Woolf*, 5:236.
18. Woolf, "Modern Fiction," 160, 161.
19. *Letters of Virginia Woolf*, 5:167.
20. Garber, *Use and Abuse of Literature*, 225. For a discussion of the generic hybridity—even indeterminacy—of *Flush* in the context of life writing, see Herman, *Narratology Beyond the Human*, 157–70.
21. Woolf, "Modern Fiction," 161.
22. *Diary of Virginia Woolf*, 4:40.
23. Ibid., 4:133–34.
24. See, for example, Reid, *Art and Affection*, 355; Rosenthal, *Virginia Woolf*, 206.
25. Woolf, "Character Sketch," 255.
26. As Woolf explains in an endnote, the historical Flush "was stolen three times; but the unities seem to require that the three stealings shall be compressed into one" (*Flush*, 167n). She thus recounts only the third and longest episode, which occurred just eleven days before Elizabeth Barrett's secret marriage to Robert Browning. While Flush was recovered relatively quickly after his first two dognappings, this time he was held captive for five days, even after Barrett's brother Henry paid the ransom. An alarmed Elizabeth,

accompanied only by her personal maid, traveled to Whitechapel, where she pleaded with the dognapper's wife to persuade her husband to release Flush. Flush was later returned to the Barrett residence.
27. Woolf, *Flush*, 80, hereafter cited parenthetically in the text.
28. Snaith, "Of Fanciers, Footnotes, and Fascism," 622. See also Squier's chapter on *Flush*, which treats the novel as "a serious critique of the values organizing London's social and political life," particularly with regard to gender and class. *Virginia Woolf and London*, 122.
29. Snaith, "Of Fanciers, Footnotes, and Fascism," 624.
30. Adams, *Shaggy Muses*, 238.
31. Woolf, "Modern Fiction," 160.
32. Kennedy-Shaw, "Horse and Hound," 7. Early Kipling biographer Nella Braddy notes tellingly that Boots's "dog language . . . is as puzzling to read as the Uncle Remus dialect is to one who was not brought up in the South." *Rudyard Kipling*, 256.
33. Weil, *Thinking Animals*, 83.
34. Herman, *Narratology Beyond the Human*, 166, 164.
35. De Waal, "Anthropomorphism and Anthropodenial," 261.
36. Sewell, *Black Beauty*, 13, 4.
37. Saunders, *Beautiful Joe*, 14, 304.
38. Butterworth, introduction to *Beautiful Joe*, 7.
39. *Letters of Virginia Woolf*, 5:161–62, 167.
40. Garber, *Use and Abuse of Literature*, 215.
41. London, *Call of the Wild*, 5.
42. Ibid., 12, 13.
43. London, "Other Animals," 10.
44. London, *Call of the Wild*, 22.
45. Ibid., 63.
46. Sheehan, *Modernism, Narrative, and Humanism*, 124.
47. Bergson, *Creative Evolution*, 43.
48. London, *Call of the Wild*, 15, 23, 79.
49. Auerbach, *Male Call*, 94–95.
50. London, *Call of the Wild*, 6, 36, 85, 88, 87.
51. Doctorow, *Jack London, Hemingway, and the Constitution*, 18–19.
52. London, *Call of the Wild*, 21.
53. Ibid., 85.
54. Ibid., 79, 80.
55. Quoted in Labor and Leitz, introduction to *Call of the Wild*, xv.
56. London, *White Fang*, 275–76.
57. Ibid., 187, 278, 280.
58. Lorenz, *Man Meets Dog*, 25.
59. Woolf, *Room of One's Own*, 4.
60. Ibid.
61. Haraway, *Companion Species Manifesto*, 88.
62. Wolfe, *Animal Rites*, 8.
63. Woolf, *Room of One's Own*, 50.
64. Ibid., 3.
65. Goldman, "'Ce Chien Est à Moi,'" 82; Woolf, *Room of One's Own*, 59; Boswell, *Life of Samuel Johnson*, 244.
66. Squier, *Virginia Woolf and London*, 122, 124. Faris similarly contends that Woolf and her Bloomsbury peers employ animals as symbolic "markers of neglected topics"—among them, presumably, the topic of women and fiction. "Bloomsbury's Beasts," 115.
67. Scott, *In the Hollow of the Wave*, 174.
68. Woolf, "Women Novelists," 315.
69. Alden, *Social Mobility in the English Bildungsroman*, 99.
70. Lawrence, *Sons and Lovers*, 319.
71. Alden, *Social Mobility in the English Bildungsroman*, 99.
72. The racialized portraits in this comparison signal Woolf's critique of how dog breeds served to naturalize human racial and ethnic categories and reinforce the taboo against miscegenation in the Victorian era. Further, Woolf's Orientalist language points to the need to look beyond white, Anglocentric representations to develop a fuller understanding of the human/dog relationship in its diverse expressions—a need I discuss in more detail in the coda.
73. Smith, "Across the Widest Gulf," 353.
74. *Letters of Virginia Woolf*, 4:49, 34.

75. Smith, "Across the Widest Gulf," 353.
76. See Adams, *Shaggy Muses*, 223–32.
77. Castle, *Reading the Modernist Bildungsroman*, 9.
78. McHugh, *Animal Stories*, 133.
79. *Letters of Virginia Woolf*, 3:253.
80. *Letters of Vita Sackville-West*, 122.
81. *Letters of Virginia Woolf*, 3:331, 228.
82. Ibid., 5:41.
83. Woolf, *Passionate Apprentice*, 243; Adams, *Shaggy Muses*, 211.
84. Woolf, *Passionate Apprentice*, 234, 228.
85. Adams, *Shaggy Muses*, 211.
86. Woolf, *Passionate Apprentice*, 270–71.
87. Adams, *Shaggy Muses*, 211.
88. *Letters of Virginia Woolf*, 1:351.
89. Rohman, *Stalking the Subject*, 129.
90. Lawrence, *Women in Love*, 244.
91. Haraway, *When Species Meet*, 4.
92. Castle, *Reading the Modernist Bildungsroman*, 26–27, 198, 214–15.
93. Quoted in Adams, *Shaggy Muses*, 22.
94. Ibid., 13, 19.
95. Castle, *Reading the Modernist Bildungsroman*, 27.
96. See, for example, Garber, *Dog Love*, 47; Griffiths, "Almost Human," 166–67.
97. Weil, *Thinking Animals*, 85.
98. Horowitz, *Inside of a Dog*, 219–20. Horowitz notes that while dogs persistently fail the mirror test, "there are other dog behaviors suggestive of their self-knowledge," including scent marking and play behavior (220).
99. Quoted in Adams, *Shaggy Muses*, 22.
100. Ryan, *Virginia Woolf*, 164. Herman similarly highlights *Flush* as exemplary of narrative's capacity for what he terms "*Umwelt* modeling," arguing that Woolf "leverages modernist techniques as an imaginative aid or modeling tool—that is, as a resource for modeling how the biophysical structure as well as the life histories of nonhuman agents might impinge on their ways of engaging with environments inhabited, in other ways, by human agents." *Narratology Beyond the Human*, 167.
101. Heidegger, *Fundamental Concepts of Metaphysics*, 176.
102. Uexküll, *Worlds of Animals and Humans*, 96–97.
103. Ibid., 96.
104. Horowitz, *Inside of a Dog*, 89.
105. Ibid., 233.
106. Weil, *Thinking Animals*, 83.
107. Derrida, *Animal That Therefore I Am*, 32.
108. Abel, Hirsch, and Langland, introduction to *Voyage In*, 10.
109. Castle, *Reading the Modernist Bildungsroman*, 244, 198.
110. Herman, *Narratology Beyond the Human*, 26.
111. Castle, *Reading the Modernist Bildungsroman*, 236.
112. Ibid., 24.
113. London, *Call of the Wild*, 86.
114. Quoted in Adams, *Shaggy Muses*, 35.
115. Castle, *Reading the Modernist Bildungsroman*, 244.
116. Haraway, *When Species Meet*, 4.
117. Ryan, *Virginia Woolf*, 160.
118. Castle, *Reading the Modernist Bildungsroman*, 197.
119. Woolf, *Mrs. Dalloway*, 152–53.
120. *Diary of Virginia Woolf*, 4:318, 317.

Chapter 3

1. Woolf, *Flush*, 139. Nero survived the fall and lived for almost ten more years; he died, apparently following several months of suffering, after being run over by a butcher's cart (Ireland, *Life of Jane Welsh Carlyle*, 259). Writing a few months after Nero's "suicide attempt," Carlyle complained of London, "There has been a dreadful racket here this season—worse, I think, than in any London season I ever lived through—it has seemed to me sometimes as if the town must burst into spontaneous combustion. . . . People dare not let themselves think or feel in this centre of frivolity and folly; they would go mad if they did, and universally

commit suicide." *Letters and Memorials of Jane Welsh Carlyle*, 373.
2. I use the terms "working dog" and "working breed" in a broader sense than do the British and American Kennel Clubs. Whereas these clubs use the term "working" to refer to breeds distinguished from the sporting/gundog, hound, terrier, toy, nonsporting/utility, and herding/pastoral groups, I use it generically to refer to breeds traditionally used for hunting, herding, guarding, and other specialized tasks. In other words, I differentiate working breeds from companion breeds, while recognizing that these two functions are not mutually exclusive.
3. Dalgliesh, "Collie," 98.
4. Leighton, *New Book of the Dog*, 168, 577.
5. Ibid., 168, 172; Dalgliesh, "Collie," 98, 106.
6. Dalgliesh, "Collie," 107.
7. Compton, *Twentieth Century Dog*, 1:79.
8. Litvag, *Master of Sunnybank*, 6.
9. Terhune, *Lad: A Dog*, 100, hereafter cited parenthetically in the text.
10. Litvag, *Master of Sunnybank*, 111.
11. Ackerley, *My Father and Myself*, 232.
12. Litvag, *Master of Sunnybank*, 146; *Letters of J. R. Ackerley*, 115, 110n.
13. Quoted in *Letters of J. R. Ackerley*, 114.
14. Quoted in ibid., 308n.
15. Litvag, *Master of Sunnybank*, 197.
16. Ibid., 194, 197, 196.
17. See ibid., 88–89. The real Lad's only foray into the ring was at a Fourth of July dog show in Hawthorne, New Jersey, in 1916. "Terhune Memorial Park," Township of Wayne, NJ, https://www.waynetownship.com/terhune-park.html.
18. Worboys, Strange, and Pemberton, *Invention of the Modern Dog*, 7.
19. Compton, *Twentieth Century Dog*, 1:89.
20. Ritvo, *Animal Estate*, 89, 93.
21. London, *Call of the Wild*, 6.
22. Woolf, *Flush*, 32.
23. Ibid., 32, 134, 135.
24. Litvag, *Master of Sunnybank*, 55, 182.
25. This event precipitates one of the rare lapses in Lad's obedience—lapses that occur only when Lad knows better than the Master. In this case, Lad, knowing that Lady is innocent, growls at the Master and accepts the punishment on her behalf. Lad's devastation at having to disobey the beloved Master only reinforces the depth of his fidelity: "It was the supreme misery, the crowning hell, of Lad's career. For the first time, two overpowering loves fought with each other in his Galahad soul. And the love for poor, unjustly blamed, Lady hurled down the superlove for the Master" (16).
26. Compton, *Twentieth Century Dog*, 1:79.
27. Dalgliesh, "Collie," 107.
28. Claude Morrison, quoted in Compton, *Twentieth Century Dog*, 2:33.
29. Dalgliesh, "Collie," 111.
30. Leonard, *Care and Handling of Dogs*, 252.
31. Ritvo, *Animal Estate*, 88.
32. Davies, *Kennel Handbook*, 113–14.
33. Ritvo, *Animal Estate*, 88.
34. London, *Call of the Wild*, 22.
35. Ironically, some of Terhune's neighbors regarded him as a pretentious upstart not unlike Glure. While much of Terhune's writing positions him as "the old settler" who watches in dismay as "newcomers mov[e] in around him" (Litvag, *Master of Sunnybank*, 111), in fact the Terhune family purchased the property they christened Sunnybank only a few years before his birth, and the house they built there served only as a summer retreat for several years while the family resided in Newark. Thus Terhune's self-characterization as one of the area's authentic residents was somewhat misleading. As one long-time resident explains, "Pompton Lakes was and is a mill town, a town of blue-collar working people. Many of them enjoyed the fame

that Bert Terhune brought the town and respected him for it, but others resented him and felt he was putting on airs" (quoted in ibid., 190–91). Another acquaintance remembers Terhune as "a good man until he got delusions of grandeur. As the years went on, he became a figment of his own imagination" (quoted in ibid., 191).
36. Terhune rebuts this view more extensively in another collection, titled *Bruce*. Most of the Bruce stories take place in France, where the titular character serves as a war dog in World War I—pure fiction, as the real dog he was modeled after spent the war years comfortably at Sunnybank. Bruce's achievements, moreover, surpass even Lad's in implausibility. As Litvag puts it, "Bruce outshone General Pershing as he almost single-handedly defeated the Germans and made the world safe for democracy" before returning to The Place "as a wounded hero." *Master of Sunnybank*, 124.
37. Leighton, *New Book of the Dog*, 172.
38. Litvag, *Master of Sunnybank*, 89, 111.
39. Compton, *Twentieth Century Dog*, 1:1.
40. Burrows, "How to Train a Collie," 17–18.
41. Sloan, *My Years with General Motors*, 165, 163; Litvag, *Master of Sunnybank*, 141.
42. While Lad's victory might seem to demonstrate the fancier's appreciation for the true thoroughbred, Terhune is careful to point out that the Kennel Club has "engaged [McGilead's] services for this single occasion" and is unlikely to do so again, as his possession of "a knowledge of collies such as is granted to few men . . . made him a wretchedly bad dog-show judge" (117).
43. Fielder, Poor, and Nicoll, "Rabies in the City of New York," 143; Litvag, *Master of Sunnybank*, 195.
44. See Litvag, *Master of Sunnybank*, 89, 142.
45. Ritvo, *Animal Estate*, 93.
46. Anti-German sentiment in inter- and postwar America and Britain led to the substitution of "masquerade names such as 'Alsatian' and 'police dog'" for the original German sheepdog or German shepherd. See Tenner, "Citizen Canine," 75–76.
47. Ackerley, *My Dog Tulip*, 4, hereafter cited parenthetically in the text.
48. Ackerley, *We Think the World of You*, 169, 191. The page citations in the following four paragraphs are also to this source.
49. Ibid., 95, 59.
50. McHugh, "Marrying My Bitch," 36. Ackerley alludes to the problematic effects of this concept on canine bodies when he calls Tulip "degenerate" and attributes her chronic digestive problems to "inbreeding." *My Dog Tulip*, 95.
51. Srinivasan, "Biopolitics of Animal Being," 113.
52. McHugh, "Marrying My Bitch," 36.
53. Kiang, "Friendship," 142.
54. Leighton also acknowledges the widespread use of such methods when he discusses the problem that arises when a bitch, like Tulip, refuses "to mate herself with the dog that we have chosen, yet exhibits a mad desire for one with whom we would not on any account have her mated"; he speculates that "enforced and loveless mating is accountable for the small and feeble litters which frequently occur in many of our modern breeds. To send a bitch who is in temporarily delicate condition boxed up in a railway van on a long journey, and to assist her immediately on her arrival to a strange and possibly abhorrent dog cannot be good; yet this is very frequently done." *New Book of the Dog*, 581.
55. McHugh, "Marrying My Bitch," 38.
56. Nordau, *Degeneration*, 500.
57. McHugh, *Animal Stories*, 133, 132.
58. Brutal as this plan sounds, culling is a routine practice in the history of

dog breeding. Great Dane fancier E. P. Joachim, for example, recommends destroying "foul-marked puppies" ("Great Dane, or German Boarhound," 86). Borzoi fancier S. P. Borman warns that a bitch "should not be allowed to suckle more than five—or, if a strong, big bitch, six—pups. If the litter is larger, it is better to destroy the remainder." "Borzoi, or Russian Wolfhound," 186.
59. Flegel, *Pets and Domesticity*, 11. Flegel's analysis of pets' roles and status in the Victorian family suggests that Ackerley's relationship with Tulip could itself be interpreted in heteronormative culture as a sign of Ackerley's sexual deviancy: "Those who remain single or childless . . . are open to question, their sexuality and choice of intimate/physical relations subject to scrutiny, particularly when a pet vividly attests to the non-reproductive capacity of the home. Representations of single people or queer people and their pets, therefore, must be understood within a social construction of sexuality that is always tied to reproductivity, one that inevitably perceives 'families' made up of a single human or a non-reproductive couple and their pets as a sign of social failure and deviant sexuality" (11).
60. McHugh, "Marrying My Bitch," 36.
61. Parker, *Ackerley*, 329.
62. Grier, *Pets in America*, 4. Srinivasan similarly contends that "castrating or removing the ovaries and uterus of an otherwise healthy animal is certainly a biopolitical act in that it intervenes in basic life processes—sexuality and reproduction—on the basis of a set of truth discourses about the regulation of the wellbeing of dog individuals and populations." "Biopolitics of Animal Being," 113.
63. McHugh, "Marrying My Bitch," 36.
64. Grier, *Pets in America*, 4.
65. Holmberg, *Urban Animals*, 2, 3.

66. Kiang, "Friendship," 132.
67. *Letters of J. R. Ackerley*, 105. In *My Dog Tulip*, Ackerley claims that dogs' habit of "smelling one another's bottoms," though regarded by prudish humans as "perverse and unhygienic," is actually a means of "investigating . . . that secretion of the anal glands . . . which provides them with information" (46).
68. Horowitz, *Inside of a Dog*, 83.
69. Ibid., 84.
70. Ibid.
71. Ibid., 23.
72. Kiang, "Friendship," 133.
73. Horowitz, *Inside of a Dog*, 283.
74. Ackerley, *We Think the World of You*, 88–89, 162, 172, 95.
75. Haraway, *Companion Species Manifesto*, 34.
76. Ackerley, *We Think the World of You*, 163.
77. Ackerley, "I Am a Beast," 69.

Chapter 4

1. Beckett, *How It Is*, 47.
2. Beckett, *Watt*, 82–83.
3. Sheehan, "Zoomorphism," 663.
4. Beckett, *Three Novels*, 89, 78, hereafter cited parenthetically in the text.
5. Begam, "Samuel Beckett and Antihumanism," 302.
6. Levy, "Living Without a Life," 91. In a 1992 essay, W. J. McCormack counters the common characterization of Beckett as misanthrope, objecting that he "has been not so much accused of misanthropy, as declared manifestly guilty of that offence or something so similar that precise details need hardly be supplied" ("Samuel Beckett and the *Negro Anthology*," 73). Levy provocatively insists that the "Beckettian repugnance for humanity goes deeper than mere misanthropy," and his analysis makes an implicit but important distinction between humanist delineations of the subject, which are the real targets of Beckett's satire, and actual human beings, who

inevitably fail to complete "the rational process of self-actualization" that such delineations mandate. "Living Without a Life," 80, 88.
7. Moorjani, "Dancing Bees in Samuel Beckett's *Molloy*," 174.
8. Yeoh, "Beckett's Persistent Humanism," 115.
9. Boulter, *Beckett*, 13, 15.
10. Wolfe, *What Is Posthumanism*, xv.
11. My use of gendered terminology throughout this chapter is deliberate, for it is typically Beckett's male characters who find themselves unable to make sense of their species membership, indicating that the humanist subject in question is always-already male.
12. Beckett, *Watt*, 85.
13. Sheehan, *Modernism, Narrative, and Humanism*, 184.
14. For early studies that read Beckett's animals as emblems of degraded humanity, see Chambers, "Artist as Performing Dog"; Solomon, "Samuel Beckett's *Molloy*." For more recent scholarship that reflects a growing interest in animals within the field of Beckett studies, see Bryden, *Beckett and Animals*.
15. Connor, "Beckett's Animals," 29.
16. Weller, "Not Rightly Human," 212, 214, 216.
17. Puchner, "Performing the Open," 21.
18. Wolfe, *Animal Rites*, 8.
19. Weller, "Not Rightly Human," 219.
20. Derrida, *Animal That Therefore I Am*, 31, 34.
21. One exception is Belacqua in *Dream of Fair to Middling Women* (Beckett's first novel, written in 1932 but published posthumously): "Dogs, for their obviousness, he despised and rejected, and cats he disliked, but cats less than dogs or children" (128). The association of canine bodies with grotesque sexuality is visible in a number of texts. In *How It Is*, the narrator describes a dog "lower[ing] its snout to its black and pink penis too tired to lick" (30) and later remarks, "my spinal dog it licked my genitals" (85). At the beginning of Beckett's *Mercier and Camier*, an awkward embrace between "our heroes" is rendered even more so by the presence of two dogs "copulating, with the utmost naturalness," a few feet away (9). Molloy describes his sexual relationship with Edith, a woman he meets "in a rubbish dump," in canine terms: "She bent over the couch, because of her rheumatism, and in I went from behind. . . . It seemed all right to me, for I had seen dogs, and I was astonished when she confided that you could go about it differently." *Three Novels*, 56–57.
22. Connor, "Beckett's Animals," 30. Connor attributes this response to "the presence of animals" more generally, as the scenes in question involve dogs and sheep (30). Below, I discuss the special significance of dogs in such multispecies assemblages.
23. Haraway, *Companion Species Manifesto*, 12.
24. Derrida, "'Eating Well,'" 279.
25. Levinas, "Name of a Dog," 153; see also Atterton, "Dog and Philosophy," 69. In the recent edited collection *Face to Face with Animals*, co-editor (with Tamra Wright) and contributor Peter Atterton makes several changes to Seán Hand's original English translation of "The Name of a Dog, or Natural Rights," which has been the basis for most animal studies scholarship on Levinas. Throughout this chapter, I quote Hand's translation except where Atterton's changes produce a significantly revised understanding of Levinas's intended meaning. In the passage just quoted, Atterton replaces Hand's "For him, there was no doubt that we were men" with "For him—it was incontestable—we were men." Whereas in Hand's translation, the absence of

doubt concerns the prisoners' status as men, Atterton's translation indicates that it is Bobby's *recognition* of the prisoners' humanity that Levinas deems "incontestable."

26. Derrida, "'Eating Well,'" 278.
27. Weller, "Not Rightly Human," 214.
28. Beckett, *More Pricks Than Kicks*, 20, 22.
29. Descartes, "To Mersenne, 11 June 1640."
30. Beckett, *More Pricks Than Kicks*, 22.
31. Bentham, *Principles of Morals and Legislation*, 283n. Both Peter Singer and Tom Regan include the larger passage from which this statement is extracted in their arguments for animal ethics, indicating the central significance of suffering for both Singer's utilitarianism and Regan's deontological ethics. Singer, *Animal Liberation*, 7; Regan, *Case for Animal Rights*, 95. For Derrida's analysis of Bentham's seminal question, see Derrida, *Animal That Therefore I Am*, 27–29.
32. Beckett, *Nohow On*, 20–22. Biographer Anthony Cronin notes that this passage depicts "one of the traumas of [Beckett's] childhood." *Beckett*, 21.
33. Weller, "Not Rightly Human," 214–15.
34. The expression of donkeys also proves compelling for Belacqua in *Dream of Fair to Middling Women*: "The appearance of domestic animals of all kinds he disliked, save the extraordinary countenance of the donkey seen full-face" (128). Beckett's mother, May, owned a number of donkeys, and at least one of them—Kisch, named by Beckett and his brother—was purchased from an abusive owner. Cronin, *Samuel Beckett*, 22.
35. Beckett, *Watt*, 91, 95, 100, 93.
36. Descartes, *Discourse on the Method*, 120.
37. Beckett, *Watt*, 115, 116, 117.
38. Ibid., 112.
39. Ibid., 117, 116, 91, 100, 91. On the notebooks, see Ackerley and Gontarski, *Grove Companion to Samuel Beckett*, 146.
40. Deleuze and Guattari, *Thousand Plateaus*, 240. By extension, this characterization of Teddy relegates Lousse to a position likewise disparaged by Deleuze and Guattari: the pet-keeping elderly woman. To elucidate their privileged category of "the anomalous"—an "exceptional individual" with whom one form of becoming-animal can be achieved—they contrast Ahab's Moby-Dick with "the little cat or dog owned by an elderly woman who honors and cherishes it" (243–44). Haraway excoriates this passage for its palpable "misogyny, fear of aging, incuriosity about animals, and horror at the ordinariness of flesh," demonstrating how these trappings contradict a theory ostensibly "opposed to the strictures of individuation and subject." *When Species Meet*, 30.
41. Beckett, *Murphy*, 98.
42. Beckett, *More Pricks Than Kicks*, 167.
43. Katz, "Beckett's Measures," 250. Cronin notes that Beckett "took care never to own an animal and take responsibility for its well-being or its love" (*Samuel Beckett*, 21). Beckett not only viewed pet-keeping as a weighty responsibility but "contemplated suicide" (248–49) following the death of one of his mother's Kerry Blues—the one killed in the accident, by Katz's account—and later grieved the death of another with whom he had taken many walks and who appears in *More Pricks Than Kicks* and *Krapp's Last Tape* (258). In the latter case, he regretted not being able to "be with her at the end, to try and make it perhaps a little easier," and had difficulty persuading his distraught mother "to take a reasonable view of what oneself could not take a reasonable view of." Quoted in Knowlson, *Damned to Fame*, 244–45.
44. Beckett, *Watt*, 172–73.
45. Levinas, "Name of a Dog," 153; see Homer, *Odyssey*, 364.

46. Levinas, "Name of a Dog," 153; Atterton, "Dog and Philosophy," 67.
47. Levinas, "Name of a Dog," 153.
48. Nash, "Animal Nomenclature," 101.
49. Derrida, *Animal That Therefore I Am*, 9.
50. Levinas, "Name of a Dog," 152.
51. Levinas, "Is Ontology Fundamental," 9.
52. See Kendall, "Face of a Dog," 192–93; Levinas, "Name of a Dog," 152; Atterton, "Dog and Philosophy," 66. The original sentence reads: "A l'heure suprême de son instauration—et sans éthique et sans logos—le chien va attester la dignité de la personne." Atterton replaces Hand's "his" with "humanity's" (among other, more minor changes) to clarify that the dog is not the referent of what appears in the original French as "son."
53. This is a translation of the title of his 1972 book *Humanisme de l'autre homme*, sometimes translated simply as "Humanism of the Other." As we will see, though, Levinas has in mind an exclusively human other.
54. Levinas, *Totality and Infinity*, 21.
55. Ibid., 251.
56. Levinas, *Entre-Nous*, 59.
57. Levinas, "Animal Interview," 5.
58. Levinas, "Substitution," 94.
59. Levinas, "Humanism and An-archy," 127.
60. Atterton, "Ethical Cynicism," 61. Matthew Calarco provides a fuller discussion of the posthumanist potential of Levinas's emphasis on alterity, arguing that "Levinas's ethical philosophy is, or at least should be, committed to a notion of *universal ethical consideration*, that is, an agnostic form of ethical consideration that has no a priori constraints or boundaries." *Zoographies*, 55.
61. Rohman, "On Singularity and the Symbolic," 67.
62. Levinas, *Totality and Infinity*, 194.
63. Derrida, *Animal That Therefore I Am*, 117.
64. Levinas, "Animal Interview," 4.
65. Clark, "On Being 'the Last Kantian,'" 166.
66. Levinas, "Name of a Dog," 153. Atterton and Wright replace Hand's "maxims and drives" with "the maxims of its drives." Atterton and Wright, "Editors' Introduction: Extending the Boundaries of 'The Ethical,'" in *Face to Face with Animals*, xxiv.
67. Derrida, *Animal That Therefore I Am*, 115.
68. Nash, "Animal Nomenclature," 101.
69. Levinas, "Animal Interview," 5.
70. Darwin, *Descent of Man*, 74, 84; Darwin, *Expression of the Emotions*, 63.
71. Levinas, "Animal Interview," 4–5.
72. Ibid., 4; Levinas, "Is Ontology Fundamental," 8, 10.
73. Levinas, "Animal Interview," 4.
74. Ibid., 3–4. The first ellipsis in this passage is in the original; the rest are mine.
75. Ibid., 4.
76. Ackerley, "'Despised for Their Obviousness,'" 187.
77. Solomon, "Samuel Beckett's *Molloy*," 85, 91. Chris Ackerley's more recent analysis of dogs in *Watt* and *Molloy* takes their dogginess more literally, yet he ultimately deems it "self-evident . . . that dogs in their obviousness, in their demented particularity, frequent the Beckett country and are an intrinsic part of the fundamentally absurd." "'Despised for Their Obviousness,'" 186.
78. Derrida, *Animal That Therefore I Am*, 11.
79. Beckett, *Waiting for Godot*, 19.
80. Beckett, *Watt*, 28.
81. *Basic Writings of St. Thomas Aquinas*, 1:20.
82. Beckett, *Watt*, 117, 199.
83. Connor, *Samuel Beckett*, 56–57.
84. Descartes, *Discourse on the Method*, 120.
85. Levinas, *Entre-Nous*, 14–15.
86. Ibid., 14; Derrida, *Animal That Therefore I Am*, 81.
87. Derrida, *Animal That Therefore I Am*, 135.

88. Levinas, *Entre-Nous*, 14.
89. Levinas, *Totality and Infinity*, 195.
90. Ibid., 213.
91. Derrida, *Writing and Difference*, 112, 113, 147.
92. Uhlmann, *Beckett and Poststructuralism*, 161, 165.
93. Beckett, *Watt*, 83.
94. Beckett, "German Letter of 1937," 172–73.
95. Jacobs, "Grammar of Zoopoetics," 65. Jacobs examines Oskar Panizza's *From the Diary of a Dog* (1892) and Franz Kafka's *Investigations of a Dog* (1922).
96. Wordsworth, preface to *Lyrical Ballads*, 611.
97. Wordsworth, "Ode ('There Was a Time')," line 28; Beckett, *Murphy*, 99.
98. Beckett, *Endgame and Act Without Words*, 11.
99. Beckett, *Watt*, 46–47.
100. Wordsworth, "Ode ('There Was a Time')," line 33.
101. Levinas, "Name of a Dog," 151.
102. Adams, *Sexual Politics of Meat*, 14, 51.
103. Levinas, *Entre-Nous*, 13.
104. Clark, "On Being 'the Last Kantian,'" 170.
105. Llewelyn, "Am I Obsessed by Bobby," 235.
106. Levinas, "As If Consenting to Horror," 487.
107. Clark, "On Being 'the Last Kantian,'" 171.
108. Levinas, "Name of a Dog," 151.
109. Derrida, *Animal That Therefore I Am*, 24, 26.
110. In *Malone Dies*, too, the eponymous narrator tells the story of Lambert, "a connoisseur of mules" (212) with a "gift" for "sticking pigs" (201), and he later imagines "the last stage of the horse" as it stands at the gates of the slaughterhouse (230). The Unnamable's location corresponds to that of a room Beckett rented near the cattle market in Camden Town, London, in 1932, and in *Murphy*, Celia rents a room in the same neighborhood "between Pentonville Prison and the Metropolitan Cattle Market." Knowlson, *Damned to Fame*, 195, 63.
111. Burt, "Conflicts Around Slaughter," 126.
112. Ibid., 127, 128.
113. Müller, "Electric Stunning of Animals," 166.
114. Hill, "Electric Methods," 53.
115. Burt, "Conflicts Around Slaughter," 131.
116. Derrida, *Animal That Therefore I Am*, 26.
117. Clark, "On Being 'the Last Kantian,'" 170.
118. McHugh, *Dog*, 34.
119. Clark, "On Being 'the Last Kantian,'" 169.
120. Levinas, "Name of a Dog," 151.
121. Haraway, *Companion Species Manifesto*, 5, 29, 31.
122. Haraway, *When Species Meet*, 17.
123. Derrida, "'Eating Well,'" 278.
124. Haraway, *Companion Species Manifesto*, 45.

Coda

1. Woolf, *Flush*, 176.
2. I am indebted to Susan McHugh's incisive review of a manuscript draft of this book for the designation "literary canine studies."
3. Chez, *Victorian Dogs, Victorian Men*, 2.
4. Kreilkamp, "Anthroprosthesis, or Prosthetic Dogs," 37.
5. Wallen, *Whose Dog Are You*, 4, 28, 21.
6. Ibid., 28.
7. Kreilkamp, *Minor Creatures*, 16.
8. Chez, *Victorian Dogs, Victorian Men*, 20.
9. Kreilkamp, *Minor Creatures*, 2, 13, 180.
10. Ibid., 180.
11. Rohman, *Stalking the Subject*, 27.
12. Wallen, *Whose Dog Are You*, 28.
13. Fijn, "Dog Ears and Tails," 87, 89, 82, 84.
14. Srinivasan, "Biopolitics of Animal Being," 106.
15. Ibid.; Derrida, "'Eating Well,'" 278. In Britain, the Dogs Act of 1906 granted

police the authority to seize and detain any apparently stray dog, with unclaimed dogs subject to destruction after seven days. While subsequent legislation and collaboration with animal welfare organizations have promoted nonlethal methods of dog control like sterilization and adoption, unowned, free-roaming dogs continue to be legally defined as "*out of place*" and subject to "dispos[al]." Srinivasan, "Biopolitics of Animal Being," 109.

16. Srinivasan, "Biopolitics of Animal Being," 106. The treatment of both owned and unowned dogs in India is legally prescribed by the Prevention of Cruelty to Animals Act of 1960, to which were added in 2001 the ABC (animal birth control) rules that make it illegal to kill or remove street dogs, instead requiring municipalities to work with animal welfare organizations to spay/neuter and return the dogs.

17. Weaver, "Becoming in Kind," 692.

18. The Dangerous Dogs Act of 1991 prohibits the breeding and ownership of so-called pit bulls in the United Kingdom. In the United States, no such nationwide or statewide breed-specific legislation exists, but local ordinances ban or restrict pit bull breeding and ownership in numerous communities.

19. Dayan, *With Dogs at the Edge of Life*, xv, 5.

20. Boisseron, *Afro-Dog*, 91.

21. For an analysis of the Creole dog in the work of Césaire and other black Atlantic writers, see ibid., 81–119.

22. Weheliye, *Habeas Viscus*, 8.

BIBLIOGRAPHY

Abel, Elizabeth, Marianne Hirsch, and Elizabeth Langland, eds. *The Voyage In: Fictions of Female Development*. Hanover: University Press of New England, 1983.

Ackerley, C. J., and S. E. Gontarski, eds. *The Grove Companion to Samuel Beckett: A Reader's Guide to His Works, Life, and Thought*. New York: Grove Press, 2004.

Ackerley, Chris. "'Despised for Their Obviousness': Samuel Beckett's Dogs." In *Beckett and Animals*, edited by Mary Bryden, 177–87. Cambridge: Cambridge University Press, 2013.

Ackerley, J. R. "I Am a Beast." *Orient/West Magazine*, March–April 1964, 67–72.

———. *The Letters of J. R. Ackerley*. Edited by Neville Braybrooke. Chatham, UK: Duckworth, 1975.

———. *My Dog Tulip*. 1956. New York: New York Review of Books, 1999.

———. *My Father and Myself*. 1968. New York: New York Review of Books, 1999.

———. *We Think the World of You*. 1960. New York: New York Review of Books, 2000.

Adams, Carol J. *The Sexual Politics of Meat: A Feminist-Vegetarian Critical Theory*. 1990. 10th anniversary ed. New York: Continuum, 2000.

Adams, Maureen. *Shaggy Muses: The Dogs Who Inspired Virginia Woolf, Emily Dickinson, Elizabeth Barrett Browning, Edith Wharton, and Emily Brontë*. New York: Random House, 2007.

Alden, Patricia. *Social Mobility in the English Bildungsroman: Gissing, Hardy, Bennett, and Lawrence*. Ann Arbor: UMI Research Press, 1986.

Aquinas, St. Thomas. *Basic Writings of St. Thomas Aquinas*. Vol. 1. Edited by Anton C. Pegis. New York: Random House, 1945.

Armstrong, Tim. *Modernism, Technology, and the Body: A Cultural Study*. Cambridge: Cambridge University Press, 1998.

Atterton, Peter. "Dog and Philosophy: Does Bobby Have What It Takes to Be Moral?" In *Face to Face with Animals: Levinas and the Animal Question*, edited by Peter Atterton and Tamra Wright, 63–89. Albany: SUNY Press, 2019.

———. "Ethical Cynicism." In *Animal Philosophy: Essential Readings in Continental Thought*, edited by Matthew Calarco and Peter Atterton, 51–61. New York: Continuum, 2004.

Atterton, Peter, and Tamra Wright, eds. *Face to Face with Animals: Levinas and the Animal Question*. Albany: SUNY Press, 2019.

Auerbach, Jonathan. *Male Call: Becoming Jack London*. Durham: Duke University Press, 1996.

Baker, Steve. *The Postmodern Animal*. London: Reaktion Books, 2000.

Barnes, Djuna. *Nightwood*. 1936. New York: New Directions, 1961.

Beckett, Samuel. *Dream of Fair to Middling Women*. New York: Arcade, 1992.

———. *Endgame and Act Without Words*. Translated from the French by Samuel Beckett. New York: Grove Press, 1958.

———. "German Letter of 1937." Translated by Martin Esslin. In *Disjecta: Miscellaneous Writings and a Dramatic Fragment*, edited by Ruby Cohn, 51–54 (German), 170–73 (English translation). New York: Grove Press, 1984.

———. *How It Is*. Translated from the French by Samuel Beckett. New York: Grove Press, 1964.

———. *Mercier and Camier*. Translated from the French by Samuel Beckett. New York: Grove Press, 1974.

———. *More Pricks Than Kicks*. 1934. New York: Grove Press, 1972.

———. *Murphy*. 1938. New York: Grove Press, 1957.

———. *Nohow On: Company, Ill Seen Ill Said, Worstward Ho*. 1989. New York: Grove Press, 1996.

———. *Three Novels: Molloy, Malone Dies, The Unnamable*. Translated from the French by Patrick Bowles and Samuel Beckett. New York: Grove Press, 1955.

———. *Waiting for Godot*. Translated from the French by Samuel Beckett. New York: Grove Press, 1954.

———. *Watt*. 1953. New York: Grove Press, 1970.

Begam, Richard. "Samuel Beckett and Antihumanism." *REAL: Yearbook of Research in English and American Literature* 13 (1997): 299–312.

Bentham, Jeremy. *An Introduction to the Principles of Morals and Legislation*. Edited by J. H. Burns and H. L. A. Hart. Oxford: Oxford University Press, 1996.

Berger, John. *About Looking*. New York: Vintage, 1991.

Bergson, Henri. *Creative Evolution*. Translated by Arthur Mitchell. New York: Henry Holt, 1911.

Boisseron, Bénédicte. *Afro-Dog: Blackness and the Animal Question*. New York: Columbia University Press, 2018.

Borman, S. P. "The Borzoi, or Russian Wolfhound." In *The New Book of the Dog: A Comprehensive Natural History of British Dogs and Their Foreign Relatives, with Chapters on Law, Breeding, Kennel Management, and Veterinary Treatment*, by Robert Leighton, 180–87. London: Cassell, 1907.

Boswell, James. *The Life of Samuel Johnson*. 1791. New York: Penguin Books, 2008.

Boulter, Jonathan. *Beckett: A Guide for the Perplexed*. New York: Continuum, 2008.

Bowler, Peter. *Charles Darwin: The Man and His Influence*. Cambridge: Cambridge University Press, 1990.

Braddy, Nella. *Rudyard Kipling: Son of Empire*. New York: J. Messner, 1941.

Broe, Mary Lynn, ed. *Silence and Power: A Reevaluation of Djuna Barnes*. Carbondale: Southern Illinois University Press, 1991.

Bryden, Mary, ed. *Beckett and Animals*. Cambridge: Cambridge University Press, 2013.

Burkhardt, Richard W., Jr. *Patterns of Behavior: Konrad Lorenz, Niko Tinbergen, and the Founding of Ethology*. Chicago: University of Chicago Press, 2005.

Burroughs, John. "Real and Sham Natural History." *Atlantic Monthly*, March 1903, 298–309.

Burrows, William. "How to Train a Collie for the Show Ring." *Dog Fancier*, February 1922, 17–19.

Burt, Jonathan. "Conflicts Around Slaughter in Modernity." In *Killing Animals*, edited by the Animal Studies Group, 120–44. Urbana: University of Illinois Press, 2006.

Butterworth, Hezekiah. Introduction to *Beautiful Joe: An Autobiography*, by Marshall Saunders, 7–9. Philadelphia: Charles H. Banes, 1894.

Calarco, Matthew. *Zoographies: The Question of the Animal from Heidegger to Derrida*. New York: Columbia University Press, 2008.

Carlyle, Jane Welsh. *Letters and Memorials of Jane Welsh Carlyle*. Edited by James Anthony Froude. New York: Harper and Brothers, 1883.

Castle, Gregory. *Reading the Modernist Bildungsroman*. Gainesville: University Press of Florida, 2006.

Chambers, Ross. "The Artist as Performing Dog." *Comparative Literature* 23, no. 4 (1971): 312–24.

Chez, Keridiana W. *Victorian Dogs, Victorian Men: Affect and Animals in*

Nineteenth-Century Literature and Culture. Columbus: Ohio State University Press, 2017.

Clark, David. "On Being 'the Last Kantian in Nazi Germany': Dwelling with Animals After Levinas." In *Animal Acts: Configuring the Human in Western History*, edited by Jennifer Ham and Matthew Senior, 165–98. New York: Routledge, 1997.

Clark, Edward B. "Roosevelt on the Nature Fakirs." *Everybody's Magazine*, June 1907, 770–74.

Compton, Herbert. *The Twentieth Century Dog.* 2 vols. London: Grant Richards, 1904.

Connor, Steven. "Beckett's Animals." *Journal of Beckett Studies* 8 (1982): 29–44.

———. *Samuel Beckett: Repetition, Theory, and Text.* Aurora, CO: Davies Group, 2007.

Cooper, Frederic Taber. "Primordialism and Some Recent Books." *Bookman*, November 1909, 278–82.

Coppinger, Raymond, and Lorna Coppinger. *Dogs: A Startling New Understanding of Canine Origin, Behavior, and Evolution.* New York: Scribner, 2001.

Caughie, Pamela L. "*Flush* and the Literary Canon: Oh Where Oh Where Has That Little Dog Gone?" *Tulsa Studies in Women's Literature* 10, no. 1 (1991): 47–66.

Cowan, S. A. "Echoes of Donne, Herrick, and Southwell in Eliot's *The Waste Land*." *Yeats Eliot Review* 8, nos. 1–2 (1986): 96–102.

Cronin, Anthony. *Samuel Beckett: The Last Modernist.* New York: Da Capo Press, 1997.

Dalgliesh, James C. "The Collie." In *The New Book of the Dog: A Comprehensive Natural History of British Dogs and Their Foreign Relatives, with Chapters on Law, Breeding, Kennel Management, and Veterinary Treatment*, by Robert Leighton, 98–111. London: Cassell, 1907.

Darwin, Charles. *The Descent of Man.* 1871. Edited by James Moore and Adrian Desmond. New York: Penguin Books, 2004.

———. *The Expression of the Emotions in Man and Animals.* 1872. Edited by Francis Darwin. Mineola, NY: Dover, 2007.

———. *On the Origin of Species.* 1859. Edited by Gillian Beer. New York: Oxford University Press, 2008.

Davies, C. J. *The Kennel Handbook.* London: John Lane, 1905.

Dayan, Colin. *With Dogs at the Edge of Life.* New York: Columbia University Press, 2016.

Deichmann, Ute. *Biologists Under Hitler.* Translated by Thomas Dunlap. Cambridge: Harvard University Press, 1996.

Deleuze, Gilles, and Félix Guattari. *A Thousand Plateaus: Capitalism and Schizophrenia.* Translated by Brian Massumi. Minneapolis: University of Minnesota Press, 1987.

Derrida, Jacques. *The Animal That Therefore I Am.* Translated by David Willis. New York: Fordham University Press, 2008.

———. "'Eating Well,' or the Calculation of the Subject." Translated by Peter Connor and Avital Ronell. In *Points . . . Interviews, 1974–1994*, edited by Elisabeth Weber, 255–87. Stanford: Stanford University Press, 1995.

———. *Writing and Difference.* Translated by Alan Bass. Chicago: University of Chicago Press, 1978.

Descartes, René. *Discourse on the Method of Rightly Conducting One's Reason and Seeking the Truth in the Sciences.* Translated by Robert Stoothoff. In *The Philosophical Writings of Descartes*, vol. 1, edited and translated by John Cottingham, Robert Stoothoff, and Dugald Murdoch, 111–51. Cambridge: Cambridge University Press, 1985.

———. "To Mersenne, 11 June 1640." Translated by Anthony Kenny. In *The Philosophical Writings of Descartes*, vol. 3, edited and translated by John

Cottingham, Robert Stoothoff, Dugald Murdoch, and Anthony Kenny, 148. Cambridge: Cambridge University Press, 1991.

De Waal, Frans B. M. "Anthropomorphism and Anthropodenial: Consistency in Our Thinking About Humans and Other Animals." *Philosophical Topics* 27, no. 1 (1999): 255–80.

Diamond, Jared. *Guns, Germs, and Steel: The Fates of Human Societies*. New York: W. W. Norton, 1999.

Doctorow, E. L. *Jack London, Hemingway, and the Constitution: Selected Essays, 1977–1992*. New York: Random House, 1993.

Eliot, T. S. *The Waste Land*. 1922. In *Collected Poems, 1909–1962*, 61–86. London: Faber and Faber, 1963.

Faris, Wendy B. "Bloomsbury's Beasts: The Presence of Animals in the Texts and Lives of Bloomsbury." *Yearbook of English Studies* 37 (2007): 107–25.

Fielder, Frank S., Daniel W. Poor, and Matthias Nicoll Jr. "Rabies in the City of New York: Its Suppression a Civic Duty." *Monthly Bulletin of the Department of Health of the City of New York*, June 1914, 129–48.

Fijn, Natasha. "Dog Ears and Tails: Different Relational Ways of Being with Canines in Aboriginal Australia and Mongolia." In *Domestication Gone Wild: Politics and Practices of Multispecies Relations*, edited by Heather Anne Swanson, Marianne Elisabeth Lien, and Gro B. Ween, 72–93. Durham: Duke University Press, 2018.

Flegel, Monica. *Pets and Domesticity in Victorian Literature and Culture: Animality, Queer Relations, and the Victorian Family*. New York: Routledge, 2015.

Freud, Sigmund. *Civilization and Its Discontents*. 1930. Translated by James Strachey. New York: W. W. Norton, 2005.

Fudge, Erica. *Pets*. Durham, UK: Acumen, 2008.

Garber, Marjorie. *Dog Love*. New York: Simon and Schuster, 1996.

———. *The Use and Abuse of Literature*. New York: Anchor Books, 2011.

Gerstenberger, Donna. "Modern (Post) Modern: Djuna Barnes Among the Others." *Review of Contemporary Fiction* 13, no. 3 (1993): 33–40.

Goldman, Jane. "'Ce Chien Est à Moi': Virginia Woolf and the Signifying Dog." *Woolf Studies Annual* 13 (2007): 49–86.

Graham, Sylvester. *A Defense of the Graham System of Living: or, Remarks on Diet and Regimen*. New York: W. Applegate, 1835.

Grandin, Temple, with Catherine Johnson. *Animals in Translation: Using the Mysteries of Autism to Decode Animal Behavior*. New York: Simon and Schuster, 2005.

Grier, Katherine C. *Pets in America: A History*. Chapel Hill: University of North Carolina Press, 2006.

Griffiths, Jacqui. "Almost Human: Indeterminate Children and Dogs in *Flush* and *The Sound and the Fury*." *Yearbook of English Studies* 32 (2002): 163–76.

Grosz, Elizabeth. *The Nick of Time: Politics, Evolution, and the Untimely*. Durham: Duke University Press, 2004.

Groves, Colin P. "The Advantages and Disadvantages of Being Domesticated." *Perspectives in Human Biology* 4, no. 1 (1999): 1–12.

Gubar, Susan. "Blessings in Disguise: Cross-Dressing as Re-Dressing for Female Modernists." *Massachusetts Review* 22, no. 3 (1981): 477–508.

Haraway, Donna. *The Companion Species Manifesto: Dogs, People, and Significant Otherness*. Chicago: Prickly Paradigm Press, 2003.

———. *When Species Meet*. Minneapolis: University of Minnesota Press, 2008.

Hare, Brian, Alexandra Rosati, Juliane Kaminski, Juliane Bräuer, Josep Call, and Michael Tomasello. "The Domestication Hypothesis for Dogs' Skills with

Human Communication: A Response to Udell et al. (2008) and Wynne et al. (2008)." *Animal Behaviour* 79, no. 2 (2010): e1–e6.

Heidegger, Martin. *The Fundamental Concepts of Metaphysics: World, Finitude, Solitude.* 1983. Translated by William McNeill and Nicholas Walker. Bloomington: Indiana University Press, 1995.

Herman, David. *Narratology Beyond the Human: Storytelling and Animal Life.* New York: Oxford University Press, 2018.

Hill, Leonard. "Electric Methods of Producing Humane Slaughter." *British Veterinary Journal* 91 (1935): 51–57.

Holmberg, Tora. *Urban Animals: Crowding in Zoocities.* New York: Routledge, 2015.

Homer. *The Odyssey.* Translated by Robert Fagles. New York: Penguin Books, 1996.

Hopwood, Aubrey. "The Old English Sheepdog." In *The New Book of the Dog: A Comprehensive Natural History of British Dogs and Their Foreign Relatives, with Chapters on Law, Breeding, Kennel Management, and Veterinary Treatment,* by Robert Leighton, 112–23. London: Cassell, 1907.

Horowitz, Alexandra. *Inside of a Dog: What Dogs See, Smell, and Know.* New York: Scribner, 2009.

Hovanec, Caroline. *Animal Subjects: Literature, Zoology, and British Modernism.* Cambridge: Cambridge University Press, 2018.

Ireland, Mrs. Alexander [Annie E.]. *Life of Jane Welsh Carlyle.* London: Chatto and Windus, 1891.

Jacobs, Joela. "The Grammar of Zoopoetics: Human and Canine Language Play." In *What Is Zoopoetics? Texts, Bodies, Entanglement,* edited by Kári Driscoll and Eva Hoffman, 63–79. New York: Palgrave Macmillan, 2018.

Joachim, E. P. "The Great Dane, or German Boarhound." In *The New Book of the Dog: A Comprehensive Natural History of British Dogs and Their Foreign Relatives, with Chapters on Law, Breeding, Kennel Management, and Veterinary Treatment,* by Robert Leighton, 84–91. London: Cassell, 1907.

Kalaidjian, Andrew. "The Black Sheep: Djuna Barnes's Dark Pastoral." In *Creatural Fictions: Human-Animal Relationships in Twentieth- and Twenty-First-Century Literature,* edited by David Herman, 65–87. New York: Palgrave Macmillan, 2016.

Katz, Daniel. "Beckett's Measures: Principles of Pleasure in *Molloy* and 'First Love.'" *Modern Fiction Studies* 49, no. 2 (2003): 246–60.

Kendall, Karalyn. "The Face of a Dog: Levinasian Ethics and Human/Dog Coevolution." In *Queering the Non/Human,* edited by Noreen Giffney and Myra J. Hird, 185–204. Burlington, VT: Ashgate, 2008.

Kendall-Morwick, Karalyn. "Jack London, Nature Fakery, and the Stakes of Animal Narrative." *Evolutionary Review* 4, no. 1 (2013): 67–75.

Kennedy-Shaw, F. S. "Horse and Hound in Kipling's Works." Part 2. *Kipling Journal* (April 1944): 7–8.

Kermode, Frank. *The Sense of an Ending: Studies in the Theory of Fiction.* 1966. New York: Oxford University Press, 2000.

Kiang, Shun Yin. "Friendship; or, Representing More-Than-Human Subjectivities and Spaces in J. R. Ackerley's *My Dog Tulip.*" In *Creatural Fictions: Human-Animal Relationships in Twentieth- and Twenty-First-Century Literature,* edited by David Herman, 127–48. New York: Palgrave Macmillan, 2016.

Knowlson, James. *Damned to Fame: The Life of Samuel Beckett.* New York: Simon and Schuster, 1996.

Kreilkamp, Ivan. "Anthroprosthesis, or Prosthetic Dogs." *Victorian Review* 35, no. 2 (2009): 36–41.

———. *Minor Creatures: Persons, Animals, and the Victorian Novel*. Chicago: University of Chicago Press, 2018.

Kuzniar, Alice. *Melancholia's Dog: Reflections on Our Animal Kinship*. Chicago: University of Chicago Press, 2006.

Labor, Earle, and Robert C. Leitz III. Introduction to Jack London, *The Call of the Wild, White Fang, and Other Stories*, edited by Earle Labor and Robert C. Leitz III, ix–xxii. Oxford: Oxford University Press, 1990.

Lawrence, D. H. "Him with His Tail in His Mouth." In *Reflections on the Death of a Porcupine and Other Essays*, 127–41. Bloomington: Indiana University Press, 1963.

———. *Sons and Lovers*. 1913. New York: Penguin Books, 2006.

———. *Women in Love*. 1920. New York: Penguin Books, 1995.

Leighton, Robert. *The New Book of the Dog: A Comprehensive Natural History of British Dogs and Their Foreign Relatives, with Chapters on Law, Breeding, Kennel Management, and Veterinary Treatment*. London: Cassell, 1907.

Leonard, John Lynn. *The Care and Handling of Dogs*. New York: Doubleday, 1928.

Levinas, Emmanuel. "The Animal Interview (1986)." Translated by Peter Atterton and Tamra Wright. In *Face to Face with Animals: Levinas and the Animal Question*, edited by Peter Atterton and Tamra Wright, 3–5. Albany: SUNY Press, 2019.

———. "As If Consenting to Horror." Translated by Paula Wissing. *Critical Inquiry* 15, no. 2 (1989): 485–88.

———. *Entre-Nous: On Thinking of the Other*. Translated by Michael B. Smith and Barbara Harshav. New York: Continuum, 1998.

———. "Humanism and An-archy." In *Collected Philosophical Papers*, translated by Alphonso Lingis, 127–39. Dordrecht: Martinus Nijhoff, 1987.

———. "Is Ontology Fundamental?" Translated by Simon Critchley, Peter Atterton, and Graham Noctor. In *Emmanuel Levinas: Basic Philosophical Writings*, edited by Adriaan T. Peperzak, Simon Critchley, and Robert Bernasconi, 1–10. Bloomington: Indiana University Press, 1996.

———. "The Name of a Dog, or Natural Rights." 1963. In *Difficult Freedom: Essays on Judaism*, 151–53. Translated by Seán Hand. Baltimore: Johns Hopkins University Press, 1990.

———. "Substitution." 1968. Translated by Alphonso Lingis, Robert Bernasconi, and Simon Critchley. In *Emmanuel Levinas: Basic Philosophical Writings*, edited by Adriaan T. Peperzak, Simon Critchley, and Robert Bernasconi, 79–96. Bloomington: Indiana University Press, 1996.

———. *Totality and Infinity: An Essay on Exteriority*. Translated by Alphonso Lingis. Pittsburgh: Duquesne University Press, 1969.

Levy, Eric P. "Living Without a Life: The Disintegration of the Christian-Humanist Synthesis in *Molloy*." *Studies in the Novel* 33, no. 1 (2001): 80–94.

Lewis, Wyndham. *Tarr: The 1918 Version*. Edited by Paul O'Keeffe. Santa Rosa, CA: Black Sparrow Press, 1996.

Litvag, Irving. *The Master of Sunnybank: A Biography of Albert Payson Terhune*. 1977. Lincoln, NE: iUniverse, 2001.

Llewelyn, John. "Am I Obsessed by Bobby? (Humanism of the Other Animal)." In *Re-Reading Levinas*, edited by Robert Bernasconi and Simon Critchley, 234–45. Bloomington: Indiana University Press, 1991.

London, Jack. *Before Adam*. 1907. Lincoln: University of Nebraska Press, 2000.

———. *The Call of the Wild*. 1903. In *The Call of the Wild, White Fang, and Other Stories*, edited by Earle Labor and Robert C. Leitz III, 1–88. Oxford: Oxford University Press, 1990.

———. "The Other Animals." *Collier's*, September 1908, 10–11, 25–26.

———. *White Fang*. 1906. In *The Call of the Wild, White Fang, and Other Stories*, edited by Earle Labor and Robert C. Leitz III, 89–291. Oxford: Oxford University Press, 1990.

Lopez, Barry. *Of Wolves and Men*. 1978. New York: Simon and Schuster, 2004.

Lorenz, Konrad. "Companions as Factors in the Bird's Environment." 1935. In *Studies in Animal and Human Behaviour*, 1:101–258. Translated by Robert Martin. London: Methuen, 1970.

———. Foreword to *The Wild Canids: Their Systematics, Behavioral Ecology, and Evolution*, edited by M. W. Fox, vii–xii. New York: Van Nostrand Reinhold, 1975.

———. *King Solomon's Ring: New Light on Animal Ways*. 1952. Translated by Marjorie Kerr Wilson. London: Routledge, 2002.

———. *Man Meets Dog*. 1954. Translated by Marjorie Kerr Wilson. London: Routledge, 2002.

———. *On Aggression*. Translated by Marjorie Kerr Wilson. New York: Harcourt, 1966.

Lukács, Georg. *The Theory of the Novel: A Historico-Philosophical Essay on the Forms of Great Epic Literature*. 1920. Translated by Anna Bostock. Cambridge: MIT Press, 1971.

Lundblad, Michael. "From Animal to Animality Studies." *PMLA* 124 (2009): 496–502.

McCormack, W. J. "Samuel Beckett and the Negro Anthology." *Hermathena: A Trinity College Dublin Review*, quatercentenary issue (1992): 73–92.

McHugh, Susan. *Animal Stories: Narrating Across Species Lines*. Minneapolis: University of Minnesota Press, 2011.

———. *Dog*. London: Reaktion Books, 2004.

———. "Marrying My Bitch: J. R. Ackerley's Pack Sexualities." *Critical Inquiry* 27, no. 1 (2000): 21–41.

Meedom, Peter J. "Impersonal Love: *Nightwood*'s Poetics of Mournful Entanglement." In *What Is Zoopoetics? Texts, Bodies, Entanglement*, edited by Kári Driscoll and Eva Hoffman, 213–33. New York: Palgrave Macmillan, 2018.

Moorjani, Angela. "The Dancing Bees in Samuel Beckett's *Molloy*: The Rapture of Unknowing." In *Beckett and Animals*, edited by Mary Bryden, 165–76. Cambridge: Cambridge University Press, 2013.

Müller, Max. "The Electric Stunning of Animals for Slaughter from the Humane Standpoint." *British Veterinary Journal* 85 (1929): 164–66.

Nash, Richard. "Animal Nomenclature: Facing Other Animals." In *Humans and Other Animals in Eighteenth-Century British Culture: Representation, Hybridity, Ethics*, edited by Frank Palmeri, 101–18. Burlington, VT: Ashgate, 2006.

Nel, Philip. *The Avant-Garde and American Postmodernity: Small Incisive Shocks*. Jackson: University Press of Mississippi, 2002.

Nordau, Max. *Degeneration*. 1892. Edited by George L. Mosse. Lincoln: University of Nebraska Press, 1968.

Parker, Peter. *Ackerley: A Life of J. R. Ackerley*. New York: Farrar, Straus and Giroux, 1989.

Peterson, Clell T. "London and Lorenz: A Brief Note on Men and Dogs." *Jack London Newsletter* 12 (1979): 46–49.

Plumb, Cheryl J. Introduction to *Nightwood: The Original Version and Related Drafts*, by Djuna Barnes, vii–xxvi. Normal, IL: Dalkey Archive Press, 1995.

Puchner, Martin. "Performing the Open: Actors, Animals, Philosophers." *Drama Review* 51, no. 1 (2007): 21–32.

Regan, Tom. *The Case for Animal Rights*. 2nd ed. Berkeley: University of California Press, 2004.

Reid, Panthea. *Art and Affection: A Life of Virginia Woolf*. Oxford: Oxford University Press, 1996.

Rilke, Rainer Maria. "Black Cat." 1908. In *Ahead of All Parting: The Selected Poetry and Prose of Rainer Maria Rilke*, edited and translated by Stephen Mitchell, 71. New York: Modern Library, 1995.

———. "A Meeting." In *Ahead of All Parting: The Selected Poetry and Prose of Rainer Maria Rilke*, edited and translated by Stephen Mitchell, 283–85. New York: Modern Library, 1995.

———. Preface to *Mitsou: Forty Drawings*, by Balthus. 1921. In *Ahead of All Parting: The Selected Poetry and Prose of Rainer Maria Rilke*, edited and translated by Stephen Mitchell, 304–7. New York: Modern Library, 1995.

Ritvo, Harriet. *The Animal Estate: The English and Other Creatures in the Victorian Age*. Cambridge: Harvard University Press, 1987.

Rohman, Carrie. "On Singularity and the Symbolic: The Threshold of the Human in Calvino's *Mr. Palomar*." *Criticism* 51, no. 1 (2009): 63–78.

———. *Stalking the Subject: Modernism and the Animal*. New York: Columbia University Press, 2009.

Rosenthal, Michael. *Virginia Woolf*. New York: Routledge and Kegan Paul, 1979.

Ryan, Derek. *Virginia Woolf and the Materiality of Theory: Sex, Animal, Life*. Edinburgh: Edinburgh University Press, 2013.

Sackville-West, Vita. *The Letters of Vita Sackville-West to Virginia Woolf*. Edited by Louise DeSalvo and Mitchell A. Leaska. San Francisco: Cleis Press, 1984.

Sandburg, Charles A. [Carl]. "Jack London: A Common Man." 1906. Reprinted in *Jack London: A Study of the Short Fiction*, by Jeanne Campbell Reesman, 227–31. New York: Twayne, 1999.

Saunders, Marshall. *Beautiful Joe: An Autobiography*. Philadelphia: Charles H. Banes, 1894.

Sax, Boria. *Animals in the Third Reich*. New York: Continuum, 2000.

Scott, Bonnie Kime. *In the Hollow of the Wave: Virginia Woolf and Modernist Uses of Nature*. Charlottesville: University of Virginia Press, 2012.

Seitler, Dana. "Down on All Fours: Atavistic Perversions and the Science of Desire from Frank Norris to Djuna Barnes." *American Literature* 73, no. 3 (2001): 525–62.

Sewell, Anna. *Black Beauty*. 1877. New York: Penguin Books, 2011.

Sheehan, Paul. *Modernism, Narrative, and Humanism*. Cambridge: Cambridge University Press, 2004.

———. "Zoomorphism." In *The Grove Companion to Samuel Beckett: A Reader's Guide to His Works, Life, and Thought*, edited by C. J. Ackerley and S. E. Gontarski, 662–63. New York: Grove Press, 2004.

Shipman, Pat Lee. "Do the Eyes Have It?" *American Scientist*, May–June 2012, 198–201.

Singer, Peter. *Animal Liberation*. 3rd ed. New York: HarperCollins, 2002.

Sloan, Alfred P., Jr. *My Years with General Motors*. New York: Doubleday, 1990.

Smith, Craig. "Across the Widest Gulf: Nonhuman Subjectivity in Virginia Woolf's *Flush*." *Twentieth-Century Literature* 48, no. 3 (2002): 348–61.

Snaith, Anna. "Of Fanciers, Footnotes, and Fascism: Virginia Woolf's *Flush*." *Modern Fiction Studies* 48 (2002): 614–36.

Snow, C. P. *The Two Cultures*. 1959. Cambridge: Cambridge University Press, 1998.

Solomon, Philip Howard. "Samuel Beckett's *Molloy*: A Dog's Life." *French Review* 41, no. 1 (1967): 84–91.

Squier, Susan Merrill. *Virginia Woolf and London: The Sexual Politics of the City*. Chapel Hill: University of North Carolina Press, 1985.

Srinivasan, Krithika. "The Biopolitics of Animal Being and Welfare: Dog Control and Care in the UK and India."

Transactions of the Institute of British Geographers 38, no. 1 (2013): 106–19.

Tenner, Edward. "Citizen Canine." Wilson Quarterly 22, no. 3 (1998): 71–79.

Terhune, Albert Payson. *Lad: A Dog*. New York: E. P. Dutton, 1919.

Thayer, Gwyneth Anne. *Going to the Dogs: Greyhound Racing, Animal Activism, and American Popular Culture*. Lawrence: University Press of Kansas, 2013.

Thomas, Elizabeth Marshall. *The Hidden Life of Dogs*. New York: Houghton Mifflin, 1993. Reprint, New York: Mariner Books, 2010.

Uexküll, Jakob von. *A Foray into the Worlds of Animals and Humans*. 1934. Translated by Joseph D. O'Neil. Minneapolis: University of Minnesota Press, 2010.

Uhlmann, Anthony. *Beckett and Poststructuralism*. Cambridge: Cambridge University Press, 1999.

Wallen, Martin. *Whose Dog Are You? The Technology of Dog Breeds and the Aesthetics of Modern Human-Canine Relations*. East Lansing: Michigan State University Press, 2017.

Warren, Diane. *Djuna Barnes' Consuming Fictions*. Burlington, VT: Ashgate, 2008.

Weaver, Harlan. "Becoming in Kind: Race, Class, Gender, and Nation in Cultures of Dog Rescue and Dogfighting." American Quarterly 65, no. 3 (2013): 689–709.

Weheliye, Alexander. *Habeas Viscus: Racializing Assemblages, Biopolitics, and Black Feminist Theories of the Human*. Durham: Duke University Press, 2014.

Weil, Kari. *Thinking Animals: Why Animal Studies Now?* New York: Columbia University Press, 2012.

Weller, Shane. "Not Rightly Human: Beckett and Animality." *Samuel Beckett Today / Aujourd'hui* 19 (2008): 211–21.

Wolfe, Cary. *Animal Rites: American Culture, the Discourse of Species, and Posthumanist Theory*. Chicago: University of Chicago Press, 2003.

———. *What Is Posthumanism?* Minneapolis: University of Minnesota Press, 2010.

Woolf, Virginia. "Character in Fiction." 1924. In *The Essays of Virginia Woolf*, vol. 3, edited by Andrew McNeillie, 420–38. London: Hogarth Press, 1988.

———. "A Character Sketch." 1920. In *The Essays of Virginia Woolf*, vol. 3, edited by Andrew McNeillie, 255–58. London: Hogarth Press, 1988.

———. *The Diary of Virginia Woolf*. Edited by Anne Olivier Bell and Andrew McNeillie. 5 vols. London: Hogarth Press, 1977–84.

———. *Flush: A Biography*. 1933. New York: Harcourt, 1983.

———. *The Letters of Virginia Woolf*. Edited by Nigel Nicolson and Joanne Trautmann. 6 vols. New York: Harcourt, 1977–82.

———. "Modern Fiction." 1921. In *The Essays of Virginia Woolf*, vol. 4, edited by Andrew McNeillie, 157–65. London: Hogarth Press, 1994.

———. *Mrs. Dalloway*. 1925. New York: Harcourt, 1981.

———. *A Passionate Apprentice: The Early Journals, 1897–1909*. Edited by Mitchell A. Leaska. New York: Harcourt, 1990.

———. *A Room of One's Own*. 1929. New York: Harcourt Brace, 1991.

———. "Women Novelists." 1918. In *The Essays of Virginia Woolf*, vol. 2, edited by Andrew McNeillie, 314–17. London: Hogarth Press, 1987.

Worboys, Michael. "Inventing Dog Breeds: Jack Russell Terriers." *Humanimalia: A Journal of Human/Animal Interface Studies* 10, no. 1 (2018): 44–73.

Worboys, Michael, Julie-Marie Strange, and Neil Pemberton. *The Invention of the Modern Dog: Breed and Blood in Victorian Britain*. Baltimore: Johns Hopkins University Press, 2018.

Wordsworth, William. "Lines Written a Few Miles Above Tintern Abbey." 1798. In *William Wordsworth: The Major Works*, edited by Stephen Gill, 131–35. New York: Oxford University Press, 2008.

———. "Ode ('There Was a Time')." 1815. In *William Wordsworth: The Major Works*, edited by Stephen Gill, 297–302. New York: Oxford University Press, 2008.

———. Preface to *Lyrical Ballads*. 1802. In *William Wordsworth: The Major Works*, edited by Stephen Gill, 595–615. New York: Oxford University Press, 2008.

Yeoh, Gilbert. "Beckett's Persistent Humanism: Ethics and Epistemology in *Molloy*." *AUMLA: Journal of the Australasian Universities Language and Literature Association* 103 (2005): 109–35.

INDEX

Abel, Elizabeth, 86
Ackerley, Chris, 146
Ackerley, J. R., 18, 94–96, 110–28
    on Alsatians, 95, 110–28
    background, 95–96
    compared with Terhune, 95, 113, 127–28
    as a dog owner, 111
    and homosexuality, 95–96, 118
    on interspecies relationships, 126
    My Dog Tulip, 18, 95, 111–26
    "New Dog," 123, 128
    and *Umwelt*, 125–26
    We Think the World of You, 95, 111–26
Alden, Patricia, 73
Alsatian (breed), 18, 45, 95, 110–26
American Kennel Club, 12, 96
Anglocentrism. *See* Eurocentrism
animal control practices, 11
animal cruelty, 60–61, 64
Animal Estate, The (Ritvo), 98–99
animal narrative tradition, 60–70, 77–78
Animal Stories (McHugh), 15, 23–24, 57
Animal That Therefore I Am, The (Derrida), 3, 131–32
animals
    animal origins of humanity, 5, 53, 168
    animal studies, 166–67
    Cartesian binary (human vs. animals), 131
    communication, 82–86
    ethical treatment of, 143–44
    fictional portrayals of, 22
    in heat, 74–75
    human repression of animality, 52
    human/animal divide, 9, 57
    kinship with humans, 6–7
    and limited human understanding (*Umwelt*), 80–82, 85–86
    man as animal, 141–42
    as metaphor for dehumanization, 4, 131
    in modernism, 15, 92–96
    as nonlinguistic beings, 4
    as Other, 2, 158–64
    as sacrificial, 158–64
    self-awareness, 79–81
    significance of animality in humans, 2
    sterilization, 119–21
    suffering of, 60–61, 64, 134–35, 143–44
    and the unconscious, 52
    in zoos/captivity, 9–10
Animals in the Third Reich (Sax), 44
anthropocentrism, 61–63
antihumanism, 148–58
Aristotle, 85, 131
Armstrong, Tim, 5, 7
Atterton, Peter, 132
Auerbach, Jonathan, 37–38, 67
Aureus (dog breeds), 41, 44, 45–47, 53

Baker, Steve, 15, 16
Barnes, Djuna, 1–4, 16, 19
Beames, Thomas, 60
Beautiful Joe (Saunders), 17, 55–56, 61–64
Beckett, Samuel, 4, 18–19, 129–65
    and animals as metaphors, 131
    and antihumanism, 129–30, 148–58
    Company, 134–35
    and Catholicism, 149–50
    depiction of animal suffering, 134–38, 158–64
    depiction of dogs, 131–32, 133, 135–38, 146–61, 164–65
    depiction of equines, 135
    and the human/animal boundary, 131
    and humanism, 129–30, 156–58
    on language, 154–56
    and Levinas, 132, 140
    and posthumanism, 130–31, 133, 157–58
    Malone Dies, 129, 135, 153–54
    Molloy, 18, 129, 131–32, 146–50, 151–54, 154–58
    on slaughterhouses, 158–64
    and species identity, 129, 149
    Three Novels, 129–30, 137–38, 152–53, 154–58

Beckett, Samuel (*continued*)
　The Unnamable, 129, 152–54, 154–56
　Waiting for Godot, 149
　Watt, 18, 129, 132–33, 135–37, 149–50, 159
Before Adam (London), 24, 25–29, 32
　and canine domestication, 25–29
　on dogs and human evolution, 27, 32
　humanoid characters in, 25–27
　and the Pinocchio hypothesis, 36
Begam, Richard, 129
Bell, Clive, 74
Bell, Quentin, 74
Bentham, Jeremy, 134
Berger, John, 9–10
Bergson, Henri, 66
bestiality, 1–2
Bildung. *See* bildungsroman
bildungsroman, 67–69, 77–88
Biologists Under Hitler (Deichmann), 42
Black Beauty (Sewell), 17, 55–56, 61–64
"Black Cat" (Rilke), 10–11
Boulter, Jonathan, 130
Bowler, Peter, 5–6
breeders. *See under* breeding
breeding, 110–26
　and the aristocracy, 102–3
　breeders, 96–97
　as depicted by Terhune, 105–6
　dogs as status symbols, 98–99
　and domestication, 13, 32–41
　excesses of, 106–7
　and industrial modernity, 14–15, 92–96
　and physical beauty, 101–2
　resultant mental degeneration, 47–48
　standards of, 11, 12–13
　thoroughbreds, 100–103
　utility in the modern world, 103–5
　and working dogs, 110–11
　See also individual breeds; kennel clubs
British Kennel Club. *See* Kennel Club (British)
Browning, Elizabeth Barrett, 55, 61, 78, 81, 88
Browning, Robert, 55
Burkhardt, Richard W. Jr., 42–44
Burroughs, John, 22

Call of the Wild, The (London), 21–24
　as an allegory, 21–22
　and bildungsroman, 67–69
　compared with Terhune's *Lad: A Dog*, 99, 103
　compared with Woolf's *Flush*, 64–70
　critical reception of, 21–22
　on dogs and human evolution, 27, 32–34
　dogs as protectors in, 29
　domestication/coevolution in, 32–34, 36–40, 52–53
　and domestication as degeneracy, 47–51, 69
　and dogs' relationships with humans, 39–40
canines. *See* dogs
Cartesianism, 57, 131, 134, 136–37, 141, 143, 150–53
Castle, Gregory, 77
cats, 10–11, 139–40
Césaire, Aimé, 171–72
Chapman, Frank, 56
cheetahs, 7–8
Chez, Keridiana, 38–39, 167–68
chow (breed), 40–41, 44, 45, 47
city life. *See* modernity; urbanization
Civilization and Its Discontents (Freud), 12, 27
Clark, David, 143
cocker spaniel (breed), 17, 55, 73–74, 78, 84, 87
coevolution of dogs and humans. *See under* evolution
Coleman, Emily, 1, 3
collie (breed), 18, 93, 94–95, 96–110
Companion Species Manifesto (Haraway), 16
Company (Beckett), 134–35
Compton, Herbert, 12, 13, 93–94
concentration camps, 132–33, 139–40
Confessions of a Young Man (Moore), 73
Connor, Steve, 131–32, 150–51
Conrad, Joseph, 2, 19
contingent mutability of species, 5
Coppinger, Lorna, 23, 24, 33–34, 35, 46–47
Coppinger, Raymond, 23, 24, 33–34, 35, 46–47
Cowan, S. A., 4

Dalgliesh, James C., 92–94

"Dante and the Lobster" (Beckett), 134
Darwin, Charles, 2, 4–6, 17, 33–34, 35, 43
    See also Darwinism; Social Darwinism
Darwinism, 4–6, 17, 19, 20, 34, 59–60, 144
    See also Darwin, Charles; Social
        Darwinism
Davies, C. J., 103
Dayan, Colin, 171
Degeneration (Nordau), 11–12
Deichmann, Ute, 42
Deleuze, Gilles, 10, 14
Derrida, Jacques, 3, 6, 16, 85–86, 131–33, 139–40, 142–43, 146, 147–48, 152, 154, 161
Descartes, René, 131, 134, 150–51
Diamond, Jared, 7–8
dog breeders. *See* breeding
dog fanciers. *See* breeding
Dog Love (Garber), 57
dog shows, 96–97, 106–7
    as an allegory for modern life (Terhune), 107–10
dogs
    as blurring the species boundary, 4–5
    and breed-based superiority, 100–101
    breeds of, 14
    as coevolutionary partners of humanity, 7–10, 14–16, 24, 29–31, 32–41, 51–52, 133–34
    commercial dog food, 11
    communication with humans, 8–9, 84–86
    and deconstruction of the human, 20
    domestication of, 7–10, 25–29, 32–41, 77–78
    domestication as degeneration, 41–51, 69–70
    domestication of humans, 7–10, 29–31
    early dogs and humans, 24–32
    evolution of, 176–77
    as family members, 13, 39
    in heat, 74–75, 115, 120–21
    human suppresion of the sexual agency of, 117–20
    as hunters 35–36
    and industrialization, 11–12, 92–96
    language of, 62
    and limited human understanding (*Umwelt*), 80–82, 85–86
    love for humans, 40
    marking of territory (urination), 123–25
    as a mirror for human narcissism, 10, 14–15
    and modernism, 7, 15, 19–20
    overdomestication, 56–57, 69–70
    overpopulation, 120–21
    and pack mentality, 31–32, 36, 39–40, 44–45
    as protectors of humans, 29–31
    public regulation of dog waste, 121–22
    puppy breeding, 11
    as reinforcing racial/social hierarchies, 172
    self-awareness, 79–81, 180
    sense of smell, 12, 80, 86, 123
    and slaughterhouses, 163–64
    sterilization, 119–21
    stray dogs, 10
    as symbols of degradation in literature, 131–32
    and the pet-prosthesis model, 180–81
    and the Pinocchio hypothesis, 33–34, 36
    and their masters, 38–39, 84–85, 167, 177
    in urban spaces, 18, 60–61, 92–96, 110–28
    in the Victorian era, 166–67
    and violence against other animals, 133–34
    and "working breeds," 181
domestication, 7–9
    and brain size, 8–9
    as degeneration (overdomestication), 41–51, 69–70
    as depicted by Jack London, 25–29, 32–41, 69–70
    as depicted by Virginia Woolf, 77–78
    sterilization, 119–21
Doyle, Freddie, 95

Eliot, T. S., 2, 4, 19
Eurocentrism, 170–72, 179
Everybody's Magazine, 24
evolution, 6–7, 14–15
    canine evolution, 17, 36–37
    coevolution of dogs and humans, 7–10, 14–16, 24, 27, 29–32, 32–41, 51–52
    as depicted by Jack London, 25–29

evolution (*continued*)
   as depicted by Lorenz, 29–32, 40–41, 44, 53–54
   early dogs and humans, 24–32
   Pinocchio hypothesis (of dog origin), 33–34, 36
   See also Darwin, Charles; Darwinism

Faulkner, William, 16, 17
feminism, 70–77
Flush (Woolf), 4, 17, 55–91, 166
   and the animal narrative tradition, 60–70
   animal suffering in, 60–61, 64
   compared with London's *Call of the Wild*, 64–70
   compared with London's *White Fang*, 68–69
   compared with Terhune's *Lad: A Dog*, 99
   compared with Woolf's other works, 58–59, 77–78, 86, 89
   critical response to, 56–58, 89–91
   domestication, 69–70, 77–78
   as a feminist allegory, 59, 70–77
   and male privilege and feminism, 70–77
   and multispecies connections, 66, 77–88
   narrative techniques in, 61–62, 64–70, 80–82
   and nonhuman experience, 57–58
   as social commentary, 56, 92
   as subversively queer, 73–75
   summary of plot, 55–56
   Woolf's hesitancy regarding the project, 55–56
Forster, E. M., 96
Freud, Sigmund, 12, 27, 61–62
Fudge, Erica, 15

Garber, Marjorie, 57, 58, 64
German shepherd (breed). *See* Alsatian
German Society for Psychology, 42
Gerstenberger, Donna, 4
Goethe, Johann Wolfgang von, 67
Goldman, Jane, 71
Graham, Sylvester, 43
Grandin, Temple, 9
Great Dane (breed), 183
greyhound (breed), 175

Grier, Katherine C., 120–21
Groves, Colin, 8
Grosz, Elizabeth, 6
Guattari, Félix, 10, 14
Guns, Germs, and Steel, 7

Haraway, Donna, 3, 4, 8, 9, 10, 16, 132
heat. *See under* animals; dogs
Heidegger, Martin, 81, 85, 131, 141, 160–61
Herman, David, 20, 86
heteronormativity, 73–75
   subversion of, 74, 75, 118, 169, 183
   See also sexuality
Holmberg, Tora, 123
Holocaust: compared with slaughterhouses, 160–61
   See also concentration camps; Levinas, Emmanuel; Nazism
Homo sapiens, 8, 25–26, 27, 30
Horowitz, Alexandra, 79–80, 123–25
Hovanec, Caroline, 20
humanism, 6, 18, 67–68
   and moral education, 67–68
   and Samuel Beckett, 129–30
   and Western constructions of the animal, 3–4
hunting, 18
Hurston, Zora Neale, 171–72

Ice Age, 35
industrialization, 11
Inside of a Dog (Horowitz), 79–80, 123–24
interspecies relations, 5
Invention of the Modern Dog, The (Worboys et al.), 14

jackals, 29–32, 34–36, 44
Jaensch, Erich, 42
Joyce, James, 4, 17, 73

Kalaidjian, Andrew, 2–3
Kantianism, 131, 132, 139, 141, 143, 163
Katz, Daniel, 138
Kennel Club (British), 12, 102–3
kennel clubs, 13–14
   See also specific club names
Kermode, Frank, 19
Kiang, Shun Yin, 117, 123, 125

King Solomon's Ring (Lorenz), 23, 36, 40–41,
   canine agency in evolution, 40–41,
      53–54, 168
   dog breeds, 44–45, 46–47
   domestication of dogs, 44
Kipling, Rudyard, 61–62
Knight, Eric, 94
Kreilkamp, Ivan, 20, 167–68
Kuzniar, Alice, 40

Labor, Earle, 22
Lacan, Jacques, 79, 85, 131, 141
Lad: A Dog (Terhune), 94–95, 96–110
   as an allegory for the modern city, 107–10
   based on Terhune's dog, 97–98
   breed of, 97–98, 99–100
   compared with Ackerley's *We Think the World of You*, 113, 127–28
   compared with London's *Call of the Wild*, 99, 103
   compared with Woolf's *Flush*, 99
   depictions of the aristocracy, 102–3
   idyllic setting of, 94–95, 96, 100
   as inspiration for Lassie, 94
   and the modern world, 103–5, 107–10, 127
   as questioning the excesses of breeding, 106–7
   and "snobbery," 99–101, 103
   and thoroughbreds, 100–103, 105–6
Lassie, 94
Lawrence, D. H., 2, 15–16, 19
Leighton, Robert, 12, 13, 93–94
Leitz, Robert, 22
lesbianism, 75
   See also sexuality
Levinas, Emmanuel, 18–19, 131, 132–65
   and antihumanist ethics, 132, 141–43
   and Beckett, 132, 140
   and Cartesianism, 151–53
   on concentration camps, 132–33, 139–40
   and Darwinism, 144–45
   and Derrida, 152
   depiction of dogs, 132–33, 139–40, 146, 164–65
   and Descartes, 151–53
   ethics of alterity, 132
   and humanist ethics, 132, 141
   and Kantianism, 131, 132, 139, 141, 143, 163
   man as animal, 141–42
   and neohumanist ethics, 146, 151–52
   and the Other, 141, 142–43, 153–54
   and posthumanist ethics, 133
   on the relationship between humans and animals, 142–43, 144–46
   human self-consciousness, 152, 154–55
   on language, 153–54
   on slaughterhouses, 159–64
   on vegetarianism, 159–60
Levy, Eric P., 130
Lewis, Wyndham, 11–12
literary canine studies, 166–72
Llewelyn, John, 160
London, Jack, 16–17, 21–54
   ambivalence about domestication, 41, 47–51, 69–70
   and American naturalism, 21
   backlash against, 22–23, 24, 55
   Before Adam, 24, 32, 36
   and bildungsroman, 67–69
   The Call of the Wild, 21–24, 32–34, 36–40, 48–51, 52–53, 64–70
   canine characters of, 24
   critical reception of, 21–23
   and the human-dog relationship, 24, 25
   influence of, 23
   as juvenile fiction, 21
   and Lorenz, 23, 31
   as a "nature faker," 22–23, 24, 55
   and Terhune, 94–95, 99, 103
   White Fang, 24, 36–40, 47–51, 68–69
   and Woolf, 64–70
Lopez, Barry, 22
Lorenz, Konrad, 16–17, 21–54
   ambivalence about domestication, 41–51, 53–54
   and coevolution, 29–31
   and dogs as protectors, 30, 31
   and the human-dog relationship, 24
   and the influence of Jack London, 23, 31, 40
   King Solomon's Ring, 23, 36, 40–41, 44, 53–54
   Lupus vs. Aureus breeds, 44–47

Lorenz, Konrad (*continued*)
    Man Meets Dog (Lorenz), 23, 29–32,
        34–36, 40–41, 44, 52, 53–54
    and Nazism, 42–44
    and the Nobel Prize, 43–44
    On Agression, 23
    theory of canine origins, 24, 44
Lukács, Georg, 19–20
Lupus (breeds), 41, 44, 45–47, 53, 69

Madison Square Garden, 107
male privilege, 70–77
Malone Dies (Beckett), 129, 135, 153–54
    and animal labor, 135
    and species identity, 129
Man Meets Dog (Lorenz), 23, 29–32
    coevolution in, 29–31, 52, 53–54
    dog breeds, 40–41, 44–45, 46–47
    domestication of dogs, 34–36, 44
Marc, Franz, 15–16
marking of territory. *See under* dogs
master (of a dog). *See under* dogs
McHugh, Susan, 15, 19–20, 23–24, 57, 118, 120
Meedom, Peter, 2
"Meeting, A" (Rilke), 10–11, 14–15
Minor Creatures (Kreilkamp), 20
Mitford, Mary Russell, 55, 78
"Modern Fiction" (Woolf), 58, 61
modernism
    and the canine condition, 1–20, 92–96
    dogs as metaphors, 4
    and literary canine studies, 166–72
    narration in, 20
    novels, 20
    significance of dogs in, 7, 15
    and the species problematic, 5
Modernism, Narrative, and Humanism
    (Sheehan), 5, 19
Modernism, Technology, and the Body
    (Armstrong), 5
modernity
    and dog breeding, 14–15, 92–96
    dogs in the urban setting, 110–28
    and fragmentation/alienation, 11, 53
    and overcivilization/degeneration, 41,
        51–52, 53, 92–96
Molloy (Beckett), 18, 129, 131–32, 146–50,
    151–54, 154–58
    depiction of dogs, 132–33, 146–50, 157–58

    depiction of slaughterhouses, 158
    and dogs as Other, 131–32
    and language, 154–56
    and species identity, 129, 149
Moore, George, 73
Moorjani, Angela, 130
Mrs. Dalloway (Woolf), 58–59, 77–78, 86, 89
mutts, 175
My Dog Tulip (Ackerley), 18, 95–96, 111,
    114–26
    as analogy for suppressed homosexual
        desire, 118
    animal sexuality, 115–20
    breeding, 115–18
    dogs in the urban setting, 111, 114–15
    and images of the working class, 114
    marking of territory, 123–25
    overpopulation of dogs, 120–21
    plot of, 114–18
    on the public regulation of dog waste,
        121–22
    and *Umwelt*, 125–26

"The Name of a Dog, or Natural Rights"
    (Levinas), 132, 139–40, 143–44
narcissism, 10, 14–15
Nash, Richard, 139, 144
National Socialism. *See* Nazism
natural selection, 6
    See also Darwin, Charles
nature: human subordination of, 9–10
Nazism, 42–44, 132–33, 139–40
Neandertals, 8
neohumanism, 18
neutering. *See* sterilization
New Book of the Dog, The (Leighton), 12, 13,
    92–94
    See also breeding
Newton, Isaac, 6
Nightwood (Barnes), 1–4, 16
Nordau, Max, 11–12, 118

On Aggression (Lorenz), 23
On the Origin of Species (Darwin), 6–7,
    33–34
organic repression, 12, 52
    See also Freud, Sigmund

pack mentality, 31–32, 35–36, 39–40, 44–45, 67–68, 176
    See also under dogs
patriarchy, 70–77
Payson Terhune, Albert. *See* Terhune, Albert Payson
pedigree. *See* breeding
Pemberton, Neil, 14
pets. *See* cats; dogs
phallocentrism, 2, 60, 69, 71, 77, 89–90, 183
phallus, 183
Pinocchio hypothesis (of dog origin), 33–34, 36
Portrait of the Artist as a Young Man, A (Joyce), 73
posthumanism, 15, 130–31
Postmodern Animal, The (Baker), 15, 16
postmodernism, 15
Pound, Ezra, 17
Puchner, Martin, 131
purebred. *See* breeding

Queenie (J. R. Ackerley's character/dog), 95–96, 120, 125–26
    as metaphor for homosexuality, 95–96
    sterilization of, 120
    in the urban setting, 95–96, 111
    See also Ackerley, J. R.
queer subversion of heteronormativity, 73–75, 118, 169, 183
    See also sexuality

Rilke, Rainer Maria, 10–11, 14–15
Ritvo, Harriet, 98–99
Rohman, Carrie, 2, 4, 5–6, 15, 19, 52, 133, 169
Room of One's Own, A (Woolf), 70–72
Roosevelt, Theodore, 22
Ryan, Derek, 57

Sackville-West, Vita, 75
Saint Bernard (breed), 57
Sandburg, Carl, 21–22
Saunders, Marshall, 17, 55–56, 61–64
Sax, Boria, 44
Scott, Bonnie Kime, 56
Scottish terrier (breed), 47
Seitler, Dana, 4
Sense of an Ending, The (Kermode), 19
Sewell, Anna, 17, 55–56, 61–64

sexuality
    animal, 74–75, 115
    heteronormative, 73–75
    homosexuality, 95–96
    lesbian, 75
    queer, 73–75, 118, 169, 183
    suppression of, 118–19
Sheehan, Paul, 5, 19, 66
Shipman, Pat, 8
show dogs, 13
slaughterhouses, 133, 135, 158–64
sled dogs, 37–38, 176
    See also dogs
Smith, Craig, 56–57
Snow, C. P., 21
Social Darwinism, 5
    See also Darwin, Charles; Darwinism
Solomon, Philip Howard, 4, 147
spaying. *See* sterilization
Stalking the Subject (Rohman), 2, 5, 15
Stein, Gertrude, 17
Stephanitz, Max von, 110–11
Stephen, Julia, 56
sterilization: moral implications of, 119–21
    See also under animals; dogs
Strachey, Lytton, 58
Strange, Julie-Marie, 14
stray dogs. *See under* dogs

Taber Cooper, Frederic, 21–22
Tarr (Lewis), 11–12
Terhune, Albert Payson, 18, 94–110, 127–28
    and the American Kennel Club, 96
    antiurbanism/antimodernism of, 96, 103–5, 107–10, 127
    background, 94–97
    and collies, 18, 94–95, 96–110
    compared with Ackerley, 95, 113, 127–28
    compared with London, 99, 103
    compared with Woolf, 99
    depictions of the aristocracy, 102–3
    as a dog fancier/breeder, 96–99
    idealization of human/dog relationship, 94–95, 96, 170
    influence of Jack London, 94–95
    Lad: A Dog, 94–95, 96–110
    questioning the excesses of breeding, 106–7
    rise to fame, 97

Terhune, Albert Payson (*continued*)
  on thoroughbreds, 100–103, 105–6
Third Reich. *See* Nazism
thoroughbred. *See* breeding
Three Novels (Beckett), 129–30, 152–53, 154–58
  depiction of dogs, 137–38
  and language, 154–56
To the Lighthouse (Woolf), 58–59
Twentieth Century Dog, The (Compton), 12, 13, 93–94, 98
  See also breeding

Uexküll, Jakob von, 80–82
Ulysses (Joyce), 4
Umwelt, 80–82, 85–86, 125–26
Unnamable, The (Beckett), 129, 153–54, 154–56
  and the dissolution of self, 153
  and language, 154–56
  and species identity, 129
urban life. *See* modernity
urbanization, 11, 60–61, 92–96, 107–10, 110–28
urine marking. *See under* dogs

vegetarianism, 43, 159–60
Victorian Dogs, Victorian Men (Chez), 167
Victorian era, 6, 14, 17, 19
  dogs as status symbols, 98–99
  representations of dogs, 167
  sexual mores of, 56
Victorian realism, 20
"Violence and Metaphysics" (Derrida), 154
Voyage Out, The (Woolf), 58–59, 77–78

Waiting for Godot (Beckett), 149
Wallen, Martin, 14, 167
Waste Land, The (Eliot), 4
Watt (Beckett), 18, 129, 149–50, 159
  depiction of dogs, 132–33, 135–37
  depiction of agriculture, 159
  pun of Watt/What, 129
  and species identity, 129
We Think the World of You (Ackerly), 18, 95, 111–14, 125–26
  compared with Terhune's *Lad*, 113
  dogs in the urban setting, 111, 113–14
  plot of, 112–14

Weil, Kari, 62, 79, 84–85
Weller, Shane, 131, 134–35
Western humanism, 18, 130, 132–33
Westminster Kennel Club, 12, 106–7
When Species Meet (Haraway), 10, 16
White Fang (London), 24
  canine agency in evolution, 36–40
  compared with Woolf's *Flush*, 68–69
  dogs as protectors in, 29
  and dogs' relationships with humans, 39–40
  and domestication as degeneracy, 47–51
Whose Dog Are You? (Wallen), 167
"Why Look at Animals?" (Berger), 9
Wolfe, Cary, 16, 71–72, 130, 131
wolves, 7, 23, 35, 44
"Women Novelists" (Woolf), 74
women writers: struggles of, 70–77
  See also feminism; Woolf, Virginia
Woolf, Virginia, 4, 16, 17–18
  and the animal narrative tradition, 60–70
  approach to novel writing, 58–59
  compared with London, 64–70
  compared with Terhune, 99
  critical response to, 56–58, 89–91
  diary of, 55–56, 57–58, 89–91
  and the female experience, 58–59
  Flush, 55–91, 166
  lesbianism, 75
  on male privilege and feminism, 70–77
  Mrs. Dalloway, 77–78, 86, 89
  on multispecies connections, 66, 77–88
  narrative techniques employed by, 61–62, 64–70
  pet dog (Pinka), 74–76, 90
  rejection of anthropocentrism, 61–63
  A Room of One's Own, 70–72
  The Voyage Out, 77–78
  on women writers, 70–77
Worboys, Michael, 12–13, 14
Wordsworth, William, 158–59
World War II, 18, 129, 132–33, 142

Yeoh, Gilbert, 130

Zola, Émile, 118
zoos, 9–10

CPSIA information can be obtained
at www.ICGtesting.com
Printed in the USA
BVHW031920240222
629743BV00001B/4

9 780271 088020